Prince Gwyn

Prince Gwyn

Gwyn Nicholls
and the First Golden Era
of Welsh Rugby

David Parry-Jones

seren

seren is the book imprint of
Poetry Wales Press Ltd
Wyndham Street, Bridgend, CF31 1EF, Wales

The right of David Parry-Jones to be identified as the
Author of this Work has been asserted in accordance with
the Copyright, Designs and Patents Act, 1988.

ISBN 1-85411-262-7

A CIP record for this title is available from
the British Library

*The publisher works with the financial assistance of the
Arts Council of Wales*

Printed in Plantin by WBC Book Manufacturers, Bridgend

Prince Gwyn

Author's Preface

Acknowledgements

I should like to thank the following for information about Gwyn Nicholls and for helping me to understand him:

Gwyn Williams, of Ontario, Canada, grandson

Mrs Dorothy Picton and Mrs Enid Williams, nieces of Gwyn Nicholls and daughters of his brother-in-law Bert Winfield

Jeff Nicholls, great-nephew of Gwyn Nicholls

Claire Whythe, niece of Gwyn Nicholls

Trevor Lewis, right-hand man at Victoria Hygienic Laundries

Billy Neill, son of Nicholls' team-mate of the same name

Tom Collins, Dinas Powys Golf Club

John Jenkins, Bow Street, Ceredigion: research

Mrs Di Landon, Westbury-on-Severn: Nicholls' birthplace

John Mulford, Hon Archivist, New South Wales Rugby Union

Bryn Jones and the staff, Cardiff Central Library

Nomenclature

For the sake of simplicity I have used modern terminology or that which enjoys widest currency in cases where names or titles have changed down the century.

Thus I refer to *Cardiff Rugby Football Club* and *RFC* despite its having begun life as *Cardiff Football Club*. Similarly, in the Press the *Welsh Rugby Union* was often referred to as the *Welsh Football Union*; I choose the first version. *Llanelli* was once spelt *Llanelly*; I use today's spelling.

On his birth certificate Nicholls' Christian name is given as *Gwynne*, a spelling employed by the Press well into his playing

7

days as, occasionally, was *Gwynn*. I use the version which came to be universally known known and used: *Gwyn*.

Title: Prince Gwyn

Percy Bush, a Cardiffian who played under Gwyn Nicholls' captaincy, stated that team-mates called the skipper 'Prince' – no doubt a touch sardonically in the manner of Rugby men.

But it was the club's Hon Secretary, Charles Arthur, who accorded the nick-name its imprimatur, in 1908. In his *History* of Cardiff RFC's early decades he names the match of 29 February 1908 against London Welsh as being particularly worthy of note since it featured "...that Prince of Centres Gwyn Nicholls", emerging briefly from retirement.

That is likely to have been the first instance when this extravagant epithet was used of our subject. Certainly, I never encountered it in Press reportage of the heyday of Nicholls' career. After his retirement, and in the obituaries, the term was frequently employed.

David Parry-Jones, Radyr, Cardiff, 1999

Foreword

Having hung up their boots, distinguished modern players with something to say about Rugby football, and the confidence to say it, frequently pick up the pen or the microphone. Ieuan Evans, Barnes, Carling, Ackford, Hignell, Farr-Jones and Zinzan Brooke are among the many stars of our time who now twinkle in the media. They write newspaper columns. Television and radio channels use them to contribute insight and expertise to coverage of big games. Their authority comes across; fans want to know what they think.

They also write career books in which great matches, victories and tries are recalled – as well as lifting the lid on all manner of lurid activities in motels, bars, banqueting suites and similar locations. Midnight oil is burned as they seek to deliver the required candour without overly offending one-time team-mates still active in the game. They settle a few scores and make a few quid. "This is me," they tell the reader – sometimes assisted by professional writers, sometimes through their own doggedness and determination. Such volumes permit their admirers to know and understand them well.

With a very few exceptions such as Wavell Wakefield's *Rugger* and *Rugby Reminiscences* by Rowe Harding (both mainly technical works leavened with some personal observations and comment) none of these volumes dates from before the middle of the twentieth century, by which time Rugby's refining, process was fully seventy-five years old. The first books to be primarily personality-driven did not appear until the Fifties, when Hennie Muller and Bleddyn Williams published volumes which focussed inwards – on their subjects' viewpoints, lives and times besides their expertise.

To hazard a guess at the reason: during its earlier eras the game's dominant ethics and attitudes were still those of public schoolboys and the adults they grew up to be. It would have been considered by such people *infra dig* and vainglorious to blow their own trumpets in print. Hence it was onlookers, reporters and would-be analysts, not players, who wrote the Rugby books of the day.

Good examples include the Reverend F. Marshall's work *Football: the Rugby Union Game* (Cassell, 1892), undoubtedly a classic. E.H.D. Sewell was good for a couple of volumes a decade while 'Dromio' – W.J.T. Collins of the *South Wales Argus* – was another to put between hard covers the strong views he held. Captain H.B.T. 'Teddy' Wakelam, the BBC's first Rugby match commentator, edited a book about the game.

So much is not to say that great players were allowed by publishing houses to remain idle once their active days were over. But what they wrote was the 'how to play' type of manual, whose subject matter was not people, memories and controversy but skills and methods. It might be fleshed out with an appendix reproducing the Laws of the Game. Works by the Englishmen D.R. Gent, W.J.A. Davies and C.J.L. Marriott fall into this category. Haydn Tanner and Cliff Jones of Wales wrote in similar vein.

So, too, did Erith Gwyn Nicholls after his retirement early in 1907 from representative Rugby. His volume was called *The Modern Game and How to Play It*. The book enshrines its author's in-depth and original thinking about the challenge and possibilities held out by Rugby football, and the fresh principles which he inculcated into men who came under his influence. It is part of the Nicholls legacy to the Welsh game and its players.

But in keeping with similar publications that were to appear in due course, its revelations about the inner man are minimal. It gives away practically nothing of what Nicholls thought about the world around him. For a decade he was a colossus bestriding the evolving sport of Rugby football. Unstinting praise was heaped upon him as he collected his 24 international caps at centre during a dozen seasons in first-class Rugby. He was supreme at blending gifted players into hugely successful Cardiff or Wales teams; but from his book we learn little of his general opinions and aspirations, or how it felt to experience adulation on the grand scale. Nor is more light shed on such things in the technical articles written by him for magazines, programmes and books in later years. The image that reaches us from these sources is, inevitably, less than three-dimensional.

Other problems which confront the would-be biographer of Gwyn Nicholls include the loss of an assortment of papers which his family believe were placed with Cardiff RFC but which are missing from its archives. The sad explanation for their absence is to be found in *Cardiff Rugby Club: History and Statistics 1876-1975* by Danny Davies. He writes that newspaper cuttings and much other historical data stored in the Clubhouse were severely damaged as a result of the flooding of Cardiff Arms Park on 4 December 1960 after the River Taff had burst its banks; tragically, they had to be disposed of as waste. Thus although members of the family retain random memorabilia, the bulk of their forebear's paper are no longer extant.

Another hurdle in the path of the researcher is the nature of Press coverage a century ago. To be sure, as the size and enthusiasm of Rugby crowds grew, newspaper editors were encouraging sports writers by granting them ever more space for their match reports.

For the most part, however, the accounts of the day were unremittingly factual and blow-by-blow. This was only to be expected and indeed, in days before film and videotape, desirable. Reportage by 'Welsh Athlete', 'Dromio', 'Old Stager' and the rest was substance of record, instant history. On the other hand the personality pieces and 'profiles' commonplace today do not figure in the broadsheets published at the turn of the century. Hence some aspects of Nicholls' life have to be best guessed. For example, the metropolitan attractions and night life of Cardiff at the turn of the century can be listed; but we do not know which of these found favour with him and his pals. Other gaps in his story concern his education, and the manner of his return from Australia in 1899.

Nonetheless, the main elements of an outstanding Rugby career are faithfully recorded by the journalists of the day. A century on the wide range of Nicholls' skills, vision, and grasp of tactics can be readily perceived. Writers in the Welsh Press praised him so fulsomely, and consistently, that calculated ingratiation might be suspected were it not for the parallel, and sustained, plaudits of English writers.

Then there is the respect of his peers, friends and foes alike. Often as captain, Nicholls was in teams which beat the best sides on earth. His quality was acknowledged by contemporary observers the world over, including Australians, Kiwis, South Africans and assorted Europeans. He led Wales into a first Golden Era of successful and brilliant Rugby football. And yet his character did contain flaws, reassuring us that for all his majestic status in the game as played in his day, this was still a human being.

You may have seen, perchance, the beautiful wrought-iron gates that have graced the approach to Cardiff Arms Park during half a century – for long opposite Quay Street but latterly enjoying refurbishment and a move to the entrance opposite the Angel Hotel. Our subject is that man whom they commemorate. They are the 'Gwyn Nicholls Gates'.

One

Since the M4 was completed, along with the two bridges which transport road traffic between Wales and England, the valley of the River Severn from Chepstow to Gloucester has re-discovered the quietude and charm of a century ago. Among the few events which shatter its peace is the passage of the Bore each spring. Visitors gather on the river banks at vantage points like Newnham, Stonebench and Arlingham to watch tidal waves three to nine feet high roll upstream.

Partly explaining this phenomenon is the series of extravagant meanders in the river's course just before it broadens significantly at The Noose. One of them takes it close to Westbury-on-Severn with its pretty church and a seventeenth century water-garden which summer tourists enjoy visiting. A short distance to the west looms Nottswood Hill, marking the Forest of Dean's fringe. Busy little rivulets like Westbury brook tumble towards the Severn through fertile land dotted with small farms. Their owners still rear dairy cattle; in days gone by they also grew flax for local linen-makers. Apple orchards, often run-down now, are a reminder of the cider produced in this part of Gloucestershire.

One of the farmsteads is still called Wintles, though today it is a base for vehicle restoration and repair. A comfortable, even ample house built of brick and now partly whitewashed, it stands a mile-and-a-half inland from Westbury. In the late nineteenth century trains stopped five hundred yards away at Grange Court halt on the newly-completed Great Western Railway line between Gloucester and Newport.

Wintles is the birthplace of Gwyn Nicholls, one of the greatest players Rugby football has known. He was destined to win 24 International caps. But not for the land of his birth. For its neighbour. Wales.

The baby boy was the fifth child of Hartley and Jane

Nicholls, who came of stolid Gloucestershire stock with roots on both sides of the Severn. His birth certificate gives the date as 15 July 1874. Next to it 'Edith' is first inscribed, and then hastily crossed out with the name 'Erith' substituted. In addition, the child's second Christian name is spelled 'Gwynne', an anglicised form of the Welsh word for white. At the outset of his Rugby career, reporters used 'Gwynne', 'Gwynn' and 'Gwyn' as the mood took them. It is a fair guess that to avoid confusion and achieve consistency Nicholls the adult suggested that they adhered to the correct form, Gwyn. That is how Wales has known him since (at his wedding thirty years on the Registrar was obliged by law to use the spelling shown on the birth certificate).

Why this good Gloucestershire family should choose a Welsh forename for a son is hard to fathom. Equally, 'Erith' is inexplicable – the name of a London suburb on the south bank of the Thames near its mouth. It can only be surmised that these were names which Hartley Nicholls encountered as he travelled through rural Britain in his capacity as a farm supervisor.

Hartley's origins were humble. His father, Thomas, was a Slimbridge labourer who married a local farmer's daughter, Eleanor, and by 1865 was running the farm himself. On the certificate for his marriage that year to Jane Eliza Millard, Hartley too is described as farming, at Barnwood. His bride's father was also a farmer. This suggests a capacity in the family to recognise a main chance and move up in the world, one that is certainly exemplified later in the careers of its menfolk.

Gwyn's mother's family had French blood, and an intriguing background. An earlier generation had changed the spelling of their name from Maillard to Millard, perhaps because of the ancestor who killed a man in a duel and was forced to flee to Ireland. There, some family papers suggest, he fell out with a daughter-in-law whose bed he set on fire when she was in it: "...no idea what happened," is the scribbled addendum.

As good Victorians Hartley and Jane applied themselves swiftly to the production of offspring. Clara came first, and would be the only girl. She and Sidney – henceforth known to the world as Sid – were born at Barnwood and Hartpury respectively before the parents moved to Wintles Farm, where Thomas, Douglas and Gwyn soon came along. It is a reasonable surmise that Hartley began using the Grange Court station to move livestock, milk, vegetables and fruit to the markets at Cardiff, a Welsh port which was beginning to experience a dramatic boom as it exported coal from South Wales to the wider world. Is it possible that there, perhaps, he made a business friend named 'Gwyn' whose name seemed suitable for a son?

Mrs Nicholls had her hands full with child-rearing. Little Gwyn was safe in the farmyard and could play hide and seek in the big barn which sheltered the animals. Out of the red-brown lias stone from which the barn was built, a craftsman had fashioned a larger-than-life toadstool on which the toddler would have loved to perch – and which still stands at Wintles. Sometimes his mother might walk him across the fields as far as the village of Blaisdon to fetch his brothers and sister from school. In the other direction lay the railway station where the children could marvel at the mighty steam trains and greet their father on his return from business trips to the Midlands or South Wales.

These were daily becoming more important. For the year in which Gwyn was born also saw the enlargement of the local workhouse, lifting its capacity to 300. Shadows had fallen across the agricultural landscapes of Wales and England in the shape of imported food produced in bulk. Across the Atlantic the United States' central plains yielded huge harvests of grain which could reach Britain speedily in the holds of giant steamships. Wool from Australia's great flocks dwarfed the output of the home country's sheep farms. Soon refrigeration would mean that meat from the Empire could reach the shops at competitive prices.

The farmers of Britain were thus being squeezed, and the agricultural community shrank by a quarter between 1861 and 1901. The cosy countryside flanking the Severn was not immune to these influences. Writing in the RASE journal a local historian, Lydney-based Christine Martyn, notes the 1882 conclusion of a Government Commission on Agriculture chaired by the Duke of Richmond, that "no legislation could control the main causes of this depression".

Hartley Nicholls, however, was ahead of the field. The six mouths he already had to feed were a burden difficult to support in a deteriorating economic climate. He saw that farming's Golden Age was over and the future for many rural folk now lay in moving to the booming new industrial cities. As their populations mushroomed, so guaranteed deliveries of basic foodstuffs were needed, from any available source. Someone who identified the right urban place to be at this time, and could shrewdly exploit and profit from trading trends, would weather the storm. If our hunch is right and Hartley Nicholls had often visited Cardiff to sell produce, the town must have struck him as a good base from which to launch a fresh career. In Wales were people who could advise and help him.

Strategic conferences with Jane Eliza, herself attuned to the realities of agricultural economics, pointed to the only possible conclusion. The family sold up, and moved lock, stock and barrel to Roath, then on the eastern outskirts of Cardiff. The exact date when this took place is uncertain; but it must have been between Gwyn's birth and that of a sixth child, Ivor John, recorded in 1878 at Cardiff. The youngest member of the family, Garnett, was born in 1880.

Two of these offspring play little or no further part in our story. Thomas, born at 'Wintles' in June 1870, was drowned at sea twenty-five years later together with his wife and two children. Nor will there be further mention of Ivor John, although Gwyn would christen his first-born son Ivor.

Hartley had evidently used his Welsh connections, and his own thrustfulness, to secure an influential job at the local abattoir. This flair for business, allied to the agricultural contacts he maintained, made a potent combination. He played a successful middle-man role and, by 1891 would be described in the Census as an 'Inspector of Cattle'

The family's new address was 180 Constellation Street, part of the freshly-constructed suburban grid between the docks and the Newport Road. Here, when he was old enough, Gwyn attended a junior school in the town – later a city – where he would spend most of his life. Influenced by his father, the boy would retain an awareness of, and even an obligation towards,

Gloucestershire but his memories of Westbury naturally faded fast. Now, as the children grew up, the Nicholls family was developing a commitment to its new base: Cardiff, in Wales.

So much explains why, many decades later when the obituaries were being composed, the Rugby writers of the day would state: "In everything except birth, Gwyn Nicholls was a true son of Wales. Even in birth he can, hopefully, be claimed as a Silurian".

Two

Three quarters of a century before the Nicholls family moved in, Cardiff was no more than a village whose population was below 2000 and which had changed little since the Roman occupation. In that period regular convoys of gold and silver leaving British shores for the imperial capital were protected from pirates by flotillas of fighting vessels based on the outpost near the estuary of the Taff. Norman invaders a millennium later upgraded Roman ruins to strong-point status. There was some excitement when the Welsh patriot Owain Glyndwr stormed Cardiff's Keep in the late middle ages, and subsequently when Civil War actions were fought nearby. But the erstwhile fort on the Taff – Caer Dydd – seemed unlikely ever to become more than a small, sleepy market-town.

The abundance of coal unearthed in the Valleys to the north during the second half of the nineteenth century transformed Cardiff by an expansion which, in pace and extent, bears comparison with that of Chicago. At the time of Gwyn Nicholls' birth, in 1874, its population was around 60,000; by the time he was captaining Welsh Rugby teams twenty-five years later it was above 160,000. While the earlier growth had been Welsh-driven, Hartley Nicholls and his family found themselves among a host of English newcomers from their own county, Gloucestershire, as well as Somerset, Devon and Cornwall, seeking jobs in shipping or commerce.

The principal landowners in south east Wales were the Butes, Scottish aristocrats who had married into the Welsh Herberts and consequently owned a vast proportion of the mineral rights in the coalfield. It was the Second Marquess who took the all-important gamble and built docks to export those minerals, primarily coal, out of Cardiff. He thus guaranteed the town's steady rise towards city status.

Lord Bute's fortune was enhanced by his heir, who used it to indulge creative impulses. The Third Marquess flamboyantly restored the Castle, and refurbished the hill-fort north of the town known as Castell Coch, the 'red fortress'. Although a patrician, he sought to exert a benign influence on the design of the town's mushrooming suburbs, insisting, for instance, upon the laying-out of little parks between houses, plus space for gardens. Here, mainly to the west of the Taff, settled the captains and crews of the ships which moved huge cargoes of coal and iron to the ends of the earth. An entrepreneurial fever gripped Cardiff.

Residing in Roath, Mr and Mrs Hartley Nicholls and their children had become part of Cardiff's eastward expansion. Here the majority of properties were leased from the Tredegar estate. The latter's planners and managers were evidently not moved by the philanthropic and aesthetic considerations which motivated Bute employees; there is little to commend the appearance of the properties which were being thrown up on their lands to cope with the inflow of newcomers. For example, many front doors of the period in Roath, Splott, Adamsdown and Tremorfa open straight onto pavements. Nor are there convenient back lanes allowing easy disposal and collection of household refuse. South and east of today's City Road terraced housing, rather than detached and semi-detached, is the norm.

The up-side of all this is good neighbourliness. The young Gwyn Nicholls was growing up next door to a heady mixture of professional men and wage-earners, businessmen, tradesmen and a wide variety of shopkeepers. Near his home were foundries, engine works, a wire-rope plant that also made submarine cables. After he had entered his teens the Dowlais iron works became established locally, destined to produce a tough breed of south Cardiffian for a century.

We have to indulge in some guesswork to account for Gwyn's schooling. There is no mention of it in his own later writings, in sundry tributes to him and obituaries, in the 'Who's Who' volumes published by the *Western Mail*, or in the surviving family papers. A conspiracy of silence might almost be suspected, were it not that his hand-writing, vocabulary and ability to present an argument make it clear that he was more than adequately taught. It is likely that the little boy attended one of the elementary schools set up as a result of the 1870 Education Act. Within easy walking distance of Constellation Street were Adamsdown Gardens and Splotlands Board schools and a Church of England establishment at Metal Street. A sprinkling of 'Dame's Schools' was also to be found in the inner areas around Charles Street and Pembroke Terrace.

Not far away, either, was the new school of Higher Grade at Howard Gardens. Doomed to be blitzed in World War II this establishment stood where the high-rise Chartered Trust building now dominates Newport Road. Its entry lists held in Cardiff Record Office, covering the critical years when Gwyn would have been a potential entrant, appear to be incomplete and do not include the youngster's name. We are thus obliged to surmise that Howard Gardens was the secondary school which he attended; we do know that his youngest brother Garnett entered it in 1890, which suggests that his parents had found it to be satisfactory.

He would not have learned his Rugby at the school, however, which intriguingly opted for Association Football as its boys' winter game. On one occasion when lessons terminated early to allow pupils time to reach Cardiff Arms Park and watch Wales in action it was Association Football that was being played. Possibly such an attempt to manipulate pupils' taste was reaction to a local climate which overwhelmingly favoured the Rugby game. In the north, Association Football had caught imaginations and Wrexham was its Welsh capital. Southern Wales' choice of code was influenced by returning Oxbridge graduates enthused by the Rugby School approach to 'football', and by the stream of immigrants from England's west country where a handling code was already pre-eminent. But the old adage has Rugby as a game for hooligans, with soccer as the sport of gentlemen. Since Cardiff's early headmasters of secondary schools for boys were bent on producing the latter, soccer was clearly the preferable team game. It would be the nineteen-twenties before this regime changed.

Out and about the town, however, there was no doubt which code was paramount. For a start Cardiff City AFC would not be formed until 1899, by which time the town's Rugby club had been building a power-base and acquiring charisma for nearly twenty-five years. Just as coal had put Cardiff on the industrial map, so Rugby football was fashioning its sporting reputation. Its flagship club travelled to Dewsbury, Liverpool, Moseley and London – whose clubs drew big crowds to Cardiff Arms Park on their return visits.

There were 'international' games too. When Gwyn Nicholls was nine years old Ireland came for the first time to Cardiff, where they lost, while two years on, in 1886, Scotland were successful on their inaugural visit. England did not play at the Arms Park until their defeat of 1893. When Nicholls was approaching 14 the first overseas touring XV played Wales: the New Zealand 'natives', mainly comprising Maoris. The natural readiness of a small boy to be impressed by heroes and their deeds was fortified by the presence in the victorious home team of big brother Sid.

While soccer had yet to achieve more than a few column inches in the Press of South Wales, newspapers like the *Western Mail* and its rival *South Wales Daily News* recognised Rugby's primacy with blanket coverage of weekend fixtures which regularly occupied two broadsheet pages on Monday mornings. Writers sheltered behind pen-names like 'Welsh Athlete' and 'Forward'. They wrote highly detailed match reports, to ensure the accuracy of which they employed small boys to dash around the touch-lines and ascertain who had scored tries or made important tackles. There was candid comment and blunt criticism.

Newspapers carried advertisements, too, directed at the Rugby fraternity. "Do you wish to be strong men, fleet of foot, strong in limb and with nerves of steel?" demanded one. "If so...the best tonic yet discovered is Gwilym Evans's Quinine Bitters." Anderson, Cox and Co drew attention to their "large and varied stocks of footballs and boots" – adding the extra inducement, "Match ball given free with order of 15 or more jerseys." A. Calder was a gents' outfitter whose name survives in Cardiff. Describing himself as "late of London Caledonians FC" this Scot offered "special estimates for football and cricket club caps, jerseys and hose" at his premises in Castle Arcade.

If Cardiff Arms Park was the centre point of the town's Rugby society, a busy outer network of clubs was evolving at venues which members could easily reach, on foot, by rail or via a successful and well patronised tramway system. Penarth was founded in 1879, Dinas Powys in 1882. Cardiff Quins played at Roath, appeared from time to time on Cardiff RFC's fixture lists in the early days, and survived as a suburban side until the nineteen-thirties. Also, there was Cardiff Star, the junior club with which Gwyn Nicholls was to serve his apprenticeship. Why it was named 'Star', rather than 'Stars', will probably never be known, though Cardiffians may be put in mind of the title given some years ago to south Cardiff's recreation complex, the 'Star' centre. Its name is an acronym, formed from the first letters of the four suburbs which the establishment was to serve: Splott, Tremorfa, Adamsdown and Roath. The nineteenth century Cardiff Star was perhaps a Rugby precursor.

In family notes which she left, Erith Williams (née Nicholls, Gwyn's daughter) speculated that the Star RFC was a 'feeder' club for Cardiff itself. If, as has been noted, Cardiff's young men could not learn Rugby at secondary school it was inevitable that clubs would spring up to meet the demand from youngsters eager to emulate local sporting heroes. The Star ran two XVs and reports say that "such was Gwyn Nicholls' enthusiasm that in his first year at 17 he would play centre for the reserves before lunch, and then race to the club's Sophia Gardens pitch to play half back for the Firsts in the afternoon".

It was with the Star, too, that Nicholls got his first Press notice, in the *Western Mail* during October 1891 at the age of 17 years and 3 months. The club was away to Barry, where "Jajo, Bennett, Aitken and Nicholls played in fine style for the visitors," wrote 'Welsh Athlete'. Other clubs met by the Star included Taff Vale Wanderers, Cathays and Splott Rovers, while Cardiff Rangers conceded the first try by the youngster to be reported in the media: "from a scrum Nicholls got the ball and ran well to score at the posts." The in-put of the Nicholls family to Cardiff Star, it should be added, went beyond mere heroics on the field. Its players wore plain black jerseys onto which were sewn large white stars. The seamstress was none other than Gwyn's elder sister Clara.

Another report of 1891 concerns a Dinner which took place at the Westgate Hotel when "The Star did ample justice to the sumptuous repast so generously placed at their disposal by their genial President Mr R.C. Culley." As it turned out the President was prevented from putting in an appearance. In his absence the chair was taken by a Welsh International forward who earlier that year had figured in the Welsh defeat by Scotland. On duty to see that the young guests behaved themselves and used their knives and forks correctly was the eldest of the Nicholls boys, Sid: a hero at the head of the table.

By the time the dinner took place Sid was a strapping fellow in his mid-twenties who had served a season as Cardiff vice-captain, and probably taken part in urgent discussions during the close season on the importance of the club's strengthening of its recruiting system. He would view an evening fraternising with up-and-coming members of the Star as time well spent. And he would be pleased at the maturing of his kid brother, who was now nudging six feet and beginning to broaden out. Maybe his time was not yet. But it would come.

Three

The Rugby game with which the Nicholls boys were growing up had just been through a period when it was shaped and formulated. This began with the eagerness of England's public schools to compete against each other at sport, which necessitated the adoption of codes acceptable to all parties. The English are good at devising rules and regulations, and the controlling body which they set up in 1871 drafted Laws which were based broadly on the way 'foot-ball' (as it was known) was run at Rugby School. The other Home countries soon followed suit with their own 'Rugby unions'.

For centuries the Welsh had played Cnappan, a rough-and-ready handling game pitting village against village. Urbanisation prompted the establishing of more artificial alliances, which came to be called 'clubs' from an old Norse word meaning to group together. These could perpetuate links between young men who had been at university together and wished to continue sporting friendships. They chose to play the Rugby code, on fields put at their disposal by tolerant landowners and farmers. Games were thus public occasions, observed and enjoyed by members of the local community. Some, naturally, felt keen to be allowed to join in the fun; others kept their distance from the action, and became the first spectators.

Neath (1871), Swansea and Llanelli became the senior Welsh clubs. Because of the town's size, and the initial absence of a single dominant club, Cardiff RFC was founded later and thus dates from the amalgamation of Glamorgan Football Club and Cardiff Wanderers, which took place in September 1876. Reclaimed land on the River Taff's east bank had already been made available to the town's cricketers by the Third Marquess of Bute, the Castle's owner. In the winter this was ideal for Rugby football. It still is.

Forty muscular young men formed the first Cardiff squad,

from which teams fifteen-strong were selected comprising nine forwards, two half backs, two three quarter backs and two full backs. Three matches were played in the first season: Newport were victorious in the first fixture of what was to become an enduring series, but Swansea and Merthyr were defeated. Charcoal-shaded jerseys bearing skull and crossbones insignia were the initial dress, giving way to blue and black hoops in 1877 after the pirate-style kit was condemned in some quarters for being in poor taste.

Cardiff were playing in Cheltenham and Bristol by 1878, but most opponents on a fixture list that soon featured three or four matches a month were Welsh. Next spring the club reached the Welsh Cup Final, losing to Newport at Sophia Gardens before 1000 spectators who paid to stand outside the ropes, but were annoyed to be charged gate money (for the first time) to watch Rugby. More controversy came in the 1881 Final: Llanelli proved poor losers and a player called Mitchell made off with the ball to prevent Cardiff converting a winning try. March 1882 brought a first trip to London, where Harlequins were beaten.

Though far from invincible, the club was already showing itself ready to innovate and embrace change. On 9 February 1884, Frank Hancock, who had come to Cardiff from Wiveliscombe in Somerset to brew beer, made his debut at Cheltenham as a stand-in for an unavailable three quarter. Hancock gave so good an account of himself that, although the regular player was reinstated for the following Saturday's match against Gloucester, the committee was loath to leave Hancock out, choosing him as a fourth three quarter. The alignment was not an overnight success, but Cardiff persevered with it; in time Wales adopted it; gradually the rest of the Rugby world followed suit.

The four three quarter game led to more emphasis on handling the ball in open play, which had appeal for an ever-growing number of onlookers. At Cardiff Arms Park 'stands' had become common, that is, raised boards to lift spectators' feet out of the mud. Now a 'grand' stand, or superstructure with seats, was installed beside the south touch-line and opened on Boxing Day 1885. Soon the club hired a rub-a-dub man who massaged players' muscles for six shillings a week. The twenty-year-old Sid Nicholls judged this a club that deserved his affiliation. He duly joined it, thereby virtually ensuring that once Erith Gwyn proved his mettle he would follow suit.

A little taller than Gwyn would become, Sid played in the pack and was a major influence in the Second XV's unbeaten campaign of 1885-86. A first team debut followed in 1886-87, when he is recorded as being a try scorer. The team photograph shows him with a tense facial expression which he tries to offset by placing one hand nonchalantly on a hip, while resting the other on the chair of the team-mate sitting in front. His subsequent rise was startling. In 1888 his haul of tries for Cardiff was eleven. He was in the XV which overcame the Maoris that December and a week later won a first cap against the tourists, whom Wales also beat. Sid was to play three more times for his adopted country, though each of these games ended in defeat.

At Cardiff he became vice-captain to Charles Arthur without ever advancing to the captaincy; then, suddenly, in 1892-93 his name is absent from the club's playing strength. What seems likely is that Sid chose to concentrate on his budding career as a publican and, later, hotelier. He was mine host of the Corporation Inn at Ely and before long would manage the Grand Hotel in Westgate Street.

It is certain that Gwyn Nicholls' father Hartley had also made a mark, plus a good deal of money, among the stalwart townspeople of Cardiff. By 1900 the Cardiff Directory would locate him at 'Gresleigh', number 201 Cathedral Road, the kind of house which was selling to the new professional classes in the town for several hundred pounds. Doubtless he underwrote his sons' career ambitions and would have given backing and help to Sid and his projects. It seems unlikely, however, that he had the contacts or the know-how to accelerate their sporting ambitions; and henceforth he makes few significant appearances in their careers.

For Gwyn, therefore, it was his big brother who became the role model. Sid was already a sporting hero. Now, after his retirement from the game, he stood for and was elected to the Cardiff committee, on which he was to serve for nine years. As his association with Cardiff Star suggests, Sid was very much aware of his sibling's promise. Now it could be helped towards full bloom.

Thus in 1892, at the prompting of his brother, Gwyn left the Star for Cardiff Harlequins who had just moved from Penarth Road to a field at Roath made available by Lord Tredegar. Far from being a mere suburban side the Quins were able to register wins over Bristol and Llanelli in their heyday and proved popular tourists in the west country. For a short period their teenage recruit is reported as playing at full back and scrum half as well as centre.

He might have expected to enjoy a couple more seasons on a steady learning curve with the Quins. However, at Cardiff Arms Park a disastrous 1891-92 season, when more matches were lost than were won, had prompted crisis measures combined with a full-scale trawl through the town in search of new talent.

Predictably Sid Nicholls made certain that, caught in the net, young Gwyn transferred his allegiance to Cardiff. Still only eighteen years old, he played through the 1892-93 season for the Second XV. The team was not particularly successful, winning ten games but losing twelve. There was no doubt, however, that it contained a rising star. Selected at centre, Gwyn dropped a goal and, more important, went in for seven tries. Sid would thus have been able to argue that his brother's potential value to the club was doubled overnight when the points awarded for a try were increased by the International Board at its March 1893 meeting from two to three (Ireland retained the old points system for another year or two).

As it evolved, the appearance of the game underwent change too. Always less than wholly spherical, the shape of the match ball was now acquiring an exaggeratedly oval shape, making it more easy to handle and to kick with purpose and accuracy from the hand: early in his career Gwyn is described as sending up "a beautiful screw punt that went along the line and found touch at the centre." Careful scrutiny of early photographs shows that players had learned to nail bars and later studs to the soles of boots; while their breeches gave way to 'knickers' that coyly revealed knee-caps. Not for some time would blazers and long trousers be abandoned by referees.

The latter, however, acquired new powers. Although it pained the old guard to concede that the 'umpires' of the day might be prejudiced in favour of their teams, the Welsh system of giving total control of play to impartial referees was tried out generally in 1893-94 and soon won general adoption. By eliminating conferences and argument it speeded up the action.

Techniques had altered radically too. At the scrummages of 1870 forwards set out to drive their opponents back and kick the ball in the direction of the opposite goal-line. "At that time, to heel the ball towards their half back," wrote the England forward Arthur Budd in an article of 1892, "was regarded as unfair and discreditable." By now, the desirability of supplying backs with possession was well understood, as was wheeling a scrum and dribbling as a pack.

Away from the forwards progress was also being made. For long backs had behaved as individuals, patrolling sectors of the pitch on the look-out for loose balls offering fortuitous opportunities to attack. The RFU's first Secretary recorded that he did not see a deliberate pass by a half back to a three quarter until 1881. By 1893, however, back divisions were working out ways in which to exploit the open spaces away from the forwards. Their potential as runners-in and try-scorers was acknowledged by the hard men up front.

Ever since, backs have enjoyed sharper player profiles than forwards. To the majority of onlookers, and many who write and speak in the media, the skills and élan of halves and three quarters are more clearly identifiable and able to be enjoyed than the murky labourings of forwards. So it was in the early evolving of Rugby football. England's Aston and Poulton Palmer, Ireland's Sam Lee, Scotland's A.B. Timms (a great friend of Nicholls) – these were centres whom the game's swelling armies of spectators went to watch and cheer. In Wales there was Arthur Gould, who began representing his country in 1885 before business took him outside the Principality. Though self-confessedly overweight on returning to his native Newport in 1892, he scored thirty-seven tries for the Black and Ambers and led Wales to her first-ever Triple Crown, which included a first home victory over the English. Arguments about the relative merits of Gould and Gwyn Nicholls were to rage well into the twentieth century. The critic in the best position to judge, W.J.T. Collins – 'Dromio' of the *South Wales Argus* – is not only given to superlatives; he is also frustratingly ambivalent. Thus in 1948 he wrote of Gould: "After sixty years of football criticism I think of him still as the greatest player of all time." Later in the same book, his *Rugby Recollections*, he writes: "Gwyn Nicholls was the perfect centre – the greatest exponent of the four three quarter game I have known." He watched both men in action but is tantalisingly vague.

Both were centres. What did 'Dromio' really mean? According to Terry Godwin's *The International Championship 1883-1983* Gould was the first of that elite who today are known as 'superstars'. At his height, Pressmen and other critics agree that he possessed skills and finesse which placed him above his peers and contemporaries. But those who write about him, both in books and match reports, tell more frequently of amazing individual feats, in particular the 'corkscrew' runs which brought him so many tries. We do not read of scoring passes. Gwyn Nicholls was to state, carefully, "[Gould] steered an erratic course, darting hither and thither as openings presented themselves, that was difficult to follow". It may be speculated that although 'Monkey' Gould was outstanding within the game's existing parameters, he did not influence its evolution. In other words, Gould had shown what clever runners could achieve, given possession of the ball at a distance from the swarming scrummages and mauls enjoyed by the pack. The game's next advance awaited the tactician who could refine the art of combined play and the transfer of the ball.

Four

D anny Davies's *Cardiff Rugby Club: History and Statistics* has Gwyn Nicholls making a senior debut in 1893 "with two matches for the premier team while playing for our Reserves". Unusually, for a careful historian who took a lot of his source material from the earlier Charles Arthur publication of 1906, Davies mis-dates by a season the young man's promotion. His first appearance in the Cardiff First XV, captained at the time by Norman Biggs, is recorded by Arthur as taking place at Cardiff Arms Park on Saturday 1 January 1894 against Old Merchant Taylors. As club Secretary at the time, he would have known.

Although short of his twentieth birthday, Gwyn was now six feet and one inch tall, well above the average height for the period but, at eleven stones, still without the poundage which would soon be enabling him to break tackles and knock the breath out of opponents whom he dumped on the turf. It is a bony frame that is revealed by the team photograph, the first in which he figures. The face is approaching maturity, and the high brow and wide-eyed expression would stay with him as the years advanced.

The pose, however, was to change. This same picture is one of the very few in which Nicholls is looking into the camera. As the years go by he consistently wears a fixed stare in a sidelong direction, even angling his shoulders the same way. Around the mouth there plays the merest suggestion of a smile. Was this a camera-shy superstar? Or an example of early gamesmanship: the measured cultivation of an inscrutable image, defying the world to deduce the thoughts occupying his mind and the plans taking shape? Certainly a poker-face is something that many of the game's best backs have studiously cultivated down the decades.

Before men wore numbers to assist identification, Nicholls'

height made him instantly recognisable on the field. Consider the physiques of some contemporaries: Swansea's illustrious full back W.J. Bancroft, thirty-three times capped for Wales and skipper on eleven occasions, stood just five feet and five inches in his stockinged feet (he could and did, nonetheless, kick winning goals from the touchline).

His club-mates, daring half backs Evan and David James, measured five feet seven inches and five feet six respectively. Scrum half Dicky Owen, at five feet four inches, was not surprisingly dubbed a 'midget' in the Press. Compared with them Nicholls was a giant. His other trade-mark, noted by the critic E.H.D. Sewell, was a "peculiar heels-first running action ... which is the best of all methods on an ankle-deep field". By 'ankle-deep' we may assume that the writer was alluding to mud, rather than long grass. Certainly 'heels first' would give extra purchase to a runner – especially one like Nicholls who beat defenders by a body-swerve rather than dainty side-steps.

Twenty years earlier, we learn from Charles Arthur, anything resembling training for matches was quite unknown, and a back who had suddenly to run a long way suffered disastrous results to the 'bellows'. Even in the 1890s players did not, initially, go to the lengths of succeeding generations to acquire stamina and strength. Nicholls wrote later that hard training for backs, "except at the flabby early season stage, takes the 'snap' out of a man." However he and his team-mates were happy to spend a couple of hours a week practising passing, kicking and catching. The player who had spent a little of his spare time perfecting his skills, he argued, could be spotted by the cleanness of his actions: "It is an exception to see him fumble, miskick or lob his passes."

The Cardiff club, that is, had grasped and accepted the idea that willingness to sacrifice some leisure and creature comforts could also contribute to excellence. Thus when winter evenings became too dark for practice the Cardiff 'squads' of the day would give lunch a miss and use the daylight for working on their favourite 'moves'. For a breather they stood in circles giving high, low or short passes, to take which demanded agility from the recipient.

Gwyn Nicholls' first game ended in a comfortable win for his new club, but the media were not enamoured of Cardiff's display. Twelve days later at Newport, before a 12,000 crowd, the youngster from the Second XV was chosen to play at full back. His side was heavily beaten and the Press noted that Nicholls "failed to gather as the home forwards broke." Well, many great players have found the advance of a Black and Amber pack something of a distraction as they stooped to make a loose ball safe; and if 'Welsh Athlete', writing in the *Western Mail*, considered Nicholls "nervous" he was probably not far wrong. This same, very sound, critic suggested, "Gwyn Nicholls is not a full back....as a three quarter I fancy he will turn out a real tip-topper." But after a roasting or two at this – to him – new, advanced, level of the game, the young man was probably only too glad to end the season with the Second XV, running rings around Llandaff in the Mallett Cup and racing fifty yards for a try against Bridgwater Albion.

He could look back on eight months during which he had achieved recognition and advanced his career. Meanwhile Sid Nicholls had not been idle, having acquired an interest in the Grand Hotel, Westgate Street, directly opposite Cardiff Arms Park, at which he gave his brother a job as under-manager. Doubtless Gwyn's close season was spent learning the job.

As for relaxation in the summer months, it is nowhere recorded that Gwyn played cricket and it would be many years before he took up golf. However, as a boom town Cardiff was on the United Kingdom's entertainments circuit, and it is tempting to imagine that the rising star and his new group of young friends might have celebrated his twentieth birthday with a visit to Buffalo Bill's Wild West extravaganza at Sophia Gardens. "This Show Offers Prodigious Entertainment" thundered the hoardings. "Depicting Indian Life in Every Particular...featuring 200 Indians, Mexicans, Scouts, Buck-Riders Etc. It will include Buffalo Bill's Famous combat with Yellow Hand, Chief of the Sioux." At Stoll's Panopticon the big attraction was the 'Living Doll', 19 years of age and only 19 inches tall – "the smallest human being that ever existed". You paid your money and took your choice.

The 1894-95 season got under way; but after a few weeks Cardiff's record was no more than average. Following five defeats in eighteen matches commentators in the local Press pointed to the team's shortcomings at centre. Writing off the men in possession, who included the erstwhile captain Norman Biggs, one newspaper said, "Wing Radley Thomas is a bit 'dodgy' but the club could do worse than give him a trial".

There was at this stage no deliberate lobbying in favour of Gwyn Nicholls, who was happily laying on tries for Second XV team-mates in addition to turning out on loan for Cardiff District RU against Gloucester where he lost the heel of his boot attempting (successfully) to convert a try. He did well to miss the First team games against Llanelli – "incentives to roughness are too common in this western town" frowned the *Western Mail* – and Swansea, where an incensed crowd invaded the St Helens pitch after Cardiff wiped out a half-time deficit to win by 15 points to 3.

The break-through came with the youngster's selection for the glamorous Boxing Day fixture against Emile de Lissa's recently-founded Barbarians. The amazing speed of wonder-sportsman C.B. Fry thrilled a big crowd and secured victory for the tourists when he overtook a Cardiff wing from behind to prevent a try. But Nicholls scored from a Selwyn Biggs break, leading 'Welsh Athlete' to write in the *Western Mail*: "Gwyn Nicholls may, I think, be safely set down as occupying a permanent position in the centre." He had arrived.

For Cardiff, the New Year began sadly as well as frostily. A young forward, Richard Davies, went skating on a pond beside the Penarth Road behind the GWR station, but fell through the ice and was drowned. In April the club played a charity match to raise funds for his mother. With the thaw, however, came a series of six victories in succession climaxing in a 32-0 win over Gloucester when Gwyn Nicholls got a hat-trick of tries. This euphoria was rudely dispersed at Rodney Parade. Newport's victory margin was a mere 5-3 but the Cardiff three quarters as a combination were outplayed by their opposite numbers, who included the Welsh captain of the day. The most significant remark in one of the match reports was that "Gould and Nicholls were evenly matched in the midfield". This was not only high praise; it was a very important observation, bracketing the Cardiffian as it did with a man who was about to become the most capped of International players in the Home Countries. In days long before blanket television coverage of big Rugby, committees selecting national XVs relied heavily on second-hand views and consulted Press reports avidly. For sure, therefore, Gwyn's credentials were now certain to be pencilled in by the selectors. As he adjusted to the first-class game Nicholls had briefly profited from playing inside T.W. Pearson, who won thirteen caps for Wales in the twelve years from 1891 to 1903. When the career of this gifted wing took him to an engineering job at Newport Docks he also changed clubs, moving to Rodney Parade. His successor was Vivian Huzzey, destined to be another major try-scorer who would be capped five times by Wales. In the 1895-96 season Nicholls totalled six tries, but sent his new wing in for eighteen.

Partly, no doubt, because of the very self-effacement which already characterised his game, no great publicity came his way during the early autumn. In the away draw with Cambridge University, however, his combined attack with Norman Biggs just before the final whistle almost snatched a win for the visitors. This near miss, along with his name, was noted by the Varsity's scrum half on the day, Matthew Mullineux who, in 1899, would select Gwyn in his 'English' touring side to visit Australasia. A fortnight later, in Cardiff's defeat at Blackheath, an impression was made on London's Rugby writers, who commented: "Nicholls invariably made ground when in possession and gave Huzzey a number of good passes."

The youngster's feelings can only be imagined, however, when he was summoned to appear at centre for East Wales against West Wales in the WRU's Trial match at The Gnoll, Neath. For the first time he would play next to 'Monkey' Gould, and would be marking Owen Badger of Llanelli who had been in the Welsh midfield through the previous season. In a successful Trial Nicholls nearly scored just before half time, and did run in a try at the final whistle with help from scrum-half Dan Jones. Wrote 'Welsh Athlete': "His performance was perfect. We can put Nicholls down as the best centre on view."

Though not wholly in accordance with that judgement, the Welsh selection committee now named the Cardiffian among the travelling reserves for Wales' thirteenth game against

England. After some maulings in years when they were adjusting to strict laws and strange disciplines the Welsh had beaten Scotland and Ireland, and could point to two victories over England. Arthur Boucher, Harry Packer and Arthur Gould were hard, experienced members of the successful Newport team who, along with all the principal Welsh clubs scarcely knew the meaning of defeat at the hands of English visitors. Finally, the composure of English Rugby appeared to have been upset by the secession of the Northern Union, which had made outlaws of many fine players of the Rugby Union game. As they descended on Blackheath the Welsh were full of confidence.

Alas. Robbed during the first quarter of little Badger (fractured collar-bone) and with the forward C.B. Nichol gallantly persevering despite a badly-twisted ankle, Wales leaked a woeful seven tries, the most since the opening fixture of the series in 1881. Her pack was scrummaged into the Rectory Field mud, while England's half, wrote the scribes, was penetrated no more than six times in all. That night, as the repulsed invaders licked their wounds, London's Metropole was a glum hotel. And a certain twenty-one year old reserve was thanking his lucky stars that he had not made his debut on this day.

Wales needed time to think. The selection of a XV to meet Scotland on January 1 1896 was held back a week. Nicholls had a game at Swinton in a losing Cardiff XV before being named on 16th January as one of six new caps, the other five being in the pack. As was now becoming the custom he withdrew from his club's game with Devonport in order not to risk injury. Neither his first game for Wales nor the second, in Dublin in the March, was particularly memorable. At Cardiff Scotland fell to a fourth defeat at Welsh hands in a match distinguished by Gould's outstanding form behind a beaten pack – perhaps the display of a man desperate to atone for the debacle at Blackheath. It included a try, the other Welsh score coming from Llanelli wing Cliff Bowen.

Nicholls was chosen for the end-of-term game in Dublin, doubtless enjoying the eve-of-match outings to Phoenix Park and the Zoological Gardens. At Lansdowne Road next day, though his tackle on Magee denied Ireland one try, others by Crean and Lytle gave their country a win which confirmed them as champions. At the end of his first International campaign Wales' new centre could look back on appearances which were mistake-free but not earth-shattering.

His confidence was evidently growing. At the outset of the 1896-7 season "Mr Gwyn Nicholls" (the Press called him) picked and captained a XV which played a missionary game against Grangetown in south west Cardiff before 1,000 onlookers. His developing vision is exemplified by the scoring pass he sent back inside after realising that Huzzey, outside him, was covered. And although he would never be one to waste words, he was at this stage of his career willing to be outspoken to reporters: after Cardiff's 3-0 defeat at Swansea he stated, "I scored a good try; the referee disagreed."

In the December Trial, reported the *South Wales Argus*, "Gould played with a good deal of his old dash; of the other centres Nicholls was undoubtedly the best." The two were paired for the third, and last, time in the XV named to meet England that January. Since 1883 and the first International fixture, against England, Welsh teams had been chosen almost exclusively from the quartet of powerful clubs which lay along the Bristol Channel – Newport, Cardiff, Swansea and Llanelli. A few men from Neath had been capped, and one or two from Pontypridd. But no more than three or four from Valleys clubs had won selection – and even Tom Clapp of Nantyglo was a lawyer raised in Somerset, rather than a local miner. Thus the 1896 selection of Penygraig's David Evans in the pack had represented a break-through: an acknowledgement by the Welsh selection committee that Rugby did exist in the coalfield and its denizens had much to offer the Welsh cause, especially in the frontal exchanges. In January 1897 the sturdy Evans, who had come east from Maenclochog to find work, was joined in the Welsh pack by his clubmate John Rhapps and Dick Hellings, the Llwynypia coal-cutter. In years to come they would be succeeded by others of a breed which came to be known as 'Rhondda forwards': not particularly fast about the field, but using enormous strength derived from filling trams of coal to dominate mauls and close quarter exchanges.

Their influence would match that of brilliant Welsh backs in the golden years which lay ahead, and it certainly helped Wales to take ample revenge over the English in the last International match to be played at Newport. Despite heavy going the home side ran in three tries through Pearson, Boucher and scrum half Dan Jones. The trio would have been joined by Nicholls had he not lost his footing veering in towards the posts on a change of direction. But: "He never made a mistake tackling," wrote the *South Wales Echo.* "Even on a normal day his kicking to touch would have been called magnificent; on a slippery field with a wet ball it can only be described as superb."

His partner 'Monkey' Gould led his Welshmen to what was at that time their most decisive win over England and earned good write-ups for his contribution to the home team's crisp handling. His was a remarkable display, as it happens, in the light of the crisis which he had, all unwittingly, brought upon the game in Wales and which must have been weighing on his mind.

It stemmed initially from the testimonial fund generously set up by admirers to seal what were apparently to be his final months in the game. The gesture fell foul of dyed-in-the-wool amateur lobbies in Scotland and Ireland, and outraged administrators in England determined to protect Rugby Union football at all costs from what they perceived as the major threat of professionalism. Given his senior status, Gould could afford to take a laid-back view of the turmoil that was developing around him – in fairness, only in an indirect sense his responsibility.

Frustratingly, however, it was to mean that the International career of the exciting, ambitious twenty-two year-old who had emerged as a natural successor to Gould would go onto the back-burner.

Five

As the nineteenth century drew towards a close, Welsh club Rugby was attracting huge crowds that occasionally topped twenty thousand. Money came swilling into the game, a bonanza which is commemorated by many of the stadia surviving today. (Why they have not, more than a century on, been replaced by modern, state-of-the-art clubhouses, changing rooms, grandstands and terraces is one of Welsh Rugby's best-kept secrets.)

In the early days cash in large quantities did not, however, find its way into the pockets of players. The game's ethical thrust was against the idea of remuneration for taking part in sport – even though onlookers thought it worth paying to be entertained by fellow citizens who were more energetic or youthful.

The other great team games which were now emerging, Association Football and cricket, had sanctioned a system in which professionals and 'amateurs' coexisted. Until the revolution of 1995 Rugby Union steadfastly adhered to its earliest covenant: no money for playing the game, no mixed economy. Mainly the shots were called by the RFU, whose core of middle-class players stood in no need of match fees, indeed viewed them with distaste. In Wales, whose working class had taken eagerly to the game, cash certainly found its way into boots while their owners took a post-match shower; but ingenious ways were evolved of inflating expenses so that a facade of purity could survive and permit on-going contact with other, principled nations who played Rugby football. For decades club officials were touchy about accusations of fiscal subterfuge, however generalised. When the BBC broadcaster G.V. Wynne-Jones wrote in his book *Sports Commentary* as late as 1951 that "...some clubs make a habit of remunerating their players. In Wales it does happen..." he suffered a fate amounting to excommunication – for writing what he knew and had witnessed.

A combination of the RFU's idealism, shared by Scotland and Ireland and complemented by the lip-service paid to amateurism by the Welsh establishment, was able for two decades to keep the game on an even keel rocked only by minor spats. In 1893, however, the issue of 'broken time', or wages sacrificed through sporting commitments, proved damaging, leading to the secession of many northern clubs. They formed their own Union, or League, which introduced cash payments compensating players for wages lost through taking time off to train and play Rugby. This led to total professionalism in the north, where players were now bought and paid. 'League' representatives, horror of horrors, began invading Wales to buy talented performers.

Welsh attitudes to the League game, as has been suggested, were shaped less by respect for purist principles than by a deep disgust with the market forces that began to operate in the impecunious Valleys. For decade after decade through to 1995 Rugby League 'scouts' came to lure top players away, with suitcases full of fivers dramatically flipped open under the wide eyes of their prey. Though they have hidden their feelings and wished the emigrants good luck, the Welsh have always loathed and abhorred the northern Englishmen who made mercenaries out of the grass-root idols. In the very early days, especially, scouts and agents entered South Wales at their peril. Two emissaries from Hull who visited Port Talbot bent on signing the clever scrum half Danny Jones were told to go back where they had come from or they would be mobbed. They left with jeers ringing in their ears. Feelings ran so strong at Llwynypia that Pressmen accused of helping northerners to sign Welshmen were threatened with being thrown down the nearest pit shaft. No wonder Jack Evans slipped from the village in disguise on his way to sign for Swinton.

This was the sensitive climate in which Arthur Gould announced, prematurely as it turned out, that he would retire from International Rugby. He was persuaded to return for the January 1897 game with England, but by then the seeds of a deep-seated dispute had been sown. His supporters, fronted by the *South Wales Argus* newspaper, had launched a testimonial Fund which would be used to buy a house for the twenty-seven-times capped centre for services to Welsh Rugby." Early in 1897 it stood at £650, and the WRU decided to contribute. Though they argued that the cricketer W.G. Grace had £10,000 'benefit' and yet retained amateur status, their action flew in the face of growing opposition to the scheme outside Wales, which led an anxious Welsh Athlete to comment: "Gould will be pushed from the game. We cannot afford to do without him. Put the funds in the bank until he retires."

In addition to the case of Dr Grace, England's administrators were disconcerted by the the disclosure that Richmond RFC had given their captain silver plate to the value of £50. This appeared to condone the principle that to reward special players was acceptable, and that the amount paid could thus be discretionary.

England honoured the 1897 fixture staged at Newport, which they lost by a record 11-0 margin, conceding three tries. *The Sportsman* of London wrote that "the winning forwards are the best Wales have ever turned out", and named Jack Evans of Llwynypia along with Arthur Boucher, Dick Hellings and Harry Packer for special praise. One of the Welsh eight – anonymously – waded into the English after the game: "They played a dirty, beastly game, kicking men on the floor and lying on the ball...without ever attempting to get up and play it in the manner they boast about".

Anxious to preserve a semblance of unity the International Board now took a stronger line. Wales was told to give Gould £50 worth of silver plate and donate the Fund's balance to charity. If this were not done, her fixtures for the foreseeable future would be scrubbed. When the Welsh demurred, Scotland and Ireland cancelled future fixtures with them. The RFU followed suit when Gould accepted the title deeds of a house bought with his testimonial fund – yet its members in the west country, and also the Barbarians, maintained contact with the big Welsh clubs.

Gwyn Nicholls had already been named in the Wales team to play Scotland in late January. Thus the frustration of him and his contemporaries at the cancellation of International matches can well be imagined. They just wanted to play the game, at the highest level possible. Now the chance to compete against their peers in the other Home Countries had been taken away for reasons they found arcane and puzzling.

Not that Nicholls' commitment and application eased. On January 16 he played at Morriston, running out of deep defence to give Huzzey a scoring pass in the game in which Bert Winfield made his debut for Cardiff. Born in Nottingham, this talented full back was destined to become a close friend and International team-mate of Nicholls and go into business with him.

Three weeks later, when Cardiff avenged a November defeat at Moseley, Nicholls scored his first 'dream' try. Said the *South Wales Echo* report: "The Moseley men clustered thick but Gwyn Nicholls, setting off at full speed as he grabbed the ball, cleared his man wonderfully, trickily dodged the centres and set off down the field at a pace which defied the efforts of the Moseley defenders to get to him. It was a sensational run, almost the length of the field; and when the exciting race was over and Nicholls fell across the line the crowd went wild with excitement over the finest effort of the season..."

He could make an impact off the field also. Charles Arthur's book credits Huzzey with giving Cardiff a 9-7 win at St Helens with a try – disallowed by the referee. In Swansea's archives a home win is claimed. Questioned by reporters, Nicholls was testy: "When I passed to Huzzey," he snapped, "he was four yards out from the touchline [i.e., infield]. The touch-judge did not put up his flag and indicate 'no try' to the referee, Mr England, until someone in the crowd shouted at him to do so." In those days touch judges were, ideally but not invariably, neutral. Each side supplied one.

Cardiff's season cannot be said to have petered out, finishing with nine straight wins. But February and March lacked the oxygen of what are now called Test matches to make the blood race. International players and spectators alike would have experienced a feeling of anti-climax. For Gwyn Nicholls it was relieved in the close season by the invitation from club skipper Selwyn Biggs to serve as his vice captain the following winter.

This presaged a first taste of responsibility. The marshalling of a three quarter line made it imperative to comprehend totally what was being aimed at and how it could be achieved. From his later writings, it seems that the ambition to be a director of combined attacks was what prompted Gwyn to think through and lay down basic principles that had not, as far as can be established, been articulated before.

Sometimes he would need to re-align conventional advice. For example, in an essay published in E.H.D. Sewell's *Rugby Football Up To Date* (1921) he recalls that midfield players were always exhorted to run 'straight' – which he had initially interpreted as 'parallel to the touchline'. This, he soon decided, was not realistic, since it carried a player into a bunch of opposing forwards or into the clutches of a back cutting across to help the defence: "Such advice... was first given when individualism was the greatest asset" – a throwaway line which is the closest he ever came to publicly criticising Arthur Gould.

So what was the Nicholls method? He crystallised it in his slim volume *The Modern Rugby Game* (whose publication date is uncertain but was probably 1908). What it amounted to was running a diagonal course towards the opening between the two opposing centres so as to commit one of them and distract the other: "In this way you invariably 'draw' a man and thus leave your co-centre and his wing with only one defender to contend with." To us in modern times, this was to state the obvious; but Nicholls' use of quotation marks indicates that 'drawing' a man was not at all a familiar or old-established technique. Its implications were worked out at practice sessions of the Cardiff back division.

In his essay of 1892 Arthur Budd had compared Rugby two decades earlier with the contemporary game: "Forwards, halves and three quarters played with a mutual irresponsibility, and without any notion of forming themselves into the links of the cleverly co-ordinated machine which a high-class team of the present day can manufacture," he recalled. "Passing was an unearthed treasure bequeathed to the discovery and elaboration of more modern philosophers."

Before the century was out, Nicholls had revealed scientific ways of exploiting the pass. The first half of Cardiff's 1897-98 season brought huge success: twenty victories, a draw, and one defeat, by Swansea. The All Whites scored three tries against one for Cardiff by newcomer W. Jones, nicknamed 'Pussy', from an opening made by Nicholls. The new vice captain, however, took stick for three abortive attempts to drop goals against Newport, who for the first time were to lose all four of what had now become a quartet of fixtures against Cardiff.

The trouble centring around Gould persisted; and the impasse over International matches involving Wales remained unresolved. For the moment pragmatism continued to rule at club level where, to the relief of both Welsh and English club treasurers, Cardiff, Newport, Swansea and other clubs maintained fixtures with the Devonports, the Moseleys, the Bristols and the Blackheaths (though a blanket of December fog forced the abandonment of Cardiff's game at the Rectory Field).

'Monkey' Gould himself cannot be said to have contributed to the resolution of the dispute. His nickname derived from a boyhood habit of swinging from the branches of trees; it could equally have sprung from his mischievous nature. For example, he baited the RFU by refereeing a match at Plymouth where he afterwards complimented the players on their discipline and acceptance of his decisions. Asked about the dispute over his Testimonial he told reporters, "It is a source of great anxiety to me."

On Boxing Day he accepted an invitation from Bristol to play for them, thereby raising fears about a breakaway from the RFU by its members in the west – as if the northern secession were not a grave enough development. "Bristol will side with Wales", thundered the west country Press. A 'Gloucester correspondent' wrote to the *Western Mail*: "Everyone here is anxious to avoid the splitting up of the Union, but if division should take place the natural instinct of self-preservation will force our clubs to join hands with Wales" ...language that uncannily presages disputes in our time a century later.

The influential *Sporting Life* now appealed to the IB to bury the hatchet and allow Wales to resume International matches. The newspaper feared that if denied such contests Wales would form a domestic League which would damage west country and Midlands clubs; the threat loomed larger after being sanctioned at a meeting of Welsh clubs called by the WRU.

The *Western Mail* chimed in, printing a version of an alleged interview between one of its writers and an un-named member of the RFU asking for information: "Has Gould absolutely retired?" "Yes, absolutely." "Give him the money, then. That's the end of it." "He might not be able to referee, or go on a committee." "That's rot. That'll soon die down."

English attitudes were mellowing, and it was now clear that the International Board, supported by the RFU, would permit and recommend the resumption of International fixtures if Wales asked to be re-admitted to competition and accepted the ineligibility of Gould for International games. These terms were met when the Secretary Walter Rees wrote the necessary letter. It was terse; but ultimately compliant.

This was no storm in a tea-cup. It threw into relief anomalies in the administration of Rugby which would again become apparent during the century to come. Do Unions, or their constituent clubs, have the last word on how to organise top-level Rugby football and its competitions? Is it a Union's sole job to oversee the on-field playing of Rugby as a game? Or does it have a right and a duty to determine, and rule on, the ethics of a growing spectator sport – and be obeyed? What sort of obligations do players owe clubs, country, team-mates and spectators? It would take nearly another hundred years for the game to go 'open'; and even now not all these questions have been satisfactorily answered.

As for 'Monkey' Gould, in response to the WRU's request he now bade farewell to International Rugby with twenty-seven caps to his name. However, he turned out for Newport until the 1898-99 season before retiring at 35 to spend some seasons refereeing. He died in 1919.

Six

The town of Cardiff was buzzing with energy and consumed with ambition. Underpinning a palpable feel-good factor was undreamed-of commercial success. Coal exports reached some eight million tons by 1898 when sales brochures listed two hundred varieties of coal from Abercarn Black Vein to Wyndham Red Ash. A prestige publication declared: "The countless pits belt out unceasingly a supply of fuel; the black diamonds are fed to the great engines of war and the leviathans of commerce that plough the waves of the Seven Seas. Where fire is wanted, there the Welsh coals go."

Arrogance was in the air too, as fortunes were made and honours bestowed on what was to become dubbed the 'City of Dreadful Knights.' A 'Cardiff Exhibition' was dreamed up to include cycle racing (then a very popular spectator sport), a 'street of all nations', a Welsh Fair, an Indian bazaar and a stall selling Welsh Whisky from a Frongoch, Bala, distillery "as supplied to HM the Queen". The Exhibition's Nine-a-Side Rugby tournament acquired enhanced prestige from the entry of a Cardiff IX skippered by Gwyn Nicholls which, heavily points-handicapped, lost to Roath Dolphins.

This extravaganza was staged on open ground known as Cathays, just north of Lord Bute's Castle. Coincidentally the Council was seeking a location at which a Town Hall more in keeping with Cardiff's new importance could be built. After sites at 'Temperance Town' and Adamsdown had been considered and rejected, negotiations began with the Bute estate, resulting in the acquisition of fifty-eight acres at Cathays for £160,000. A competition to design municipal buildings and law courts was won by a London firm, Lanchester, Steward and Rickards, an outcome which the *Western Mail* dismissed as 'disappointing'. Posterity has disagreed.

The Rugby fraternity's mood could not have been more upbeat. Although some dark clouds made progress hard to plan with certainty, the sport in Wales had not stood still. While thinkers like Nicholls were formulating new game-ploys and techniques, behind-the-scenes workers were attending to the game's infrastructure. At Cardiff Arms Park £1,055 had been spent on an elaborate drainage scheme for the pitch. The grandstand erected in 1885 on the south side of the ground was about to be extended; beneath it were put rooms where players' blazers and sweaters could be hung during games. Hitherto, garments had simply been handed to spectators willing to guard them.

But provision of fully equipped changing areas with baths would have to wait for the next century. The players of Cardiff and Wales, and their opponents, had been using the Queens Hotel, whose back door opened onto Westgate Street. Sid Nicholls was now running the Grand Hotel two hundred yards away and, doubtless persuaded by their committeeman, Cardiff RFC chose his premises in which to set up what the Press described as 'headquarters'. Presumably the club vice captain, Nicholls minor, looked after his team-mates well.

And now, on February 28 1898, the WRU announced that fences had been mended and their hat was back in the ring. Ireland would host Wales in March, while it was hoped that England could be met at Blackheath in April. Nicholls took in a club fixture or two, and used a Glamorgan game against Yorkshire for match practice before being named in the XV to play Ireland at the County Limerick Cricket and Lawn Tennis Club. His co-centre was to be 'Pussy' Jones, while the choice of another club colleague Viv Huzzey on the wing also gave him satisfaction. Already a baseball International, this twenty-two year old licensee had become a deadly finisher averaging twenty tries a year.

Travel to Ireland from Wales was not the one-hour joy-ride by jet that it is today. Leaving Cardiff station at half past nine in the morning the 1898 Welsh party went by train via Pontypool, Shrewsbury and the North Wales coast to Holyhead. Here they boarded the 3.30 pm ferry for a turbulent crossing into a strong headwind. The Hotel Metropole in Dublin was their Friday night base, where the IRU reported that Wales' objection on the grounds of inexperience to the appointment of Scot-

land's Graham Findlay as referee had been upheld. A.J. Turnbull of Hawick would control the game.

After bacon, eggs and coffee on the Saturday morning a train
journey of nearly three hours to the south-west still awaited the
Welsh players. All in all, this was a far-from-propitious re-entry
route after a twelve month absence from top-flight International
Rugby.

Though the Irish had sided with England and Scotland against
Wales during the crisis there could be no doubt of their genuine
delight at the renewal of fixtures with the latter nation. For
Munster in particular this was to be a first taste of International
Rugby, and the Province went out of its way to ensure a successful afternoon. Nicholls later wrote of the "fireworks, brass bands
and whirros of what appeared to be the whole populace of
Limerick" which greeted the Welshmen's arrival, with gaudy
marquees and temporary seating erected at the field. "This is the
cradle of Irish Rugby," wrote a local journalist in the Saturday
morning paper. "Our forwards are archetypically Irish; their
loose rushes are like a cavalry charge". Later part of the grandstand collapsed, and a spectator died; but news of the fatality did
not reach the players, and the match went uninterrupted.

Billy Bancroft succeeded Gould as captain on his twenty-
third appearance for Wales, converting a try by the
coal-trimmer from Cardiff Docks, Tom Dobson, to give Wales
a half time lead. The visitors built on this success when Nicholls
sent Huzzey in for a try that Bancroft was unable to convert,
but the skipper put the game beyond Ireland's reach with a late
penalty. 'Shamrock' wrote in *Athletic News* that he had never
seen a better demonstration of full back play.

Announcing Wales' XV for the next game, WRU secretary
Walter Rees stated that the Scots had declined to make a date
available for a match with Wales before 1899 (when their faces
were to be well and truly smeared with egg). England, however,
were agreeable to re-establishing a working relationship at
Blackheath on April 2. Noting that Wales had dropped Pontymister's Joe Booth in order to restore David Evans of Penygraig,
match previews in the English Press betrayed apprehension that

forwards from Evans's valley, and others, were men to be reckoned with. Early examples began to be published of a technique which was to become commonplace in the print and broadcast media: that of 'talking down' the opposition. Thus the *Sporting Life* of March 1898: "Welsh Rugby suffers from periodic attacks of hallucination for example, that the Rhondda forward is a man of superhuman power. When they appear at the Rectory field the Welsh pack will find they are giving away a great deal in the matter of weight and muscle." On this occasion, too right. A 20,000 crowd revelled in England's revenge for 1897, and although the Welsh led into the last quarter the New Zealand-bred wing Ernest Fookes scored two tries to kill them off. Fifteen rancorous months had ended gloomily for Wales.

If one criterion of sporting 'greatness' is the ability to exert innovative influence, the other vital one concerns the capacity to achieve victories consistently. This was what Gwyn Nicholls was now able to do with Cardiff, whose captain he had become for the 1898-99 season. Besides leading the Blue and Blacks to twenty-two victories and three draws out of twenty-eight games, he drew praise from the generally restrained Charles Arthur: "Nicholls' form this season was probably the best he has ever shown in all his long and brilliant football career". People evidently thought of him now as an old-established, 'ever-present'; yet that career was not much more than five years old

His team's unbeaten record lasted only until the third game and defeat at Neath; but thereafter only Gloucester and Newport, with home advantage, lowered its colours. The captain's form was tremendous. He scored twice against Bristol. He opened the scoring against Newport with a brilliant single-handed try: "showing infinite cleverness, dash and determination," wrote the Press. After his try in Cardiff's 3-3 draw at St Helens a Swansea journalist observed, "One opportunity seems to come his way in every match, and I cannot remember when he failed to use it. As a defender he is like a centre half in Association Football – always able to look after an attack that comes down the middle, in addition falling back and relieving threats on either right or left wing."

The club's three quarter line performed superbly under Nicholls' guidance. Co-centre 'Pussy' Jones scored nine tries, while wing Huzzey was sent in eighteen times by the captain, who would total sixteen tries himself. Gloucestershire, the county of his birth, mindful of his Westbury roots chose him twice during the season in what seem to have been fairly pedestrian games – including a 0-0 draw with Devon.

In Wales, the nation was girding itself for the annual tussle with England, which would return to its traditional month, January, in 1899 and take place at Swansea. Although the *Saeson* led the series 11-3, and had been cruelly superior in 1898, Wales were steadily cultivating a 'David' mentality which told them that Goliaths were there to be overthrown.

The ever-strengthening hold exercised by the Game on the Welsh imagination was acknowledged in enhanced Press coverage and build-up. Distinguished scholars, usually content to pontificate in the columns of the popular Press on the origins of Celtic words and phrases, found themselves spellbound by the new sporting magic gripping the south, and impelled to write about it. Such a figure was 'Morien', an Archdruid who contributed to the *Western Mail*. Here is his description of the media of the day in action at an International match: "Behind me sat, ranged along a long, narrow table, fifty or sixty journalists. Further back was a Grand Stand flanked on both sides by seething multitudes. On opposite sides of the field were solid rows of people forty lines deep and extending at least a distance of 200 yards...It was interesting to watch the army of nimble-fingered shorthand writers jotting down the incidents of the game. With raised face and pencils at the ready they all gazed with earnestness at the contending athletes as if a Waterloo were being fought before them."

Back at the subs' tables the efforts of the location reporters were being ever more steadfastly supported by page designers and graphic artists. A *South Wales Daily News* chart portrayed a Rugby pitch with the thirty players' names printed in their positions.

Today's media may have made it more vivid, but the excitement and expectation that accompanies the start of Rugby's European championship season can scarcely be more intense in our own day than was the case a century ago. The air is full of threat and counter-threat, boast and counter-blast, and an all-pervading tension. Hope is dominant in the minds of players and spectators alike.

At the outset of 1899 confidence east of the Severn was unusually buoyant. Largely, it would seem, this sprang from the memory of England's spectacular victory the previous spring. Said the *Sporting Life*, "We predict that England will romp through the forwards, rout their opponents, and spoil the pet Welsh game." To be sure, Wales were putting out seven new caps for this encounter at Swansea – but so were the visitors, only five of whose side had been in the big win at Blackheath a year earlier. Hence from this distance there seems no valid reason for the blind confidence of the England camp. Their personnel trickled into Swansea during the evening of January 6 from locations as diffuse as Devonport, Gloucester, Blackheath, Cambridge, Hartlepool and Aspatria.

The ever-inventive Welsh had stolen a march on their opponents. On the previous Wednesday they had gathered at Cardiff Arms Park for what would today be called a squad session in which, explained 'Old Stager', they could get some knowledge of each other's "peculiarities in style". There can be no doubt that this preparation paid off, beginning with astute decisions taken frequently during the game by the captain, Bancroft, to scrummage instead of fruitlessly contesting lines-out against taller opponents.

On the Saturday morning Swansea Bay was spray-flecked, and towards noon a stony January sky threw down some sleet flurries onto the popular terrace, which had begun filling up some three hours before kick-off time. In those days many onlookers posted themselves on the cycling embankment formed of cinders, traces of which can still be seen at the Mumbles end of the ground. Estimates of the attendance vary, but in his history of English International Rugby John Griffiths puts it as high as 25,000. In addition faces were pressed to the windows of houses which stood, and still stand, overlooking the arena.

Whipped to a frenzy by pack-leader John Daniell, England made their opponents cling on for dear life in the first quarter, when the brave tackling of bigger attackers by the ten-stone newcomers Willie Llewellyn and Reggie Skrimshire was applauded by reporters. But, once their offensive was weathered, the visitors were undermined by hesitancy and indecision. Before the interval Llewellyn scored twice in what was to be England's biggest-ever defeat, and ran in two more tries in the second half to set a record which was equalled but still unsurpassed a century later. In the course of a 'masterful' display Nicholls sent Huzzey in for the other two tries in a 26-3 victory, to which the little James brothers of Swansea had contributed cleverly at half back.

The Rugby correspondent of the *Sunday Special* wrote, "That the England line would be crossed six times must have been beyond the anticipation of even the most enthusiastic believer in the perfection to which the Welsh have brought the four three-quarter game." Some English writers, no doubt regretting their pre-match grandiloquence, put a figurative boot into their team, saying that it had been humiliated and disgraced. Other Press comments are also down to chagrin and pure disbelief. "Not so much a loss; what our American friends would call a landslide," groaned the *Daily Graphic*. The *Daily Mail* criticised England's methods as dated and haphazard. The *Morning Leader* stated that there was little left to the credit of English football – its reporter had seen "a heavy Englishman unnecessarily flinging down little Evan James." The paper carried what was probably the most perceptive observation on the result: "Wales have been showing since 1893 how scientific methods can overcome physical force." True, the Welsh were now headed for greatness. They had a long way yet to climb, however – though the two defeats suffered in the remaining Championship games perhaps owed less to their own shortcomings than to the black comedy of errors in which the Scots were now to play an involuntary lead.

The Secretary of the Scottish Rugby Union was J.A. Smith. During the Gould affair his attitude had been hawkish, and it is certain that the Scots were not only prime movers in persuading the IB to outlaw the Welsh in 1897 but also dragged their heels and made no strong attempt under Smith to resume fixtures with them during the 1898 season. Welsh newspapers waxed indignant about him: "Why this little individual should rule the roost passes people's comprehension."

However, opinion north of Hadrian's Wall was tending to the view that for the time being the Welsh had become greater crowd-pullers than England. Hence, having decided to abandon Raeburn Place as their venue for home games, the Scots chose 28 January 1898, and the match with Wales, for the opening of their new out-of-town stadium at Inverleith. But Mr Smith was about to get his come-uppance.

On 27 January the WRU Secretary Walter Rees received an early-morning telegram from the SRU stating that Inverleith was "frozen like steel", notifying the Welsh of a postponement, and suggesting the following Saturday, 4 February, for the match. But the frost did not relent; nor was there a thaw before the next date offered, the 11th. The 18th was not a possibility since Scotland were to play Ireland – who duly arrived during a brief mild spell and opened Inverleith with a 9-3 victory.

The SRU now proposed 25 February for the Welsh visit, but incredibly the elements closed in again and Mr Smith had to request a fourth postponement. If he was under fire in Edinburgh, this was nothing to the pressure Walter Rees was enduring from the major Welsh clubs, who did not know if their top players were coming or going; Cardiff, for example, had to grant leave of absence to Nicholls, Huzzey and three others for four Saturdays – all for nothing. In addition, the February weather in Wales was sunlit and balmy, leading Welsh sceptics to wonder if the Scots' main concern was to prevent the playing surface of their precious new stadium from being cut up.

Mr Smith's agony finally ended on 4 March at the fifth time of asking when 30,000 spectators saw Wales humbled 21-10. Nicholls had been hurt in his club's game against Newport a week earlier and, despite encouragement from the club doctor, probably played against his own better judgement – remember, he was still only an impetuous twenty-five years old. The *Athletic News* stated bluntly that "Nicholls was not fit."

Now, again, Wales' international campaign was to end in devastating anti-climax. If Scotland had been shame-faced in February, March brought disgrace for the WRU at Cardiff where a 30,000 gate was anticipated.

Some 1,200 excited Irishmen had sailed from Dunlaoghaire on board the ferry *Innisfallen*, all set to cheer their heroes on to a third win of the season and a Triple Crown. Although, to their huge disappointment, fog delayed the voyage by seven and a half hours they still reached Cardiff soon enough to join the throngs of fellow-countrymen celebrating victory. Having heard about the day's events at Cardiff Arms Park they may have felt relief not to have made it to the match.

After a perimeter fence gave way before the weight of late-comers seeking entry, the kick-off was put back to allow the sixty policemen on duty to restore order. But no sooner did they quieten one area than trouble flared elsewhere. There was anger in the enclosure as reserved seats were seized. Fresh waves of spectators swarmed up walls along Westgate Street and into the arena, lifting the crush to an estimated 40,000. The police abandoned attempts to keep gate-crashers at bay in favour of protecting the field of play. This proved beyond them, and the interval lasted fifteen minutes while the crowds were pushed back. Even so, the second half took place with onlookers ranged along the touch-lines within a foot of the pitch.

Gwyn Nicholls himself spoke of "a hundred or more on the grandstand roof. Trees were occupied, and walls and adjacent buildings were black with people...Billy Bancroft had his ribs broken through falling amidst the crowd." Here Nicholls was perhaps being diplomatic; Press reports averred that "Bancroft was obliged to leave the field with a cracked rib, having been late-tackled as he chased a kick ahead." Police Sergeant Bobby Brice, a powerful Aberavon forward who was in the Wales back row that day, later wrote, Bancroft was thrown heavily by Mike Ryan, the Irish 'Terror' and was injured badly, fracturing his ribs."

Brice's comments, contained in an article written for a commemorative programme in 1924, suggest that anger in the crowd at the incident had led to the first of the numerous pitch invasions. The players certainly seem to have been engaged for fully two hours, delays often occurring before lines-out where spectators were on the pitch. Miraculously, there were no fatalities.

On assuming the captaincy after Bancroft's departure, Nicholls had to make an immediate judgement on who should become the replacement full back. Though he would be criticised later for nominating Brice (who occasionally played full back for his Police XV), the Welsh pack was on top at the time and Nicholls must have reasoned that this momentum could be kept up. Doran, however, got a vital try – the sole score – for Ireland, who finished stronger than their fourteen opponents. The WRU was quick to stifle a rumour which threatened to spread during the evening that Bancroft had died of his injury. The captain was certainly in great pain until the Monday, but his life was never in danger. He would be back in charge next season, and was to win another six caps. Even in pain he was arguably better off in a sick bay than on the streets of Cardiff that night, where Welsh gloom and Irish glee were a volatile cocktail. Men caroused, fought, vomited, broke windows, caused alarm to horses pulling cabs and shouted raucously at police officers attempting to keep order. Nonconformity and Rugby football were uneasy bedfellows in southern Wales, and now *Y Tyst*, a denominational newspaper published by the Congregationalists, gorged itself on the sinfulness reported by its Man in South Wales: "The truth is there has never been witnessed in Cardiff in the memory of anyone now living such an exhibition of bestiality [*bwystfileiddiwch*] and the lower passions of human nature as were seen on Saturday. Streets were thronged until a late hour with the classes that make up the rubbish of the Valleys and South Wales."

Allowing for such malign and doubtless calculated hyperbole, the afternoon and evening on the banks of the Taff had nonetheless showed that for much of the coming century the control and safety of crowds attending big sporting events were questions needing to be addressed by administrators and keepers of the peace. In a decade's time the day of the super-stadium would arrive, and every lesson learned at venues like Cardiff Arms Park was valuable.

His assumption of the captaincy after Bancroft left the field nursing his ribs was a clear indication of the command status in Welsh Rugby now possessed by Gwyn Nicholls. It also pointed to him as his country's next leader once Bancroft called it a day. Although he would never enjoy public speaking, he was mastering the art of talking men into a game, and through it. The *Morning Leader*'s observation concerning the "scientific methods" of the Welsh were almost entirely down to his blueprint about ball transference, which was directed not only at three quarters and half backs but at forwards too.

Thus his influence on Welsh attacking play was now profound. The example he set in defence, however, should not be forgotten. E.H.D. Sewell wrote of his "superb" skills whether against a forward rush or a single advancing opponent. Surely he had become the most complete player yet thrown up by Rugby football.

Seven

Rising 25, Gwyn Nicholls could point to an impressive track record in the Rugby game. The holder of eight caps, he was accepted by both the Press and the public in Wales as one who had built on the Welsh style behind the scrum pioneered by Hancock and Gould. At club level Cardiff RFC had performed outstandingly in his first year as its captain; it had been noted by officials and fans alike that their distinguished skipper was not too proud to play for the Second XV if the need arose. When they came to choose a leader to take the club into the twentieth century, members had no hesitation in re-electing Nicholls, in his absence.

The previous January the *South Wales Daily News* had revealed the Welsh centre's acceptance of an invitation to join the British party which would tour Australia in the summer. The players had been selected by Mark Mullineux, the then scrum half of the Blackheath Rugby Football Club. By now a Reverend gentleman, he had been in the 1895 Cambridge University XV which held Cardiff to a 3-3 draw. On that November day Nicholls had all but scored a winning try for the visitors, and his calibre had not gone unremarked.

As it turned out, he would be the only Welsh representative to travel. Three Irishmen and three Scots were included, with fourteen Englishmen forming a majority. Many of these personnel were from professional, monied families, but no evidence survives to indicate how young Nicholls was able to afford a trip that would have threatened to be expensive. By this time, however, his father Hartley was installed in the substantial property in Cathedral Road, while big brother Sid was running the Grand Hotel; the two may have decided – and possessed the financial means – to subsidise the young man on what promised to be the trip of a lifetime: an enriching experience.

A second theory is offered by Malcolm Pearce, whose father

Ewart headed the firm of accountants which later dealt with Nicholls' financial affairs. He names a local businessman, J.T. Morgan, who would later provide financial assistance to Nicholls and Bert Winfield when they set up their laundry business after the turn of the century. A fervent admirer of the Cardiff skipper, Morgan may have chipped in with the funds which made it possible for the Mullineux invitation to be accepted. Nicholls' seniority on tour would be recognised by his appointment as a selector.

The party left Charing Cross railway station at 11 a.m. on 9 May 1899, co-incidentally the day on which Australia's cricketers began a tour of England at Crystal Palace (and got Jessop out for six). Its crates of kit included a bright playing strip comprising red, white and blue hooped jerseys, dark blue shorts, and blue stockings with red and white tops. Team caps were maroon, and bore kangaroo motifs. To formal functions Mullineux's men were to wear smart navy blazers, complete with a breast-pocket badge reading "The Anglo-Australian Rugby Football Team". Nicholls doubtless wore it with a good grace; but when hosts at receptions welcomed "the tourists from England, Scotland and Ireland" he insisted that his team-mates roar in unison, "And Wales!"

The British (the Home Countries on tour would not be known as 'Lions' until 1930) crossed the Channel and travelled through France to the port of Marseilles. Here they boarded the P&O liner *Oriana* for a five week voyage terminating at Adelaide. The final lap was overland again to Sydney, in good time for the first fixture on June 14. The tour was expected to finish so that members could return soon enough to participate in the opening of the new season back home.

The Monmouthshire Chartist John Frost had sad and painful memories of his years as a deported criminal doing hard labour in Tasmania midway through the nineteenth century. But by 1899 Australia had shed its role as a penal colony. Suddenly, after long dependence upon subsidies from the mother country, the 1851 discovery of gold in Victoria and New South Wales transformed the Continent's economic viability and prospects.

Next came wool production: the volume exported to the UK rose from 39 million pounds in 1850 to 300 million by 1880 –

part of that same trend in Britain which had persuaded the Nicholls family to leave the land. Australia's population, too, soared into the millions from the 350,000 at which it stood in mid century. Cities like Melbourne and Sydney took shape. There came the emergence of New South Wales, Victoria, South Australia and Queensland as powerful self-governing colonies which, two years after Gwyn Nicholls' visit, would unite to form a Commonwealth.

As a rule, first and second generation colonials cherish and nurture the mother country's values and way of life. Certainly a handling code of football was something the first settlers took with them from the Home Country. The historian Tom Hickie speculates in his history of the game in Australia *They Ran with the Ball* that some fixtures may have been played as early as the 1840s. But by now, just over a century since Captain Cook had hoisted the Union flag at Botany Bay, expatriates were beginning to prefer doing their own sporting thing. It disturbed the English establishment that Victorians, for example, were developing 'Australian Rules' football, a Gaelic variant on the handling game brought in by Irish expatriates.

Further, fans were acquiring a taste for 13-a-side professional Rugby – a code which had brought about the grievous amputation of many distinguished northern clubs from England's ruling body. The RFU was committed to upholding an amateur ethic; no wonder Mullineux was given every encouragement to go to the Antipodes and, by the quality of his side's play, maintain the Australian public's broad preference for the 15-a-side amateur game.

All was, in no way, lost. The enthusiasm that existed for Rugby Union Down Under was glowingly reflected in the Press, with newspapers like Sydney's *Sunday Times* carrying page upon page of Rugby previews, match reports and 'colour' pieces throughout the tour. It was also manifested in the parading of civic pride which, as is well known by every player who has ever toured, can be wearisome and tedious. In 1931, approving the decision of the Springboks in Britain to curtail attendance at receptions, Gwyn Nicholls recalled in print: "...and wisely so. From my own experience there is a great risk, if not of being actually killed by kindness, of playing form being seriously affected by excessive hospitality. I recollect our arrival at Melbourne where, besides being officially welcomed by the entertaining Union, we were received by five other bodies in as many hours. We travelled overnight to the town where we were to play our first fixture, arriving at seven a.m. – when we found the municipal fathers awaiting our arrival, for the inevitable reception."

That first town was Goulburn, where the British opened their account by beating a scratch XV called Central Southern. Since their arrival at Adelaide there had been non-stop rainfall, so that a winning margin of 11-3 was satisfactory in the mud. Nicholls played, in conditions that must have reminded him of Cardiff.

The tourists were in good heart as they travelled the final 100 miles north-east to Sydney where the serious exchanges would start with a match against New South Wales. They practised hard on the Friday, before visiting the great cricket enclosure which was to stage the game. Pools of water lay on the playing surface. But Saturday dawned crisp and sunny, the clouds disappeared, and a crowd of 30,000 was tempted to come and enjoy the big match: "Ladies predominated in the stands, where the bright, variegated colouring of the gowning and millinery made a picture of great beauty."

Early enthusiasm for the game in Australia had been generated by the military, and in particular its officer class which used matches to keep the troops fit. The process was carried forward by civilian settlers from northern England, Wales and the west of England. They ensured that the game took root and flourished in these 'southern colonies' by forming clubs wherever townships took shape. Next came the formation of Unions, the first and second being New South Wales (1874) and Queensland (1882) who developed a fierce and mutually beneficial rivalry. The two States hosted New Zealand sides in 1884, 1893 and 1897, and a first British team in 1888. The tourists of the latter year went unbeaten through the sixteen fixtures they undertook in Australia, squeezed between two spells in New Zealand. Now, in 1899, no New Zealand matches would interrupt progress; while for the first time there would be International matches between the British and 'all-Australia'. First, though, came a demanding game against 'the Welshmen' (part of the terminology employed by the Press when alluding to New South Wales). This made it clear that the four Tests would not be a pushover.

After a tenth minute breather when 'God Save the Queen' was played to mark the – late – arrival at the ground of the Governor, Earl Beauchamp, the British controlled the first half and took the lead at 30 minutes through a goal from a mark by Martelli, the Dubliner at full back. 'The Welshmen' spent the third quarter in control, but thanks to good defence they were held to a single try by five-eighth 'Ginger' Ward. The tourists' winning margin was 4-3.

Observers wrote that Gwyn Nicholls enjoyed his usual busy, thrustful afternoon, colliding with the referee at one stage on the point of crossing for a try. Nor did the Australian Press overlook his defensive qualities. Crediting him with having prevented two tries the *Sunday Times* commented, "Nicholls proved himself an ubiquitous, india-rubber sort of defender." Quite soon, then, he was beginning to be identified as both the team's danger-man and the player crowds loved to watch. Having seen him in action for a second time *Telegraph* critic made up his mind: "Nicholls is the great player of the side. He's a wonder on defence, worth two or three ordinary men." In the same edition of the newspaper the Cardiffian was also pen-pictured as: "clean-limbed and appearing to possess intuitively quick judgement. This leads to his invariably doing the right thing either in attack or defence.... He is beyond question quite an exceptional defender and, unlike most brilliant players, is not above performing the low, diving tackle when such a thing is necessary to save his side." On the following Tuesday, however, Mullineux' men struggled to beat a Sydney club side 8-5 and were accused by more than one Pressman of being out of condition.

If probably true, this was arguably unfair. It was still only days since their arrival at Adelaide after a six-week sea voyage during which training amounted to little more than physical jerks. Since disembarking the tourists had travelled a further 2,000 miles across south east Australia, for much of the time cooped up in spartan railway carriages. Secondly Nicholls was quoted as finding the climate strange: either burning hot, or uncomfortably damp and humid. Alarming electrical storms with brief torrential rain could interrupt training without warning; playing surfaces, both for matches and training, could be as hard as iron and, a mere day later, soggy and pudding-like.

On Saturday 24 June, however, a mere fortnight after disembarking, the British were confronted with a First Test. Thoroughly fired-up, their opponents would be taking the field for the first time as a National XV comprising nine New South Welshmen and six Queenslanders, in the process announcing Australia's arrival as an ambitious force in world Rugby. Although the match was to be refereed by a Kiwi, Mr W.G. Garrard of Canterbury, and the relationship between his country and the Australians was not unfriendly, the New Zealanders chose this same weekend to rule out a proposal emanating from Sydney to set up an 'Australasian' Rugby Union as the region's ruling body.

On the morning of the game the *Sydney Herald* carried a precious throwaway line about a skill possessed by Gwyn Nicholls which was seldom, if ever, alluded to by reporters based in the Home Countries. It was in the context of a preview in which a columnist calling himself 'The Arrow' was assessing the capability of Australia's chosen five eighth Ward, who had played and scored against the tourists a week earlier for New South Wales. Of that game the writer speculated that the tourists would have been more sorely pressed "...had Ward punted (as Nicholls often did) over the opposition three quarter line." The remark in parenthesis completes the set, so to speak, of Nicholls' array of talents. His running, handling, passing, tackling, line kicking and drop kicking are all cited by critics as being of the very highest order. Now a chance remark by an Australian onlooker indicates that the Welshman was used to being closely marked by opposing three quarter lines which lay up in defence – and well knew how to turn them by chipping over their heads. To a midfield player this is a basic skill; but journalists writing about Nicholls tend to highlight his more spectacular contributions to the action.

To encourage the Australians, a stridently partisan 30,000 spectators were expected at the Sydney Cricket Ground. Further, some key players in the tour party were on the injured list including A.B. Timms, a Scottish centre of Australian origin, whose partnership with Nicholls promised to become highly effective. Despite such handicaps, Mullineux' team went well until the final ten minutes of the game. Alexander Kelly scored the only try of the first half for the home team, but some minutes after the break the tourists drew level through a first International try by Gwyn Nicholls, who had taken the field with a heavy cold. It rounded off a sensational move by the British which included seven passes, and in which the Welsh star handled twice before using great strength to force his way across the line

The game looked certain to be drawn until ten minutes from time, when 'Lonnie' (short for Alonzo) Spragg, a wing, and the five eighth 'Poley' Evans scored for Australia, two conversions by the former extending the victory to 13-3. "We may congratulate ourselves," said selector F.C. Lea modestly at the post-match dinner that evening. Pointedly one of his colleagues, Dr Neill, observed that "the only regret arose from New Zealand's failure to assist making the winning team an Australasian one". But such considerations did not diminish the revelry that evening at the Empire Hotel, the home side's HQ, where "speech-making was punctuated by war-cries of aboriginal origin." Said the Governor, "This was a celebration of the most conspicuous triumph ever gained by an Australian XV on a Rugby field." The British kept their own counsel, joined in the fun – and quietly resolved to do better next time.

They were still not at a peak; and though comfortable winners over Toowoomba in their first match in Queensland they failed, against all expectations, to beat the state side who rose to the occasion and emerged victorious by 11-3. However, the last fifteen matches on tour would bring only one more defeat. As Gwyn Nicholls was to write later, the tour contained not a single dull moment and he retained only the happiest memories of games against smaller Queensland communities like Bundaberg and Rockhampton. Though outlandish, and connected to civilisation only tenuously by a recently-completed railroad, such townships lay in countryside of great natural beauty on a coastal plain between the rainforests and the Great Barrier Reef. Farming was the dominant industry, with sugar cane developing as an important cash-crop.

The hospitality extended by public bodies and individuals alike was generous and imaginative. One of the tour's most memorable outings took place at Brisbane whose city fathers escorted the visitors on a fifteen-mile excursion up the Condamine River in hot weather. A picnic lunch was accompanied by only one or two – inevitable – speeches. On another day the tourists were taken on a wallaby 'drive', or cull.

A crowd of 15,000 took trains, buses and cabs to the Exhibition Ground, Brisbane, for the Second Test. The British were without the injured Matthew Mullineux, for whom the English forward Moxham Stout deputised as captain. Timms, however, was fit and could be paired with Nicholls at centre where they presented their opposite numbers with big problems which were admiringly reported in the Brisbane Press. The Welsh star made breaks which led to two tries before scoring a third, decisive one himself beneath the bar after an Australian handling error. Said the *Daily Telegraph* reporter, "Nicholls played the best game on the pitch...his line-kicking was magni-ficent." An 11-0 win squared the series before the tourists travelled south again to Armidale where another tough game awaited them against New England. They snatched the result by 6-4, thus avenging their earlier 11-5 defeat by New South Wales. Here Nicholls heard how the colony acquired its name. It appears that one of the early settlers hailed from the area around Margam in west Glamorgan. The Australian coast flanking Sydney's magnificent harbour put him in mind of the terrain back home – a narrow coastal plain back-dropped by a steep escarpment of low hills. It was not quite 'south Wales', but it could justifiably claim to be 'New' south Wales.

The visitors now suffered an 8-5 reverse at the hands of the Metropolitan RFC before Australia were met again, in what was beyond doubt the tour's most enthralling contest. Oddly, the attendance was down from the 30,000 who had seen the First Test to just 15,000 despite excellent weather. Once more heavy rain had evaporated under warm sunshine, leaving just a few square yards that were greasy on the half way line.

The first half was level-pegging until its final moments. The crowd screamed excitement as Alfred Bucher, an Edinburgh Academical, kicked a loose ball behind the Australian three quarters and hared after it, hotly pursued by Sydney Miller who overtook him five yards from the goal line. Here, however, the New South Welshman essayed a fly hack that was meant to land on the cycle track beyond the dead-ball line. Instead, his complete miscue left Bucher with the simple task of flopping on the ball for a try converted by Adamson.

As the second half got under way Bucher was nearly sent in again by Nicholls: "Quick as lightning the crack Welsh three quarter disposed of the ball to Bucher, only for him to be halted at the Australian 25. Minutes later, however, the wing did succeed in scoring a second try, one which went unconverted.

Now, again, the excitement reached fever pitch as Bucher's opposite number Spragg scored and converted a try which closed the gap to 8-5, only for a combined move by the tourists to put the game out of the home team's reach. The *Sydney Herald* said, "Cookson passed to Nicholls, who ran in front of the opposing goal where he was confronted by Row and Spragg. Nicholls removed the latter from his road by feinting to pass before going straight for the line. Fearing a 'collar' he got in a clever pass to Timms, who scored.

Australia rallied briefly at the close when Spragg was awarded, and converted, a try against which the tourists appealed. They claimed that the scoring pass had been forward, but referee W.S. Corr held to his decision. The last kick of the game was a drop at goal by the Australian scrum half Ignatius O'Donnell, which drifted just wide. A crucial Test had been won by the tourists, who jumped for joy in the knowledge that they could not now lose the series.

Two more district sides were seen off before a final Test on 14 August in which the British side touched a late and impressive peak. Wrote one experienced Aussie hack, "The team simply played [sic] rings around their opponents. There was no aspect of the game in which they did not show to advantage...while their forward rushes were undeniable and their sprinters exhibited greater dash and pace". The tourists were kept at bay by Australia's first half display but once the British scrum half Adamson had opened the scoring with a try at the posts which he converted the result was not in doubt. Adamson soon majored a try by the speedy Bucher and built the winning score to 13-0 with a final penalty.

The home team were quick to acknowledge their defeat by a better side on the day. Hosting the post-match dinner J.J. Calvert, President of New South Wales RFU, light-heartedly blamed the heavy, greasy conditions for the margin of Australia's defeat adding, "We do not have any Ashes for you to take home – but you can have the mud". Regrettably the response, by the Rev Matthew Mullineux who had missed many of the tour's high-profile games through a succession of injuries, was far from being the most diplomatic ever made by a tour captain. Completely insensitive to the cordial, fare-thee-well atmosphere, he chose to lecture his men's opponents for alleged sharp practice during matches, offering them helpful hints on how to refine their game. Not surprisingly *The Telegraph* records that he "was subjected to some interruption during his speech". Significantly, Mullineux neither captained England on his return nor won a cap.

In contrast the lone Welshman in the party had earned tribute upon tribute for his skills and temperament and getting, consistently, the best Press of his career. The *Sydney Herald* noted that "even when charged by an opponent with unnecessary violence Nicholls has never once shown feeling or attempted in any way to retaliate". In the specialist publication *The Referee* a correspondent commented, "He came to us with a great reputation...the realisation was greater than the expectation...the Welshman is the greatest all-round player I have ever seen; he combines defending and attacking powers of an uncommonly high order."

In two short months Nicholls had enhanced the reputation forged back home and moved into world class. He had been the tour's leading scorer of tries. He had made them for others. He had prevented opponents from scoring. Further, because of Mullineux' unavailability for the last three Tests, he had also assumed tactical control behind the scrum.

The British were disappointed in only one respect. Since their arrival in Adelaide there had been speculation that they might play in New Zealand after their final games in Australia. The Press in Sydney had established that the 'English' players could afford the time to go on to Auckland and Canterbury to meet "the greatest exponents of Rugby in the hemisphere." This extra leg of the tour, however, was never embarked upon and a sly line in the Sydney *Daily Telegraph* of 25 July 1899 implies a reason. "The New Zealanders are admittedly the cleverest of Australasian footballers," wrote the correspondent. "The standard of football proficiency there, however, is not as high now as it has been, so that the possibility exists that the English would win there also".

Certainly, Australian Rugby men were sore that New Zealand would not join them to forge a very powerful southern hemisphere axis to compete against tourists from Home and thereby guarantee victory. The burden of the Sydney reporter's sideswipe, therefore, was that New Zealand could not stomach the prospect of defeat. In their book *100 Years of All Black Rugby* R.H. Chester and N.A.C. McMillan ignore the issue. This is odd, since it was to have a bearing on the whole evolution of southern hemisphere Rugby.

Never in their history, in any circumstances, have the All Blacks ducked a challenge. Hence it can be deduced that 'intercolony' rivalry between New Zealand and Australia (more than discernible up to our own time) bears responsibility for the waspish reportage in New South Wales. At this moment in time New Zealanders clearly felt ready to do their own thing without assistance from folk whose game was diluted by Australian Rules football and polluted by Rugby League. History's verdict is that this gut instinct was right; it has been proved so time and time again.

Consistent with this interpretation, New Zealand had ambitions that were greater than simply splashing around in their own pond. They had already been talking to the British about hosting a major inward tour in 1904 (which would materialise under the leadership of Scotland's David Bedell-Sivright). Even more dramatically, shortly before Mark Mullineux' side ended its tour the Sydney Press revealed that £3,500 has been guaranteed towards the expenses of a New Zealand team to England.

The visitors played a charity match in Sydney, beating an Australian Public Schools Past & Present XV 21-3 before travelling south to Melbourne for a final game against Victoria. The great stadium on the outskirts of the State capital possessed the acres of space demanded by the Gaelic handling code which Irishmen had brought with them to Australia and which held sway. Doubtless with the tastes of its regular readers in mind *The Age* printed no preview of the game, and only a couple of paragraphs reporting the tourists' victory. Notwithstanding, an attractive display of running Rugby was watched by 10,000 people. That was the final salute to Australia, and at the last banquet in Melbourne correct sentiments were scrupulously expressed. A Victorian official commented that the strong criticisms of Rev Mullineux in Sydney "...were valid, for they were not the whingeings of a loser." Said Mullineux, "Maybe the results were not surprising. For Rugby is a winter game; Australia is a summer country".

The evidence so far leaves no doubt that Gwyn Nicholls had become a role model both for those concerned for the image and ethics of Rugby football and for younger players eager to progress up the game's ladder. Modesty, unselfishness and a willingness to praise the efforts of team-mates would mark him out as – in modern parlance – 'squeaky clean'. And had he lived in our time a palpable charisma would have guaranteed him regular appearances on television and radio.

But it was at the end of the tour that he first showed signs of a certain waywardness which was destined to characterise his approach to both International and club Rugby for the rest of his career. To go further than this, and censure some of his behaviour as 'irresponsible', would be to judge him by the standards of later eras with their sterner insistence upon player discipline whether for club or country. In 1899 such a rigorous culture was not yet the norm. Nonetheless episodes will be recounted in Gwyn Nicholls' later seasons when administrators, selectors, team-mates and friends alike were nonplussed and felt let down because of his attitudes and actions.

What happened after the end of the tour was this: the British left Australia on or around August 21 1899, a day or two after the match against Victoria. Not until twelve days into the new century, on the morning of a home game between Cardiff and Blackheath, did Nicholls appear in his home town. By then he had been absent from nineteen of his team's fixtures in the 1899-1900 season. During that time there was no contact at all between him and his family or club in Wales; that is, he was incommunicado from late August 1899 until January 12, 1900.

Nicholls' exit from the world stage onto which he had just jumped was Lucan-like. *The Referee* reported on August 22 that "Four members of the British team are going home on *HMS Victoria*: Stout, Timms, Bucher and Simpson. Swannell has already gone home via the Cape. Today by the *Mariposa* Messrs Francombe, Cookson, Jarman, Evers, Ayres-Smith, Nicholson, Martelli, Doran, Thompson and McGown will travel via New Zealand and Francisco. Some are staying to visit friends in Victoria." Alas, no word of the lone Welshman. And once the players had left there was no mention, let alone reportage, of their journeys home.

Cardiff RFC had known that their skipper would be unable to start the domestic season. Neither of the club's historians, Arthur and Davies, discloses a reason for the captain's unavailability. In vice-captain Viv Huzzey, by now the holder of five International caps, the Blue and Blacks had an able deputy who led the First XV to fourteen victories before the end of the old century. Although doubtless puzzled by the extended absence of a star, there is no evidence of perturbation on the part of any interested parties including his family. Neither Hartley Nicholls nor Sid could shed light on his whereabouts; and even when A.B. Timms was contacted by a journalist the Scottish medical student could only reply, "Gwyn decided to make his own way home".

This lack of great concern should not, perhaps, perplex us unduly. One hundred years ago, with telecommunications in their infancy, it was the norm for brave-hearted young men, or women, who travelled to the other end of the world to be out of touch for long periods. It did not follow from the absence of cables or letters that harm had come to them. At any rate, there are no clues to Nicholls' wanderings in the scant surviving papers held by his descendants.

Therefore the only hint we have as to where he was and what he had been doing about is a statement in *A Century of Welsh Rugby Players*, by Wayne Thomas: "...[Nicholls] had gone to

South Africa to try and enlist to fight the Boers...". In the absence of documentation it may be that this was once hearsay in the Cardiff club which came to the notice of the author's father, the Rugby writer and historian J.B.G. Thomas. South African sources have been unable to verify the theory.

With a new Championship campaign looming the Welsh Rugby Union must have been anxious about the availability of their star centre. There was still no sign of him by 2 December 1899, when the selectors went ahead and staged a Trial match (in which, incidentally they outraged local sentiment by including two unknown 'exiles' in Simmonds of Northampton and Gould of Portsmouth at the expense of local favourites Reg Skrimshire of Newport and Cardiff's 'Pussy' Jones).

Next, on December 15 they named a team to play England in a game scheduled for the Kingsholm stadium at Gloucester. The *South Wales Daily News* reported that the XV had been chosen during a discussion lasting a mere forty minutes – and at right centre it contained the name of E. Gwyn Nicholls. Compared with modern practice this must rank among the Rugby game's great acts of faith. It has to be added that the Welsh media were curiously incurious about the selectors' reasoning.

The first Championship match of the twentieth century loomed nearer. Despite its venue, the England team selection (including thirteen new caps) included only one man currently playing Rugby in the west country, Bristol's Wallace Jarman. This must have contributed to a disappointingly small sale of tickets totalling barely 15,000.

Still, there was no sign of Wales' superstar, a man who could put 5,000 on a gate simply by the promise of his presence in a game. By now the Welsh Press favoured the immediate naming of a replacement, since: "Even if he suddenly appears it is difficult to see how he can get fully fit after enforced idleness for so long".

But the immediate quandary was about to be resolved. On 31 December Hartley informed Rugby writers that he had received a telegram – from whence enquirers were not told – stating that his son would not be back in Wales in time to turn out against England. The Press, in turn, informed the WRU, at the same time demanding to know who would replace him. The Union responded at once, announcing that Swansea's Daniel Rees would stand in for their first choice centre. In the *South Wales Daily News* 'Old Stager' approved of the choice, though lamenting the absence of Gwyn Nicholls. He added, "At least he is returning here. Hope had almost been abandoned that he would ever come back to Wales from southern climes".

Kingsholm was a familiar venue which held no terrors for Billy Bancroft and his men. Before the kick-off a military band played 'Men of Harlech' before 'God Save the Queen', and a goat was let loose to race nervously around the arena. Then Hodges, Boots, Brice and co tore into the England pack. Brave Dick Hellings of Llwynypia scored a first-half try, remaining on the field despite cracking a forearm early on. In the second half Billy Trew, on his debut, added another and Bancroft's place-kicking built the victory margin up to 13-3. The antipathy which is ever-present when Wales play England manifested itself afterwards: Welsh forwards nodded agreement as one of their number described England's captain as a pig.

Athletic News gave credit to the pack for Wales' win and was dismissive of the three quarters. The *Sportsman* correspondent, however, wrote that "an exposition of the three quarter back game was given which must have satisfied the great Mr Arthur Gould himself" ('Monkey' was evidently among the spectators). 'Old Stager' was happy to write positively about the two Swansea centres on their debuts.

It was the latter's newspaper which broke the news. On the morning of Saturday 13 January, under the simple headline 'Gwyn Nicholls', the *South Wales Daily News* led its sports coverage by reporting, "Gwyn Nicholls arrived in London this Thursday on his return from touring Australia with the British Rugby team. His father, Mr Hartley Nicholls, has been asked to meet the morning train from Paddington at the GWR station." The same report quoted "a member of the Welsh Rugby Union" as stating that Nicholls would play at centre three quarter in the forthcoming Championship game against Scotland on 27 January. Daniel Rees was the unlucky player who would surrender his place; but he was not to be wholly forgotten and would subsequently claim four more caps.

Sure enough, at 10.20 sharp Gwyn Nicholls stepped again onto Welsh soil. He had travelled from London with Blackheath RFC who were to play Cardiff in the afternoon and whose players left their compartments hurriedly to swell the welcoming crowd of locals at the exit. There was loud applause and hurrahs for the local hero as he appeared, lean and bronzed, while a porter perspired beneath the weight of his touring baggage.

Hartley had a horse and trap on hand in which he and his son attempted a quick getaway. The crowd, however, would have none of it. Detaching the trap, they manhandled it through Temperance Town (where the *Western Mail* building stands today) and all the way along Westgate Street to the Grand Hotel managed by big brother Sid. From the family party which ensued Hartley extracted himself briefly to assure reporters that his son was in good condition: "He is surprised to have been picked for the Scottish game while away. But he asks me to tell you that he hopes to play."

Eight

Compared with the hype which today greets a New Year, or Millennium, the Press's welcome to the twentieth century was no more than tepid. Front pages of newspapers were given over in those days to 'small ads' – notices of births, marriages and deaths – which ruled out banner headlines. So 1900 AD crept in on tip-toe.

The lead story in Wales was the home-coming of Gwyn Nicholls who would, it seemed, be a spectator at the match between Cardiff and Blackheath. As the news raced around the town trams, horse-drawn cabs and the occasional motorised vehicle jammed roads leading to Cardiff Arms Park, where the biggest gate since the previous season was now confidently expected. The club captain was cheered as he entered the grandstand shortly before kick off, where he watched his team beat the Londoners by 17 points to nil.

As he sought to leave the ground the prodigal son was mobbed by well-wishers anxious to welcome him and slap him on the back. There seems little doubt that he became genuinely alarmed. According to Billy Neill, son of a team-mate on the day, Nicholls broke away into Westgate Street, sprinted a hundred yards in even time and bolted into the newly-opened General Post Office. Here a kindly clerk allowed the fugitive to hide beneath the counter until the fans dispersed.

Nicholls spoke publicly of his 'pleasant surprise' that the WRU had picked him twice for International matches without knowing his form or even availability. At a reception hurriedly organised for him by Cardiff clubmates he reiterated that he would play against Scotland on the 27th January, assuring everybody that he would "strive to be in top condition". Swansea gravely noted that Daniel Rees was perforce discarded. He would have to wait until 1903 for another cap.

The question arises of Gwyn Nicholls' fitness to play a Test match only days after a long sea voyage, on which opportunities for exercise would have been possible but exceedingly limited. It is hard to imagine him sprinting along the boat deck without scattering deck chairs and alarming old ladies. Since his erstwhile fellow tourists had, somewhere en route, left him behind he had no-one with whom to practise passing and catching a ball. Though the phrase had yet to be coined, Rugby is a 'collision sport' in which the body needs to be hardened for match play by frequent contact with fellow players. Again, for a lone traveller this was not practicable.

Views on training a hundred years ago could scarcely be more different from those of today. Only a few months earlier 'Old Stager' had written in the *South Wales Daily News* that "our players seem to be developing a custom to do practically no training before the early games of the season." Nicholls himself stated in *The Modern Rugby Game* "It is important that one should be careful not to train too fine", and "tackling and scrummage work may be left to the actual game itself."

It seems, however, that he cannot have been what today would be described as match-fit. Perhaps he considered that he was; perhaps he was influenced by uncritical admirers, who begged him to play; perhaps he thought that Wales could not manage without him – the Scots being seen as a bigger threat than England.

My own suspicion is that he was shown the excellent Press write-ups given to the two Swansea centres after the England game – and truly feared that they would make the positions their own unless he intervened to keep Rees out of contention. He would, therefore, play. And he would get away with it. He was lucky.

Now, he had a fortnight in which to tune up, a period which included his come-back game with Cardiff against Bristol. It attracted the biggest crowd of the winter, which would see authoritative play from the captain who provided the three scoring passes for Huzzey's hat trick. 'Old Stager' reported that Nicholls "appeared to have acquired extra weight and strength which will further advantage his side." Charles Arthur's chapter on the 1899-1900 season in his *History and Statistics* singles out neither Nicholls nor the game against Bristol for mention. Do we detect disapproval at the prolonged and unexplained absence of a key member of the club, its First XV captain?

It will be remembered that the staging of Wales' last home game, against Ireland at Cardiff the previous year, had been a shambles. Walter Rees, the recently appointed Secretary (described by his President just two years earlier as "highly efficient") was determined not to make a hash of the St Helens fixture with Scotland. Two temporary grand-stands, each seating 2000 spectators, were erected raising ground capacity to 40000; and the Secretary had gone to some lengths to ascertain from the contractors that the collapses at Limerick (1897) and before the recent match at Kingsholm would not be repeated. Further, near the half way line where the crowd would be most dense, spiked iron railings were fitted to prevent any individuals invading the field of play. The winter was proving cold, and the pitch was to be protected by straw. Finally, Mr Rees issued a word of warning to those who had bought a large number of tickets for the England game of 1899 and sold them at "double or more than that of their face value." International tickets, the nation was told sternly by the Secretary, were non-transferable.

On the day, St Helens was packed out for what would be the only home International match of the season. Overnight rain stopped at breakfast time, and the sandy soil of the Swansea stadium quickly absorbed patches of residual damp. Despite not having won in Wales for eight years Scotland took inspiration from their victory of 1899 and seemed comfortably optimistic about their chances as they ran out into the sunshine to the strains of 'God Save the Queen'.

Like Wales, however, the SRU had gambled heavily against the odds in one respect. After injuring his head in an accident, the ten-times capped skipper Mark Morrison, of Royal HSFP, had asked to be replaced – only to be persuaded by the selectors to turn out. Inevitably he gave a poor performance, which included what reporters described as "an attack of influenza" at half time. However, had he been fit, well and in top form his men could scarcely have beaten off what the Welsh threw at them from the whistle.

Within minutes Nicholls' men had seized the initiative, and the first of four tries reads wonderfully well. The *Western Mail* said: "Shortly we saw such brilliant back play as has seldom been witnessed even in Welsh club games... inside Welsh territory scrum half Phillips had the ball heeled to him and, while the opposing halves watched him under the impression that he would attempt to break past them, he threw to stand off half Lloyd. The manoeuvre was successful, and Lloyd passed to Trew. The Swansea threequarter, with a feint to travel along his own touch-line, passed inside to Geo Davies, who gave to Nicholls. The Cardiffian, making that tremendous swerve for which he is famous, gave Llewellyn the ball. The fleet Llwynypian beat all opposition and made a grand try."

A sensational opening, then, with Nicholls both displaying finesse and, even more important in the circumstances, showing his old capacity to enhance a team movement. Even when Dykes scored for Scotland after local hero Billy Bancroft had misjudged a rolling ball, the crowd's confidence was not affected, and soon they were hailing another piercing Welsh move started and rounded off by Nicholls. He gathered a loose ball, picked up speed, dodged Timms and kicked ahead past Scotland's wing Tom Scott. Now Willie Llewellyn came steaming through in support and fly-hacked the ball to the in-goal area. Nicholls had followed up at top speed and just beat the visiting full back Harry Rottenburg to the touch-down

"Feet, Scotland, feet!" urged the visiting fans in kilts. "Brains, Wales – brains!" came the Welsh response as their team's dominance grew through the second half. Eventually Llewellyn was sent in for his second, and Wales' third, try while the Pontymister forward 'Buller' Williams got a fourth. *The Edinburgh Evening News* saluted the Welsh three quarters and pointed to Gwyn Nicholls as "the best of a capital lot."

Nicholls himself, doubtless relieved that he had not let the side down, preferred to give the credit to Wales' pack. He was also stern with euphoric local reporters who suggested afterwards that his team had been "all over" the Scots. "Their defence was excellent," he declared. "Remember, we could not score our third try until ten minutes from time."

It seems to have been a marvellous game of Rugby. Through

the twentieth century Rowe Harding, Bowcott, Cliff Jones, Carwyn James, John Dawes, Gerald Davies and other Welsh thinkers on the game have beseeched their country not only to win, but to win with *style*. Nicholls and his contemporaries had shown the way.

Following the win at Gloucester the four-try victory at Swansea meant that Wales were in sight of a second Triple Crown. They became Champions with a match still to play as a result of two 0-0 draws involving the other Home Countries.

Distant rumblings over the professional issue could still be heard in March 1900. The International Board issued a directive designed to crystallise what professional status actually meant. "A person is professionalised," it stated, "who receives or is given money or any valuable consideration as an inducement to play [Rugby] Football." Given that the IB had employed expensive lawyers to advise it, this was scarcely a water-tight definition. It completely omitted the payment of a retrospective fee based on an understanding reached between a club and a player.

However, Wales had other priorities and Mr Secretary Walter Rees was cracking the disciplinary whip. "No selected player should play Rugby between March 12 and the Belfast game scheduled for the 17th," he told the chosen squad. Further, he instructed team members to make themselves available as from March 15: "Our party will make the crossing on the Thursday before the game in case the Irish Sea is too rough and players need time to recover."

The visitors were also concerned about the administration and safety precautions in force at Irish grounds, for which they could well be forgiven after the Limerick fatality of 1898. However, they were quick to indicate whole-hearted approval of Balmoral Showgrounds as a venue. The confirmation that Scotland's A.J. Turnbull would referee, as he had two years earlier, also met with Welsh approval.

In his third season as captain, Swansea's W.J. Bancroft now became the first Welshman to play through two Triple Crown seasons. Since 1893 the self-effacing Swansea full back had been his country's last line of defence, besides kicking some important goals. As a captain, he had contributed ever more constructively to the Welsh tactical approach. Now, once again, his insight was decisive in a hard-fought game.

The *Western Mail* was less than complimentary: "The Shamrock Defeated", it conceded. But: "The final triumph was not a brilliant victory but one by the lowest possible score, 3-0." For once the newspaper's usual generosity had deserted it. To win on the soil of the reigning title holders (whose Triple Crown success the previous year had climaxed in Cardiff beneath the *Western Mail*'s nose) was a great feat achieved under pressure.

Especially, the report did less than justice to Billy Bancroft. Throughout a pointless first half the Welsh skipper responded to Ireland's touch kicks by taking scrums instead of lines out (as he had done twelve months before). Suddenly, early in the second half, he elected for a line out, at which Ireland left opponents unmarked. Selwyn Biggs and Bobby Brice exploited the resulting good possession by combining with Louis Phillips (later Welsh amateur golf champion) to speed Nicholls on a defence-breaking run. Reports suggest that the centre could have gone all the way to the goal-line, "but unselfishly gave the game's only try to George Davies." Brice later had a chance to send Nicholls in, but failed to see him. The game still had a long way to go, but reports make it clear that the Irish ran out of steam. St Patrick's Day had not gone well for them, and the Triple Crown was eastward bound.

Once the action is over the Irish are invariably Wales' most generous opponents, and the post-match party was lively. Nicholls was acquiring a taste for the occasional glass of Scotch, and maybe a cigar. Doubtless it was a leaden-headed squad which set off the following morning for a journey to South Wales via the Holyhead ferry. The new champions got to Cardiff just ahead of heavy snow which had pursued them during their tortuous rail journey through the Radnor uplands and across the Brecon Beacons to Merthyr Tydfil and finally Cardiff.

Nine

For the second time since their debut in a Home Countries championship, the Welsh had proved too good for the other national sides of Great Britain. Their triumph of 1893 had been a pointer to what might be; 1900 demonstrated that the foundations which had been laid were a platform on which the game in Wales had every prospect of prospering. So it would turn out. Today, Welsh Rugby looks back on its 1900 Triple Crown as the start of a first 'Golden Era.'

Cardiff, whose importance and population had overtaken those of Merthyr Tydfil and Swansea, was steering a parallel upward course. At this time the town appears to have been more certain of its Welsh identity than would be the case in later years. Such awareness had been heightened by figures like 'Morien', the Archdruid, who imported a host of fellow bards to the Gorsedd stone circle in what was now known as Cathays Park to proclaim the final National Eisteddfod of the century. He contributed a whole page in the *Western Mail* to introduce Gorsedd symbolism and bardic cloaks to the masses, who included bewildered immigrants from England and Ireland. Green robes, he explained to readers, stood for the forests of Wales, blue for the sea, white for boulders and rock. Cardiff's representatives had attended the Ffestiniog Eisteddfod of 1898 to make sure that the great and the good would travel south to their town the following year.

As civic muscles were flexed, national feeling stirred too. A Welsh Language Society was in existence, whose Secretary J.D. Brown spoke eloquently at Pontypridd: was the preservation of the Welsh language merely a sentimental aim? "It needs to be systematically taught here," he thundered. "Not to replace other languages; to be learned along with them."

There had been cultural protest, too, in a legal context. Fifty years earlier, the report of the Parliamentary Commission on the

State of Education in Wales (known as the 'Blue Books' from the colour of the leather in which its volumes were bound) had highlighted, dramatically and piteously, the absurdity and injustice of monoglot Welsh prisoners being tried and quite possibly sentenced to death – in a language which they did not understand. Yet still, as the twentieth century opened, a judge called Darling could insist on a Welsh-speaking witness using English in his court. A *Western Mail* leader said sternly, "It is high time to end this treatment of Welsh people. They have a right to use the language they prefer."

The Home Rule movement, for the time being, was shorn of some vigour. Possibly the presence in Parliament of David Lloyd George persuaded his countrymen that they now had an able champion in the corridors of power who understood Welsh aspirations, would interpret them at Westminster, and could influence politicians in their favour (he would indeed rid them of an Established Church but there were also Budgets and wars which demanded his attention). However, following the creation of a federal University in 1893 came a drive to establish other national institutions. A Library, a Museum and an Art Gallery were prioritised (and the competition to accommodate them was as fierce as that to house the Welsh Assembly a century later).

One of the Cardiff MPs, J.M. McLean, approached the Government for Welsh representation on the Union flag, arguing that the Welsh commitment to the South African war was every bit as strong as that of England, Scotland and Ireland. The reply from Lord Salisbury was terse and negative. Rebuffed, Welsh Parliamentarians recommended the re-adoption of the Red Dragon standard.

The future Henry VII had marched onto Bosworth Field under that flag, only for it to fall into desuetude with the end of the Tudor dynasty. But now, twentieth century Wales took it quickly to heart. In our time, although the Union flag is still the emblem of officialdom and bureaucracy, it is Y Ddraig Goch to which the Welsh look on days when it is necessary to stand up and be counted.

As a result of all these trends some historians seek to establish a cause-and-effect link between economic buoyancy, which was undeniable in the south Wales of a century ago, and political confidence plus sporting success. This is an attractive thesis, but probably a little facile. Certainly Welsh industry, notably coal mining and metal manufacture, was experiencing boom times and creating what is today called a 'feel-good factor'. Equally, however, the "Edwardian high noon of prosperity, optimism and confidence" as scholars have termed it, was being shared by England. Yet in the first decade of the twentieth century her teams were able to win a mere eight Championship games (only one of which was against Wales). There were also defeats at the hands of New Zealand and Australia, and a draw with South Africa.

Nicholls' feet had scarcely touched the ground since his return from the Antipodes. In between appearances for Wales, he needed to play himself back into favour with Cardiff RFC whose supporters, once the euphoria of the star's return had died down, voiced discontent at his long absence from the action. At the same time the even tenor of his family life was soon to be destabilised, as a result of a career decision by his elder brother Sid which would impact upon his own ambitions and life-style.

During this time, however, two men crossed his path who were destined to become his good friends, team-mates and, in the case of one, a business partner. Herbert Benjamin – 'Bert' – Winfield was born in Nottingham in 1879. His father Ben was a laundryman who, like Hartley Nicholls, moved to South Wales in search of business opportunities. Evidently a bold entrepreneur, in 1898 he amassed £14,000 from bank loans and friends to open the Roath Sanitary Steam Laundry in purpose-built red-brick buildings which still stand at the junction of Marlborough and Blenheim roads in east Cardiff. As a plant it seems to have been up to the minute, boasting an automatic timing device on which the thirty employees checked in. A water-extractor reached 900 revs per minute; and another machine blew hot air through clothes to dry them.

Winfield junior made his debut for Cardiff in 1897 aged 18, the last and youngest of seven full backs used by the club that winter. The number would fall to four, and then to two; but not until the second half of the 1899-1900 season did Winfield find himself an automatic first choice. This brought him into close contact with Gwyn Nicholls, and the foundation was laid for a prosperous future in harness – though one destined to be tragically short-lived.

The other eventuality, which would lead to a close and fruitful playing partnership for Nicholls, was Cardiff's resumption of matches with Llanelli. The two clubs had squabbled over alleged player-poaching and decisions by referees in 1895. Now room was found on the fixture lists for a game in Cardiff on April 7 1900. Historian Charles Arthur writes that the match was finely contested and played in the best of spirit, adding "the outstanding feature of the play being several brilliant runs by centre Rhys Gabe."

Gabe, then still two months short of his twentieth birthday, was clearly not alarmed by the prospect of marking, and being marked by, the world's number one midfield player. Respect, however, was present from the outset. In 1946 Gabe wrote, "That was the day I saw my hero Gwyn Nicholls for the first time, and it was with mixed feelings of pleasure and awe that I made my initial appearance on the Park in opposition to him... On one occasion I cut through from our own territory, raced past the full back somewhere about half way, and then went all out for the line. There was no further opposition – but, alas! I didn't score because I was grassed inches from the line. The tackler patted me on the back and said, 'Hard luck, laddie'. It was Gwyn Nicholls himself."

A couple of seasons later, Gabe would move to a teaching post in Cardiff and join the Blue and Blacks – acquiring the nick-name 'Rusty', from 'Rhys T.' He was to win the first of twenty-four caps in 1901 and play with Nicholls in the Welsh midfield on sixteen occasions.

The partnership would prove potent. Cardiff won that 1900 game with Llanelli 9-5, but seven days later a more portentous result – as far as Nicholls was concerned – was a 27 points to 12 defeat by the Barbarians. This was the tourists' revenge for an extraordinarily outspoken piece of journalism in the *Western Mail* by 'Old Stager', taking the Baa-Baas to task for their alleged class distinction: "No working man, whatever his merits as a player or how gentlemanly his behaviour, appears to have been included in teams sent out by this singular organisation...this social exclusiveness has in many quarters been called caddishness."

The accusation is not reproduced in the official *History of the Barbarians FC*. Nor does the club state that Gwyn Nicholls ever turned down an invitation to represent them. However, it is the case that, unlike the great majority of his peers, he never played in their colours. It would have been out of character for him to comment on, let alone support, the journalistic slant in the *Western Mail*. Therefore it is reasonable to suppose that the Baa-Baas' cold-shouldering of the Cardiff centre was a direct riposte to the newspaper's criticism. It was aimed at the club, in the shape of its captain, rather than at any individual. Not until 1927, as a Cardiff committeeman, was Nicholls belatedly elected a Barbarian, accepting the honour after a particularly glittering Easter fixture between Cardiff and the tourists.

During the 1900 close season following the Wales Triple Crown triumph Nicholls, as we shall see, was pre-occupied with re-directing his future business career. In July, however, he was guilty of another *faux pas* which highlights that same insouciance and insensitivity of which he had been guilty when overstaying his leave of absence in Australia – and taking up his elected position as captain of Cardiff RFC some twenty weeks late. This also involved the club.

On the 27th of the month members attending the annual general meeting at the Park Hall were presented with two candidates for captaincy of Cardiff in 1900-01. One was H.V.P. Huzzey fresh from a vice-captaincy which had included deputising for Gwyn Nicholls during more than half of the previous season. The other was Nicholls himself. Minutes after arriving in the Hall he stated that, since he had already served two seasons as captain, he would withdraw in favour of his 'loyal colleague'. This noble avowal was made before a roomful of people for whom Nicholls was an ikon.

Now, to withdraw from contention is one thing. To stage-manage that 'withdrawal' in front of two hundred avid Cardiff supporters leaves a man open to suspicion. Not for the first time, and not by a long way for the last, Nicholls appears prone to vacillation and able to be swayed by special pleading. Or else: why had he not made the decision to withdraw in the period between the end of his second term as club captain and the a.g.m.? This had lasted for fourteen weeks.

Had the members been offered Huzzey as the sole candidate there would obviously have been only one outcome. As it was, with the great man still in the gathering, emotions ran high and a noisy lobby demanded that Nicholls should stand for a third term. Acceding to this pressure, he re-asserted his candidature and was made captain once more. His election did damage, certainly to Cardiff RFC. The likeable Huzzey had been averaging twenty tries every season in 132 games for Cardiff since 1895, and had also obtained four for Wales in five appearances. Many of these scores resulted from passes laid on by Nicholls. But, rejected and hurt, Huzzey took understandable umbrage and in September 1900 signed for Oldham Rugby League club. Cardiff were to miss his vivid acceleration and dazzling side-steps

The club lost five of its first nine games in the new season. Wales may have been 'on a roll', as the moderns have it; but there was restorative work crying out to be done at Cardiff Arms Park. Whether Gwyn Nicholls could satisfactorily deal with this crisis of morale was a question which needed an answer.

Ten

The new century now gathered momentum over a broad front, beginning with warfare and with decisive victories for British troops in southern Africa. The relief of Mafeking was soon followed by the fall of Pretoria and moves towards stability and a working relationship between the British and the Boers. Closer to home Lloyd George and Keir Hardie were the stars of Welsh politics, the latter being elected to Parliament as a junior member at Merthyr Tydfil to D.A. Thomas.

But October 1900 was a month of mourning in Wales when the Marquess of Bute died suddenly. His Lordship's most recent gift to the town was the handsome estate on its northern outskirts known as Roath Park, complete with a boating lake where Cardiffians took their leisure in beautifully landscaped rural surroundings. The sports of Rugby football and cricket, of course, owed their headquarters to the Bute family and, though there is no evidence to suggest that the Third Marquess came frequently to Cardiff Arms Park or ever spectated there, his younger son Ninian liked to occupy an enclosure seat as a guest of the Rugby committee (and was to give his name to Cardiff City AFC's new headquarters at Sloper Road). As a mark of respect the game against Moseley scheduled for 13 October was called off.

Meanwhile, under Nicholls, Cardiff RFC were in some disarray. A yardstick by which supporters judged success had always been the results obtained against the team's major rivals, the other big Welsh clubs. Now, before November was out their team had been beaten twice by Newport, lost their first game at Stradey Park for six years, and been toppled 18-0 by Swansea. Oxford University had won at Iffley Road, and there was a draw at Neath. Not until December was a sustained sequence of victories was put together.

Fans were not pleased. A typical reaction appeared among

'Letters to the Editor' in the *Western Mail:* "It is time that Cardiff got some forwards together, and that they were given some attention by a person in authority" – lines which read like an early demand for the appointment of a coach. Nicholls himself, however, escaped criticism: "We cannot help wondering, what would Cardiff do without him? He seems to have the knack of doing the right thing at the right time." The critic 'Welsh Athlete' wrote, "Without Gwyn Nicholls Cardiff are 'shucks'." The only other character this century to employ the word "shucks" in print, in my experience, has been Desperate Dan in *The Dandy.* "Shucks", says the OED, are husks or shells – "hence, a term of contempt; something to be thrown away."

Christmas Eve turned out to be memorable, however, with the visit of Edinburgh University pitting Nicholls against his team-mate and good friend on the Australian tour Alex Timms. The latter won lavish praise from Welsh onlookers including Cardiff committeeman Charles Arthur, who later wrote in his club *History*, "...Timms, on several occasions, made very strong bursts and got by Gwyn Nicholls as no other player was ever able to do." The Scot was clearly moved by the warmth of his welcome for, after qualifying as a doctor, he came to practise locally and played seventeen games for Cardiff between 1903 and 1905.

Meanwhile the Welsh selectors were giving thought to the defence of their Championship title and a possible back-to-back Triple Crown. The Trial they arranged for 1 December between the Whites and the Stripes, however, proved to be a fiasco. No fewer than five front-line backs, including Nicholls, and two forwards pulled out. Of course, it is human nature that established performers lack enthusiasm for any exercise which might undermine their primacy. But, in any case, the Welsh selection panel was hardly in a radical frame of mind. The team to play England at Cardiff, announced on December 21, contained no new caps, though an injury to scrum half Louis Phillips of Newport would lead to his replacement by Aberavon's John Jones, a mere 5 feet 5 inches tall, who was to make only this single appearance for his country.

Scheduled for 5 January, the match was the first International allocated to Cardiff Arms Park since Ireland's visit two years before in search of the Triple Crown; and administrators still shivered when they recalled the crowd frenzy of that afternoon. However, at the prompting of Walter Rees, Cardiff RFC and the WRU had taken joint steps to augment spectator capacity and safety by increasing grandstand seating to 1,800 and that of the 'temporary stands' (by which was meant the terraces) to hold some 35,000 onlookers. The cost fell just below £2000, of which the Union paid £1445. Gratifyingly, *The Times* chose to compliment the WRU on the initiative: "the arrangements for the match could not be better."

Going into his last season, W.J. Bancroft led Wales to victory in what was evidently an undistinguished game. Though the Welsh backs were always in the ascendant, a gritty display by England's pack confined the margin to 13-0. Nonetheless two Welsh tries were scored by forwards, Jehoida Hodges of Newport and 'Buller' Williams of Pontymister. Nicholls scored his second try for Wales; wrote *The Times*, "The Welsh centre performed magnificently and was almost irresistible in attack. His defence was sound."

Despite the win Wales made three changes to the team for the Scottish fixture on January 26. The death of Queen Victoria (who merited a seven-page obituary in the *Western Mail*) necessitated a 14-day postponement. Welsh officials' embarrassment at the staging of the 1899 game against Ireland had been surpassed only by that of the SRU with its four postponements of the fixture between Scotland and Wales. There was, thus, unusual relief in Edinburgh at *The Times* correspondent's eve-of-match despatch stating that despite the week's frost the field of play at Inverleith had been "well protected...the turf is in excellent condition."

For their first International of the winter Scotland named eight new caps and seven Edinburgh University men including A.B. Timms. It was not to be Wales' day, Scotland advancing to a lead of 18-0 with fifteen minutes left. Llewellyn Lloyd and George Boots then scored tries for Wales and Bancroft kicked a conversion, but these replies were too little and too late.

The Scottish Press said that Nicholls "did plenty of clever things but was not seen at his best." Reports also suggested that the 'demoralised' Welsh forwards had given the game away.

Scotland were a good side, which would beat Ireland (narrowly) and England (comfortably) to take a third Triple Crown. Meanwhile the Welsh season – and the International career of Bancroft – ended at Swansea, where a 10-9 win over Ireland secured second place in the Championship. The game is also memorable for the debut of Rhys Gabe (as a wing) and R.M. 'Dicky' Owen at scrum half.

During the summer of 1901 the need arose for Gwyn Nicholls, who celebrated his 27th birthday that July, to give much thought to his future, both on and off the Rugby field. The assuming of new responsibilities advanced upon him inexorably.

His life hitherto had been fancy-free, buoyed up by the support of a successful father and encouragement from an elder brother who was inordinately proud of him. By now Sid had proved himself an entrepreneur who could, and did, make money by running pubs and hotels. But after a decade which included his part-ownership of the Grand Hotel he was bored and found himself pining for a final taste of active service in a Rugby jersey while his limbs and joints still functioned adequately.

Out of the blue, he warned Gwyn that he would soon be joining Hull Rugby League club as player-coach, and set in motion the sale of his share in the hotel. His grandson Jeff (who today lives in retirement on the Pembrokeshire coast north of Haverfordwest) states that the deal was worth 'five figures' to Sid, who left for the North at the start of the 1901-2 season. He would return to Cardiff in time to witness Captain Scott's departure for the Antarctic in 1910 and resume an active involvement in Welsh sport – though not Rugby football: in those days to sign professional forms was to be banished forever from the Union game.

Now, in 1901, his younger brother was evidently disconcerted. It was thus fortuitous that, at this critical juncture in his life, he was enjoying a developing friendship with Bert Winfield. The young full back, for his part, was thrilled to have become a confidant of the Cardiff superstar, but was now a success in his own right, having succeeded Nicholls as club captain at the remarkable age of twenty-two. Their conversations became long and intense, often taking place while they maintained close-season fitness by jogging together. A favourite route took them along the Glamorganshire Canal tow-path up as far as Radyr, returning to Cardiff Arms Park via the bank of the River Taff

Only too ready to listen, Nicholls now allowed himself to be persuaded by Winfield that laundries were service industries with a future, offering a great opportunity to a pair of young men prepared to put in the hours. With his friend, Nicholls paid visits to the Marlborough Road plant and realised that the Winfield family understood both the economics of the industry and the technology now being introduced to it. The two men agreed to set up a partnership to run their own laundry when the time was ripe.

Also exercising Nicholls' mind was the knowledge that, with Bancroft's retirement, he was certain to be offered the captaincy of Wales. He had been a successful club captain, and had turned Cardiff's fortunes round after their poor start to the previous season. Now the Press were tipping his appointment, and in his own mind Nicholls felt ready to accept responsibility for leading Wales.

Meanwhile club Rugby beckoned again. As the Cardiff captain, Bert Winfield was heartened by the arrival of a future International player in A.F. Harding – "one of the best forwards the Club ever had," wrote Charles Arthur later. Diminutive outside half Percy Bush was on hand while, to keep him on his toes, the very promising 19-year-old centre, R.A. Gibbs came on strength. Optimism was in the air, and it was thus to the Blue and Blacks' considerable chagrin that in the third game of the season Bristol won a first-ever victory over their rivals across the Severn by a try to nil.

We have seen how International Rugby could now attract huge crowds and fan their emotions to fever temperature. In South Wales, the same was true of inter-club games, as was vividly demonstrated on 26 October. The visitors to Cardiff Arms Park were Swansea, who had done the double over Cardiff the previous winter. Charles Arthur's graphic evocation of the occasion in his *History* is well worth quoting: "As Cardiff on the two previous Saturdays had defeated Devonport Albion and Newport – two very good performances – they were thought to have a very good chance of lowering Swansea's colours.

The match drew the biggest crowd that had ever attended an inter-club match at Cardiff [given the enlarged terraces and grandstands this could have been around 35,000], gate receipts amounting £472 2s 2d. Many hundreds got in for nothing by scaling the walls in Westgate Street because ticket sellers could not cope with the thousands clamouring for admittance. The match happened to be on what was called 'play-day' in the Rhondda, and several thousand Rhondda-ites were among the spectators. It is said that fully 3,000 people made the journey from Swansea."

Even for Cardiff Arms Park the ground was unusually heavy, so that back play was minimal and the huge crowd were treated to a 0-0 draw. Thereafter the Blue and Blacks' season was moderately successful, and they went through the next 20 weeks unbeaten. It was Swansea who, emphatically, ended this excellent run 15-0.

Now came a complication for the two Rugby-playing partners-to-be. Bert's father Ben Winfield decided to open a laundry in Newport, indicating that he wished his son Bert to supervise the new venture. Such a responsibility, involving early starts and evening work, was bound to conflict with the demands of captaincy made on him at Cardiff. This was when Gwyn Nicholls intervened to suggest that, since he planned to enter the laundry business with Bert, he should assist Winfield senior by overseeing the start-up of the Newport plant and, at the same time, acquire valuable hands-on experience.

His offer accepted, Nicholls took temporary lodgings on Uskside and for the remaining half of the season played for Newport RFC. In his Cardiff *History* Danny Davies contents himself with stating, "It gave great satisfaction to all his admirers when he returned to the Cardiff fold...late in the season." Wrote Charles Arthur, "He did not play for Newport in their first meeting with us after he joined their ranks, but did play on March 22 – much against his wish, no doubt – and equally there is no doubt he was the means of Newport beating us." In other words, Cardiff took a dim view of their erstwhile captain breaking ranks.

Newport, in contrast, were gracious about the world-class recruit and the eleven games in which he appeared. Wrote the veteran critic Jack Davis in *One Hundred Years of Newport Rugby* "The club undoubtedly gained the greatest centre of the day...who played the four three quarter game better than any man who ever wore a jersey.... Newport did not lose a game in which he played. He scored in eight matches and – significant fact – Charlie Lewis, who played on his wing, scored 12 tries in the eleven matches."

Nicholls bade a cordial farewell to Newport at the end of March. Never one to shirk hard work, he had absorbed the basics of the industry which he intended entering. Now, with brimming business confidence, he could return to Cardiff Arms Park in time to take part in a victory over the Barbarians during an otherwise dismal end to the season for the Blue and Blacks.

The International picture, however, was different. Under Nicholls, predictably appointed as Bancroft's successor, the Welsh had experienced renewed success and reached fresh heights.

Eleven

Soon to be a founder-member of the first-ever Welsh golf team, Bert Winfield had grown to enjoy a twice weekly 36 holes. For long his impending business partner poured cold water on this enthusiasm chiding, "I can't understand why you bother with that stupid game." Nor did cricket or tennis feature as sporting diversions for Gwyn Nicholls. Hence his summer seasons were free to formulate business plans – and devise new ways to win Rugby matches.

Some of his close-season brain-storming yielded results that strike today's reader as astonishingly modern. What is more, his theories were by no means confined to three quarter play. Take the following passage in *The Modern Rugby Game* – which would not be out of place in a contemporary coaching manual. Nicholls is writing about the "right kind of forward" who, he says, is exceedingly hard to find:

> He must be strong, fairly heavy, as fast as a three quarter, absolutely untiring, a reveller in hard work, and of an absolutely even temper. It will be as well for him to be tall, as he will have numerous opportunities for utilising his inches at the line out.
>
> A forward nowadays must possess the quality of 'handling' the ball. That is to say, he must be able to join effectively in a three quarter attack, to initiate one if necessary.

Doubtless this was the kind of doctrine with which the captain-apparent sought to influence Wales' selection committee. Certainly the team named to play England at Blackheath on 11 January 1902 bore signs of a new broom at work. Among its seven new caps, six were those 'hard to find' forwards. Llanelli's Oxford educated full back John Strand-Jones was, for the time being, the man chosen to succeed Billy Bancroft.

Ironically his opposite number might well have been Bert Winfield. Evidently experiencing a crisis of identity, the

Nottingham-born Cardiff captain had accepted an invitation to play in England's Trial at Exeter a few weeks before, where the *Western Mail*'s new Rugby writer, 'Forward', saw him make disastrous and uncharacteristic errors. The selectors fell back on Devonport's H.T. Gamlin, while a sad Winfield retreated across the River Severn. Here he nursed his injured pride, recovered his good spirits, and told journalists, "Wales is where I now earn my living. It is Wales that I will represent on the Rugby field." However, he was to be denied a cap for fourteen months through Strand-Jones's brilliance and consistency.

New caps or not, Welsh supporters evidently thought their heroes were in with a chance and made their presence felt en route to the Rectory Field. "At Charing Cross," reported the *Western Mail*, "the 'Welsh Marseillaise', Sospan Fach, was heard. Londoners looked on in amazement and listened in admiration to the dulcet strains of that doleful dirge...All along Shooter's Hill [to Blackheath] more Cymraeg than Saesneg was heard.... Many forged tickets were on sale." Billy Bancroft, out of the Welsh XV for the first time since 1890, was spotted by fans, who demanded to know if the great man had ever seen Wales in action before.

The match began well for the visitors when Strand-Jones created a spectacular try by scorning a safe touch-finder and sprinting out of defence. He rounded the England forwards, 'doubled' – i.e. stepped inside – Coopper, and sent Gabe in from 25 yards. Then things swung England's way as Dobson scored beneath the bar, for skipper Harry Alexander to convert. Before the interval Robinson bullocked the home team further ahead with an unconverted try for an ominous 8-3 lead.

"As the second half started," wrote one Fleet Street correspondent, "the tradition of failure at the ground which had previously haunted Welsh teams seemed to be in the air again...like the mist which hung over the ground." True, England had always won at Blackheath, often heavily. But their 1902 opponents were made of sterner stuff than some predecessors.

The going was hard. From the re-start England's pack came snorting into the Welsh 25, only for Gabe and Teddy Morgan – on second and first caps – respectively to keep cool and relieve the pressure. Now it was the turn of Wales' forwards, greatly encouraged, to apply pressure which was rewarded by an unconverted try scored by the powerful Mountain Ash miner W.T. Osborne. But the conversion failed, and as the minutes ticked away the Welsh could still not deal a killer blow. Morgan dropped a scoring pass, Nicholls crossed the English line only to be called back for a minor infringement, Gabe was a passenger after suffering a heavy tackle which dazed him.

Now Nicholls, determined not to finish second best in his first match as captain, took advantage of a hold up for injury to call for a last, supreme effort. In his *Book of English International Rugby* historian John Griffiths explains (in faintly disapproving language) how the tide was turned: "Only the antics of the wily Welsh scrum half R.M. Owen allowed Wales to steal a late victory. Five minutes from no-side Owen tricked his opposite number Bernard Oughtred into an offside tackle at a scrummage near the English posts, where Strand-Jones drop-kicked the resultant penalty." The strains of *Hen Wlad fy Nhadau* rose from stands and terraces, and soon referee R.W. Jeffares of Ireland, who had been jeered by home fans for his penalty decision , blew for time with Wales ahead 9-8 – and launched on a fresh Triple Crown quest.

After the match the journalists moved in to invite comment, and Nicholls responded for the first time as skipper. "Whichever side had won," he told his interrogators, "no-one could have complained. There was so little in it. I am consequently quite satisfied with the result. I prefer not to comment on the displays of individual players."

Members of his team were not so discreet. "We should have scored more," lamented Teddy Morgan (perhaps with his own lapse in mind). "The Englishmen's first try was scored off a forward pass," complained Gabe. "I would lay my life on that." But the victory had been won, and the *Western Mail* was able to promise, "The Rectory Field at Blackheath will have no future terrors for our men."

Just as an impromptu rendering of the National Anthem had sustained Wales through the last difficult minutes at Blackheath, so it was to inspire them before their second encounter of the New Year, against Scotland at Cardiff. Originally entitled 'Glan Rhondda', the words and music are the work of father and son Evan and James James of Pontypridd – though it is uncertain whether Evan wrote words which he asked his son to set to music, or whether James' music came first. But Welsh groups had been singing it with gusto for nearly half a century; and now it was happily embraced by the Rugby fraternity, seizing prime position in the inspirational hit parade of the day. At about this time it won widespread acceptance as worthy of the title 'National Anthem', uniting north and south Wales, for once, in approbation of it. For some time 'Men of Harlech' continued to be played as the National XV took the field (a tradition which was revived at Wembley during the 1998 Five Nations championship).

On February 1 the wind howled across the River Taff and the Welsh could hardly believe their luck when, after winning the toss, Scotland's captain Mark Morrison – again – chose to play into it. The singing had only just stopped when Wales took the lead. A forward thrust from the first line out scattered the Scottish forwards and a brisk heel was followed by what was evidently a copy-book scoring move. Gabe and Nicholls drew defenders and Willie Llewellyn celebrated an eleventh cap with a superb finishing burst. Minutes later the little man from Llwynypia was quick to support a solo burst by stand off half Llewellyn-Lloyd and claim a second try.

Further highlights followed in an action-packed first half. Scotland's Timms was caught in possession and a forward drive yielded good ball. Owen, Llewellyn-Lloyd and Nicholls handled beautifully to send Gabe cruising in for a third Welsh try, the fourth following after Teddy Morgan cut infield from the wing and unselfishly passed to Gabe. Strand-Jones converted the score, as did Gillespie when Fasson sent W.H .Welsh in for a smart Scottish try which reminded Wales that the game was far from decided. Against the gale, however, Nicholls' men defended soundly through a second half which was score-less.

The captain declined to give interviews after the game. But 'Forward' said it all for him in the *Western Mail*: "Of the eighteen games between Wales and Scotland this stands out as the one in which the athletic prowess and skills of Wales reached the highest point of perfection. We have never before been represented by a more skilful body of exponents of the handling code." Could such a judgement survive ordeal by fire in Dublin?

Away from Four Nations Rugby Nicholls, still with Newport, was instrumental in assisting the Black and Ambers to take Swansea's ground record, though when he attempted a snap drop at goal against Penarth the ball travelled weakly along the ground. Better things were to come in the Welsh bid for a Triple Crown at Lansdowne Road. Wales crossed the Celtic Sea with an unchanged XV from that which had beaten Scotland. Such was the excitement surrounding the game that it became the first all-ticket match in history.

Led by the 23-times-capped Bective Ranger Louis Magee, Ireland's team had lost narrowly to England before defeating the Scots. It contained a quorum of tried and tested men who gave the Welsh a torrid first half and, commented the *Irish Herald* "...did grandly for ten minutes of the second half, but fell away after Nicholls' great dropped goal.... Nicholls was the alpha and omega of the Welsh team in this match." Again, the skipper had proved able to inspire a team. His dropped goal – with the left foot, incidentally – opened the floodgates, through which raced Willie Llewellyn and Llewellyn-Lloyd for tries, one of which Brice converted. If modern-day media hype had applied, Nicholls must have been named 'man-of-the-match', for it was he who made certain of the spoils with a final try which plunged Ireland to a 15-0 defeat, their biggest ever. England now won 6-3 at Inverleith, beating Scotland for the first time since 1897; but the success was irrelevant. Wales had won a third Triple Crown. In *The International Championship* Terry Godwin notes that the winners made only two changes during the campaign, both because of injuries, thus setting a precedent: "Most countries at that time, even when winning, changed personnel with seemingly little regard for team building."

After the Dublin game Gwyn Nicholls gave his first extended interview as captain to the Press: "It is the proudest moment of my life that we have won the Triple Crown in the first year of my leadership of the Welsh. The dropped goal was my first in International games; around about an hour into the game it was too good a chance to let go."

Writing more than twenty years later, he colourfully recalled the post-match relaxation of that Dublin weekend: "A pleasing feature of this visit was the presence of the Welsh Ladies' Choir. Owing to an afternoon engagement they were unable to see the match but, of course, were anxious for our success. On our return to the Hotel 'muddied oafs' as we were, an invitation was extended to us to the Drawing Room where, on our entry, we were greeted with the National Anthem sung with great fervour. Already elated by our success, the singing appealed to us the more. I felt, and I think everyone felt, that nothing so sweet and grand had ever been heard before."

As a Rugby player Gwyn Nicholls had been victorious in the southern hemisphere, played in one Welsh Triple Crown team, and captained the next. Mountains had been climbed, summits scaled. It was now opportune, even imperative, to give thought to a career. His family was demonstrably well off, but it would have been out of character for Gwyn to seek, or endure, a life of ease at someone else's expense. For some time the hard-working management role he fulfilled at his brother's hotel seemed to offer a career frame-work, but Sid's sudden departure for Hull had focussed his mind on the challenge that a career in business would offer, and which he needed.

On one of their jogging expeditions Bert Winfield drew Nicholls' attention to a factory a couple of hundred yards from a picturesque reach of the Taff. It had manufactured matches but now, with the business's failure, the premises in Andrews Road, Llandaff North, were up for sale. The two men decided to buy the building to house their venture into laundering.

This was why Nicholls had returned to Cardiff without seeing out the Rugby season at Newport. More significantly, he did not complete his stint as overseer at Ben Winfield's new enterprise in the town. That, in turn, may have been a reason why a rather put-out Winfield senior declined to have much to do with his son's new partnership. Malcolm Pearce, of the family

1. & 2. Gwyn Nicholls's parents, Hartley and Jane Eliza, née Millward. The couple had seven children, of whom Gwyn was the fifth.

3. A group of schoolboys somewhere in east Cardiff during the 1880s. The youthful features of Gwyn Nicholls are unmistakable. He is seated rather awkwardly, at the left hand end of the second row from the front.

4. Cardiff Star, the junior side in which Nicholls played his early rugby. Elder sister Clara sewed on the stars.

5. 'Buffalo Bill' – Colonel William Cody – brought his Wild West road show to Cardiff in 1895: 'Prodigious Entertainment!' screamed the hoardings – and possibly the young Nicholls and his pals revelled in it.

6. A Cardiffian is late, the 1895-96 team photograph features fourteen men. In his third season with the club, Nicholls is seated immediately on skipper R.B. Sweet-Escott's left.

7. Spring, 1899, and Nicholls is completing a first stint as Cardiff RFC captain. His side lost only three of twenty-eight games.

8. The Cardiff headquarters where Wales full back Bert learned the business. Later he and Nicholls would set up their own laundry.

take this as an application for membership of the Newport F.C., & I thank you for the assurance of a welcome.
As regards the Swansea match — I saw Geo. Boots this morning & explained my position to him. He will doubtless tell you at your meeting tonight what transpired.
Yours faithfully
Gwyn Nicholls
T. C. Graham Esq.

Cambrian Chambers
Newport, Mon
5/12/01.

Dear Sir,
I am obliged for your letter. It is quite true that it has been my intention to offer my services to your Club at the start of the New Year (although it puzzles me to know how the press got their information). You may

9. Sent to gain experience at the Newport branch of the Winfield's laundry Nicholls joined Newport RFC for the second half of the 1901-02 season.

10. No wonder Newport were sad to wave Nicholls goodbye. They did not lose a match in which he played; he dropped two goals and scored eight tries. Cardiff blamed him for their 10-0 defeat at Rodney Parade!

11. Throughout his career Nicholls enjoyed county rugby. Here he breaks for Glamorgan against Yorkshire.

12. Cardiff at St. Helens, with a terrace of houses in the background that have stood for over a century. Swansea's Dicky Owen feeds a scrum – keeping a safe distance from the packs.

13. Photographic coverage of rugby was in its infancy when this rare picture was taken: returning as captain after an injury, Gwyn Nicholls leads Wales out.

14. Action in front of the first 'grand stand' at Cardiff Arms Park, built in 1885. On each side can be glimpsed the 1901 extensions which raised seating capacity to 1800.

15. Cardiff's new town hall takes shape in 1904. By the time it was completed the town had been promoted; the 1905 All Blacks were the first to attend a function at the *City* Hall.

16. The first pavilion at the Arms Park, backing on to the River Taff. Shared by Cardiff's cricket and rugby clubs, it was first used in 1904.

accountancy firm used by Nicholls and Winfield, states categorically that the two young men's initiative was supported by the wealthy docksman J.T. Morgan. In 1902 he became a sleeping partner of the newly-formed Gwyn Nicholls & Winfield Ltd, owners of the Victoria Hygienic Laundry.

From the outset the firm benefited greatly from the Rugby football contacts of its two principals. Contracts were secured to launder the Rugby jerseys of Cardiff RFC and Glamorgan Wanderers as well as other clubs in the district. Not far from Andrews Road were major hospitals at Rookwood and Whitchurch which would become an on-going source of business. From his office window Nicholls could see the spire of Llandaff Cathedral, whose Dean and Chapter entrusted the cleansing of choirboys' ruffs and surplices to the Victoria. This was the heyday of the starched collar, and several thousand of these were dealt with each week plus the shirts to which they were affixed – cotton ones in summer, flannel in winter.

Born in 1908, Trevor Lewis was a one-career employee who joined the Laundry straight from school at the age of 14, earning ten shillings (50p) a week plus a 2/6d bonus for arriving early to feed and harness the horses which pulled the delivery vans. By that time the firm was well-established and successful; but being steeped in the Victoria's history and traditions he well knew how it had developed and expanded. He won the confidence of management and helped devise a strategy which kept the original horse-drawn vans circulating in inner Cardiff while motor vehicles were gradually acquired to do business further afield in Lisvane, Radyr, Penarth and the Valleys. "Mr Nicholls trusted me," recalled Trevor Lewis. "He had to. Sometimes I might bring back to HQ as much as £25 in small change and notes." That would be well over £1000 in today's money. Malcolm Pearce confirms that this was another of the factors contributing to the quick success of Nicholls and Winfield: "Their's was a cash business. Customers paid on the doorstep and consequently bad debts were rare. The Laundry made substantial profits and declared generous dividends. Beyond doubt, it became the most successful laundry company in South Wales, and by the 1950s would be making five-figure profits. The formula was working, the risk was promising to pay off, and in quick succession Winfield and Nicholls boldly set up plants at Cadoxton, near Neath, and Bridgend. Winfield's re-election as Cardiff captain for 1902-03 threw extra business responsibility onto his partner's shoulders which was willingly accepted.

Inevitably, however, something had to suffer – and that was Nicholls' commitment to Rugby and the time he was able to set aside for training.

This did not go unnoticed. A little way into the new season, after Cardiff had lost three games in a row, a letter-writer to the *Western Mail,* having lambasted the Cardiff pack for being sluggish, added: "Nor did Nicholls appear as fast as last year. Those deadly break-throughs were absent." Another letter-writer confirmed the star's preoccupation with his Laundry after the loss of the club's unbeaten record at Moseley by an under-strength XV. After criticising Biggs and Percy Bush for not travelling he wrote, "I can understand Gwyn Nicholls' unavailability. He has a new business of his own to attend to." The signs were that the new business was being exceedingly well attended to. Unfortunately, Nicholls was soon able to spend more time on its good management than he would have wished.

Twelve

At the start of the 1902 season Garnett, 18, the third Rugby-playing Nicholls brother (and the youngest child of Hartley and Jane Eliza) took part in a Trial at Cardiff Arms Park. The short-lived glossy *South Wales Graphic* sent a reporter to the game who wrote that the youngster 'did nothing'. The records show that Garnett Nicholls never played for Cardiff.

The failure of this trialist with a distinguished name was symptomatic of the frustrating season, by the club's usual high standards, on which Cardiff were now embarked. Not only were results against Welsh clubs poor, Newport winning three of the winter's four matches, but English sides like Bristol, Moseley and Oxford University also won rare victories over the Welshmen. Devonport Albions even brought off a double.

It was all hard to stomach for the Blue and Blacks' supporters, a colourful and variegated microcosm of the growing town itself. Round about this time the *South Wales Echo* gave space to a guest columnist who contributed a memorable cameo centred on what he saw and heard while observing fans queueing to enter the Arms Park:

> There is the collier from the Rhondda in his go-to-meeting clothes. You can tell him by his dark, rugged, labour-stained, sometimes ill-formed visage, his bent back and too often alas by the burn on his face. He can sing like an angel, and sing like a devil. He is a bit taciturn – until he has had a few pints...Then there is the tinman, with clearer skin than the collier, with short, dark moustache, good ready-made clothes, and with a suspicion of 'bowedness' about the legs.
>
> Then there is the Cardiff workman, who is not always Welsh. He has lived in the town for years and looks with a little contempt on strangers – but soon finds, on entering conversation with them, that they know more about many things than he does himself. The Draper looks very gentlemanly by comparison; but his mouth, when opened, betrays his recent arrival from Cardiganshire. Then there is the Cardiff

'Masher': someone at the Docks – affecting to look down on everyone, but envying their ways.

Such characters make up a body of supporters who have never been slow down the years to rail publicly against their club's administrators when its playing record has been less than satisfactory. In the media such outspokenness has always acquired more prominence when bad weather has wiped out fixtures and left sports editors with big, empty columns to fill. It is then that the latter reach eagerly for readers' letters. Thus, when frost caused the cancellation of all matches in western Britain on 6 December, the *South Wales Graphic* was only too pleased to publish an outburst from 'Casual Spectator' on the subject of Cardiff RFC: "We have not witnessed such poor football in many years...the season opened with the blowing of trumpets and visions of a brilliant record strengthened by the return [from Newport] of that great centre Gwyn Nicholls. But the resourcefulness which has been a major feature of Cardiff play in recent years is entirely absent...there is a whole lack of cohesion."

When Winfield selected himself at centre to partner his great friend, he was roasted in the *Graphic*: "Winfield is not a centre; the sooner a partner can be found for Nicholls the better." Wrote a correspondent to the *South Wales Echo*, "Cardiff are a one-man team. That one man is Gwyn Nicholls."

At 28 this one man had arguably reached a peak where he would remain for long, consistently getting a good Press not just from casual letter-writers but also from professional critics, who included English Rugby writers. After seeing him play at Oxford in November the *Daily Telegraph* critic wrote, "Nicholls retains his position as the finest centre in the Kingdom." His status as the Reds' captain in the Trial scheduled by the WRU for December 6 was a formality. For all of these reasons therefore Cardiff's visit to Blackheath a week later may have been victorious but was disastrous in the longer term.

In London on that unlucky thirteenth day of the month Nicholls had been playing his usual leading role in a visiting side which had put recent reverses behind it. A lead had been built up, which would be held to the final whistle. Some minutes into the second half, however, came a major setback. Nicholls escaped his marker with an outside swerve and change of pace which took him up to Blackheath's full back, Stone. This last line of defence now put in a determined tackle which "...laid Nicholls flat. Never before have I seen Gwyn Nicholls knocked out," wrote 'Forward' in the *Western Mail.*

After regaining consciousness, the centre was clearly in great pain. Back in the clubhouse he was diagnosed by Dr Lennard Stokes, a former England full back, as having suffered a broken collar bone. Intriguingly, Stokes told reporters that he thought the bone had been damaged before. It may well be that Nicholls had suffered a hair-line fracture or crack about which he had told no-one; certainly, he was that sort of person. Wearing a sling, the captain was reported as 'more comfortable' by tea-time and caught the Paddington train home along with his team.

By Tuesday the patient was 'progressing favourably'. The bone was knitting, and giving less pain. However, it was clear that Nicholls would be sitting out the first match of the Championship season: "Of all men, Gwyn Nicholls is the one Wales can least afford to be without," wailed the *South Wales Graphic.* "His absence can only be described as a national calamity." But worse lay in store: the Welsh XV to play England at St Helens on 10 January 1903 would also lack the two leading wings of the day, Willie Llewellyn and Teddy Morgan, ruled out like Nicholls by injury.

An out-and-out gamble by the selectors saw Tom Pearson, the former Cardiff wing now with Newport, restored to the National XV after an absence of five years and made captain. Number thirteen – his thirteenth cap – proved unlucky for him: after an early try, he was obliged to limp from the field injured after a heavy tackle by England's full back Gamlin. But the visitors failed to exploit the numerical advantage that resulted, Dobson's try being their only response to five by Wales. In the *Western Mail* 'Forward' pulled no punches: "Never have I seen a game in which a professedly national team played in such a schoolboy fashion. It was pitiable to see the miserably disorganised condition of the Saxon team."

The ill fortune of Pearson (who never played International Rugby again) made room for the ebullient forward Jehoida

Hodges to immortalise himself. Speaking on radio in 1937 Gwyn Nicholls could still recall vividly how the Newport man went to play as an emergency wing: "Hodges...was drawn from the pack to take the place of T.W. Pearson...and scored four tries.... Fifty per cent of our forwards, although essentially scrummagers, were versatile and could be made wingers if the necessity arose." At 63, Nicholls was let down by his memory: Hodges scored three tries. But he remains the only forward to have scored a hat-trick in a Championship match, albeit fortuitously

A milestone in Rugby football's evolution was also passed in this game when George Travers of the suburban Newport team Pill Harriers made his debut as the first front row 'specialist'. Hitherto the homespun philosophy 'first up, first down' had done duty at scrummages. Now, the think-tanks which were influencing the Welsh game decreed that scrummage possession was too valuable to be left to chance; and Travers was selected specifically to hook.

Although Nicholls was training hard by early February he was a good way below full fitness. Once more it was a Black and Amber whom the WRU made captain in his place, their choice now falling on George Llewellyn-Lloyd. This lawyer is not numbered among the glamour boys who have played at stand off half for Wales down the century, but his record is one that bears comparison with the best. He scored three tries in twelve appearances, and was a winner seven times.

Edinburgh 1903, however, was not among his good days in a Welsh jersey. Water lay on the Inverleith pitch until just before the start, when it was swept away by teams of workmen. Rain fell all afternoon, so that the Welsh style and rapid handling by the backs was always at a disadvantage. Bill Kyle of Hawick scored Scotland's try from the second row, and Nicholls' friend Alec Timms dropped a down-wind penalty goal to send the Welsh home with tails between legs.

Cardiff RFC, and especially its star centre, greeted with delight the announcement of the Wales XV to play Ireland. The bright but short-lived International career of John Strand-Jones was over; that of Bert Winfield was beginning. The former is named in D.R. Gent's *Rugby Football* (1932) as the first

counter-attacking full back; but now, the selectors were reject-
ing his style in favour of reliable hands and feet. Is it
conceivable, we may speculate, that they had been influenced by
a certain brother-in-law? Welsh journalists were less concerned
about Winfield than the fitness of Nicholls, Teddy Morgan and
Willie Llewellyn when all three were restored for the 14 March
fixture at Cardiff. None of the three stars had been in action
since December. Would they survive the fierce exchanges,
wondered the critics. But Irish hopes to the contrary were to be
dashed.

Before hailing the match-winners who fashioned and scored
Welsh tries in this last International match of the year, let us
salute George Boots of Newport, who broke a collar bone early
in the game. Despite the pain, the Newport forward grafted his
way to the end of the first half, by which time the Irish had been
well and truly subdued. His team-mates lifted the Welsh total to
18, a figure which comprised six tries: two by Llewellyn, two by
Morgan and one each by Gabe and Brice.

But the media had no doubt who was 'man of the match'.
Thus the *South Wales Graphic*: "The figure which towered
above all the others was Gwyn Nicholls. Playing his first game
for Wales this season, he proved that he still stands alone. There
is not a centre playing to equal him, even now in his 29th year.
He is plainly a master-artist; and the way he put Llewellyn in
for the second try was an example of perfect judgement and
accuracy.... He made good runs; but, more than that, he knew
when he had his men in position, and he knew when he had
done his part." Fans and Press alike were overjoyed to see him
back in action; people felt sure that a fit Nicholls would have
led Wales to victory in Edinburgh and a back-to-back Triple
Crown.

But the centre himself may now have begun to harbour reservations about how much further he could go in the game, or
wanted to. Rhys Gabe had become a master at Howard
Gardens School in Roath, and Llanelli were resigned to his
probable transfer to Cardiff; but even the prospect of forging a
new partnership with 'Rusty' at the Arms Park seemed unlikely

to re-animate Nicholls' Rugby ambitions. He would remain loyal to his club; but his attitude to International Rugby was to become unpredictable.

The point can be made statistically. Between 1896 and 1902, if his four appearances for Mullineux' men in Australia are counted, the centre played 20 Tests, a figure which would have been greater had it not been for the Gould controversy and Wales' temporary ostracism from competition. From 1903 to 1905, in the Home Championship, he turned out in only three of the nine games played by Wales – nor were injuries by any means the sole reason for his absences. His need, evidently, was for a big new challenge or mission. A further eighteen months were to pass before it materialised.

There were consolations, notably the time now at the star's disposal in which to refine theories and speculations which were half-formed in his mind. Though the term 'man-management' was not yet familiar, it was a skill which Nicholls now began to cultivate as he sought ways in which success at Rugby could be maximised. He wondered too if the same principles could be applied to managing a Laundry.

Thus, as on the Rugby field he chose to run the Victoria from the front, by example. This meant moving from his bachelor lodgings in Roath to the Whitchurch area close to the Laundry, in order to reach work by eight in the morning, as his employees were clocking on. Trevor Lewis, his appointee, says that the boss often lingered at his office desk until 7 p.m. He worked on Saturday mornings, before leaving for Rugby or for a round of golf, to which Winfield had by now converted him. But the departure of his partner to run their new Cadoxton plant meant that the pressure on him remained high.

He was a manager who was not afraid of getting his hands dirty in the course of learning everything there was to know about laundering. Although his dress at work was formal – suit, white shirt, tie, polished shoes – he was quick to remove his jacket and move to the shop floor if unexpected orders came in or members of staff reported sick. Here he would often operate a machine, feeding it with soap, soda and powder when required, and mixing starch. He would discuss the purchase of new plant with his technical staff.

As an employer Nicholls seems to have been genuinely concerned for his workers' welfare. Certainly he would admonish, in 'a deep, intimidating voice', anyone who made a serious mistake. But Trevor Lewis's more vivid memories were of the enquiry that used to boom out from the his boss's office towards the end of the working day: "Are they happy, Trevor?"

Nicholls also had time during the summer of 1903 to reach some original, and typically provocative, conclusions about Rugby football. Possibly with his own playing contribution to the Welsh game in mind, he stated in a lecture delivered later that year that "Brilliant individuals are, in fact, hindrances rather than helps to their team. If any player, in any position in a Rugby game, stands out head and shoulders over his fellows, then is that player inevitably the *weak* point of his side. For if he be pre-eminent he will be recognised as such by his fellows, who will be impelled to play to him. The opposition will identify the method, and will spare no pains to 'mark' that man – and thereby dislocate the whole machinery.

Thus did Nicholls challenge and dismiss conventional thinking about 'star' players. My guess is that he had his tongue in cheek. He well knew that a player of his calibre demanded intensive marking by the opposition; and if he, through ability and reputation, could draw two, or three defenders onto him, the amount of space thereby made available to team-mates would be vast. This will not be the first of Gwyn Nicholls' pronouncements to catch the attention of sceptical players a century later who may observe, 'Blindingly obvious.' Very well; but someone had to work such things out, and be the first to articulate them.

The difference between Nicholls and other gifted contemporary players was his capacity to think for his team-mates, not just for himself; he wrote that Rugby football demanded the total merging of a player in a team. He also knew that a certain category of player was answerable to no discipline, and would win – and lose – matches according to his own genius.

The season gently died. The Fourth Marquess of Bute came to live in the Castle across the road from Cardiff Arms Park and, when he attained his majority, the Rugby club presented the young aristocrat with an illuminated address and a cheque for £500 which His Lordship might donate to a deserving charity. It was passed on to the new Cardiff Royal Infirmary to pay for the installation of electric light.

At the end of the winter Cardiff RFC's capacity to invest in its own future was well shown when it sponsored the establishment of the Cardiff Schools Rugby Union. The club bought all the garments necessary to supply some 600 boys with kit, including shorts and boots, for an outlay of £289. If this was self-interest, it was nonetheless enlightened – given the many distinguished players who were to graduate from the junior Union to the Blue and Blacks.

Thirteen

If it is true that Gwyn Nicholls had fallen victim to a certain *ennui*, then that was one good reason for Cardiff members to vote him in as captain for a fourth time: bestowing on him an honour that would, hopefully, be a stimulus towards restoring his game to concert pitch. A second powerful motive was that, under Winfield, the club had lost 12 of its 32 games, an unacceptable proportion; hence Nicholls was brought back to exert seniority and crack the whip. Thirdly, it is possible that a leadership crisis had resulted from the departure of the fine forward A.F. Harding to further his career in London. Since Charles Arthur describes him as a 'good leader', it may well be that he was being groomed to succeed Winfield.

But newcomers also joined. Following his move to teach in Cardiff, Gabe completed the expected transfer from Llanelli. Newly-qualified Dr Alec Timms was a recruit from Edinburgh, while the half back problem which had troubled the club for some seasons was solved when local window-cleaner Richard Davies hit it off with Percy Bush. Constable Bobby Brice, the fifteen-times-capped Aberavon forward, signed on after the Glamorgan Constabulary transferred him to the Cardiff area. How well could Nicholls marshall such an array of talent?

He made a good fist of it. The season's 23 victories included a spectacular overwhelming of the Barbarians by 41 points to 3; while no fewer than twelve opposing sides failed to score against the defensive screen Nicholls organised. One aspect of the winter, however, made the Blue and Blacks squirm: the four defeats from four games at the hands of Swansea. Cardiff is justifiably proud of the several years when it managed to win all four fixtures against Newport (a feat which Newport never replicated); those 1903-04 reverses at Swansea's hands are spoken of less frequently.

A result members preferred to remember was secured at

Stradey Park on 23 January 1904. An 8-5 victory (the first of a 'double') was obtained – with fourteen men – after Llanelli had wiped out the visitors' early lead and dominated a second half in which Cardiff were always under pressure. With four minutes left Percy Bush received good possession from a scrum inside the Scarlets' half. He sprinted past four or five Llanelli defenders in bewildering fashion and flung himself over the goal-line a few inches from the corner. The icing on the cake was Winfield's superb conversion.

This year marked the coming-of-age of Bush as a player to be reckoned with at the top level. Raised in the Rhondda, of Carmarthenshire stock, he had graduated from University College, Cardiff, and become a teacher in the town. For long he was regarded as a flashy centre three quarter, unpredictable and not to be relied upon. Now, at Nicholls' prompting, he had switched to become a worthy occupant of the outside half back position.

In an early broadcast for the infant Welsh Region of the BBC Bush recalled how he made the change: "Cardiff's recognised outside half was taken ill shortly before a match with London Welsh and I said to Gwyn, 'Let me have a go, Prince' – that's what we called him. With a twinkle, he replied, 'Do you think you can do it, Pierce-Eye?' – that was his name for me. 'Well, all right. You've tried wing, you've tried the centre – you can't do any worse at outside half.' Then, when I had taken up what I considered to be my proper position at the first scrummage I heard Gwyn's whisper, 'Kindly get out of my pocket. Perhaps you think you are playing full back?' We understood each other very well. I knew that he was talking merely to encourage me."

Soon Bush was to tour with a British side in the Antipodes, winning the confidence of Wales' selectors on his return. Capped eight times from 1905 to 1910 he gave performances which pointed forward to Cliff Jones, Cliff Morgan and David Watkins. After hanging up his boots Bush entered the diplomatic service and became an Honorary vice-consul in France. He played a part in the development of the formidable Club Rugby de Nantes, in whose colours he is reported as having scored 54 points in one game, including ten tries.

Bush was one of the stars to whom shrewd entrepreneurs

now turned to help boost their profits. He, Nicholls and the latter's vice captain Cecil Biggs were targeted by a certain Mr Rowland Houghton who ran a 'Light-Cure and Electro-Hydropathic Establishment' off Queen Street in central Cardiff. Heavily advertised in the Press, the Establishment was described as "thoroughly equipped with the latest and highest class Apparatus including Radiant Heat and Arc Light Baths, Electric Massage &c for the treatment of Football, Cycle and other Accidents." Adverts featured a faintly menacing photograph of Mr Houghton's clinic complete with an Electric Massage provider.

But his great coup was to secure testimony from the three Rugby stars. Thus Bush is quoted as finding the treatment "wonderfully soothing...and of lasting benefit." Biggs would certainly "recommend the Treatment to all footballers." And Nicholls testified to the "great benefit" he received from Houghton's work on his badly strained knee: "I feared the accident would keep me out of the field for the remainder of the season, but after a fortnight of your skilful care I was able to resume playing." Mr Houghton's was no doubt delighted to be able to print such praise; he reciprocated by placing his advert in Arthur's book, thereby helping to fund its publication.

Other endorsements from sporting stars included one from a champion cyclist based in the Cynon Valley stating that "Dr Tibble's Vi-Cocoa improves stamina and staying power." The Established Church of the day chimed in, too, with testimony from none other than the Lord Bishop of Swansea: "Our children frequently suffer from attacks of croup and we have always found Mortimer's Cough Mixture a sure and safe remedy...we gladly take an opportunity of recommending it to our friends." Other gripping adverts included the assurance by the makers of Scott's Emulsion that it could banish "athletes' cough", and the claim by a Dr Brown that "Ogilato will develop a lady's bust by six to eight inches in one month."

With the New Year, the Four Nations' Championship arrived to dominate the Rugby scene. From Cardiff Nicholls, Gabe, Winfield and new recruit Brice were named in the Welsh XV to meet England at Leicester. The local club was pleased to be awarded another International fixture following its successful organisation of the game with Ireland two years before. That match had attracted 20,000 spectators and now, before the end of December 1903, the club reported that all the city's big hotels were fully booked by fans coming to see the game against Wales.

The media profile of Rugby was growing steadily, and for the first time the number of Press passes issued rose above 100. When a cold snap was threatened the Welford Road pitch was protected with '500 bags of oat husks'. Then the icy weather gave way to low pressure, and rain fell heavily and constantly in the English Midlands. 'Forward', of the *Western Mail*, became anxious about this and telegraphed the Tigers' secretary to ask, "would the rain stop, and if it did not, what would happen?" Understandably, the latter's retort was somewhat testy: "I'm sorry it's raining so hard here. We would give you nice weather if we could, but we cannot, and there you are." It has ever been thus: a journalist asks a stupid question and the official spokesman puts him down.

'Forward' had more weighty matters to discuss when he wrote his report on the 9 January encounter. The match would be, he said, "...the subject of controversy for some time...taking the form of eccentricity in refereeing. Associated with this for all time in Rugby history will be the name of Mr Findlay of the SRU. He interpreted the Laws in a manner which confounded the Welsh players and struck consternation into the hearts of the several thousand Cymric enthusiasts present".

The facts are that, early on, a series of seven penalties was given against Wales. The luckless E.J. Vyvyan missed six attempts at goal – or else the English would have been out of sight long before the interval. Poor Dicky Owen was so discomfited by these rulings that he declined to put the ball into the scrums and insisted that his opposite number did so. In the second half Mr Findlay allowed a try by the England wing E.W. Elliott who, even the London Press agreed, was yards offside as he chased the crucial kick ahead. In the final moments Teddy Morgan was sent in by Gabe for a try disallowed for a forward pass. Morgan had scored earlier, along with Willie Llewellyn; Winfield kicked eight points to get the draw; and it might have been thought that both sides were not unhappy with such a result: England for ending a sequence of five Welsh victories in succession, Wales because they had avoided defeat on foreign soil.

Certainly the Welsh management did not provoke controversy. The fiery Gabe, possibly under orders from his captain, declined to speak to reporters. Gwyn Nicholls made a brief appearance to state, "I have nothing to say about the game." That was typical. Gabe later said in a radio broadcast, "Gwyn's disposition was such that he was never known to show the slightest disappointment or bitterness. I never heard him make excuses or find faults."

This steadfastness was to characterise Nicholls' behaviour in the final years of his playing career despite the contrasting fortunes they brought. It may be that, in some instances, he did Rugby football a disservice by not speaking out about issues on which he held firm views – or when a referee had not been up to standard, an omission which may have led to the unwelcome reappearance of Mr Findlay for Wales' critical match at Belfast in March. With his towering authority, and reputation for total sportsmanship, to comment trenchantly might sometimes have been valuable and salutary. Very often, what he truly thought or felt at the time does not emerge until years, even decades, later in specialist articles or in speeches and broadcasts.

From Leicester in January 1904 Pressmen also filed an after-the-match comment of the kind which always causes groans of disbelief in Celtic Britain that the *Saeson* – Saxons – can be so crass. In contrast to the tight-lipped silence preserved by the visitors, an England centre, Edward Dillon, chose to sound off: "The Welsh always blame the referee. They do not understand the rules [*sic*] properly. They are not educated like [*sic*] we are. In Wales you don't find the same kind of people as in England." For which many Celts will breathe a big sigh of relief.

This Dillon had been to Rugby School and Oxford University. A Blue at cricket as well as Rugby, he next joined Blackheath and was a Barbarian. His career in the City was interrupted by World War I, in which he was commissioned into the Royal West Kent Regiment, wounded, and mentioned in despatches. With a record of that kind he clearly had no time in which to acquire good manners.

In Cardiff's win the following week at Llanelli Nicholls had been the player obliged to leave the field at half time, suffering the leg strain quoted in Mr Houghton's advertisement. By the Monday he was taking light exercise and being treated by a Dr Eckford, who got the swelling down. But thereafter, despite any amount of Radiant Heat and Electric Massage, the injury would not go away, and on 4 February Nicholls met the selectors and reluctantly declared himself unfit to play against Scotland.

He need not have worried. The selectors capped Cliff Pritchard of Newport as Gabe's partner, and Nicholls was hardly missed in a 21-3 rout of the Scots at Swansea. "Once Pritchard got over early nervousness," said the *South Wales Evening Post*, "he settled down to tackle well and form a good partnership with Teddy Morgan, probably the fastest man playing the game in the four countries. A quartet of Welsh tries were scored by Gabe, Dick Jones, Teddy Morgan and Brice, Winfield's boot contributing the balance of points. Hugh Orr got Scotland's try.

Once again the post-match comment is worth quoting, this time for amusement's sake. Reporters trailed Nicholls to the changing room area, where he thanked Willie Llewellyn for deputising for him as captain and offered congratulations on the win. "Really, Willie, that was a splendid achievement," he is quoted as saying. Back comes Llewellyn's reply, in his best Rhondda Fawr English: "Thanks, old chap. I'm sorry you were not in it. That was jolly rough luck for you." At any rate, that is how the *South Wales Daily News* put it.

Nicholls was duly named in the XV to play Ireland on 12 March in Belfast, where a win would guarantee Wales at least a share of the Championship. The centre is recorded as playing for the Cardiff reserve XV on 5 March and stating afterwards that "the knee is first rate." He did, however, request permission to remain in Cardiff after the team's departure on 10 March for some final medical attention to his leg, indicating that he would travel on the Friday morning.

The Welsh were dismayed on reaching Belfast to receive an apology for lack of communication from the Irish Rugby Union along with the information that the dreaded Mr Findlay was to referee the game. Alas: to protest at this late hour would be construed as whingeing. More bad news was to follow on the evening of the 11th. With kick-off a mere seventeen hours away a brusque wire arrived from the team captain, who had not left Cardiff: "Unable to travel", it said. "Good luck. Nicholls." Fortunately Cliff Pritchard had travelled as a reserve; he was immediately informed that he would again stand in for the absentee.

It needs to be made clear that two Pritchards became forces in the Welsh game at this time, both born and bred in Gwent. Clifford Charles, who stood in for Nicholls at Swansea and would now do so again, played most of his Rugby for Pontypool (though was with Newport at this time) and was of course a back. Charles Meyrick Pritchard was a forward, selected for a first cap in this match and destined to win fourteen caps leading up to the First World War. He would then be commissioned into the South Wales Borderers and die of wounds sustained in action.

Despite the absence of Nicholls the Welsh, again under Willie Llewellyn, went into the game with high hopes. Scotland had shattered Ireland in Dublin, running in five tries, and there seemed every reason to hope Wales could get the win that would give them a clear-cut title. Mr Findlay, however, refereed in the singular style which had been a feature of the game between England and Wales, allegedly allowing an Irish try which followed a forward pass and denying a winning score for Wales by Dick Jones. Ireland's 14-12 victory at the Balmoral Showgrounds thus pointed up refereeing decisions which cost Wales a Championship title. When Scotland beat England at Inverleith the discontent knew no depths, for a Triple Crown, too, could have come Wales' way. Findlay never again refereed Wales, though he did games for the IRU involving New Zealand and France.

But what were the reasons for Gwyn Nicholls' late withdrawal from the Welsh XV? Note that his wire did not say, "Knee still bad" or "Failed to regain full fitness." Instead he worded it, "Can't get away", which suggests some other commitment, perhaps of a business nature, blocking his departure for Ireland. This seems a further example of an unsatisfactory attitude on Nicholls' part to a Union which had behaved generously to him, placing great reliance on his playing ability and leadership qualities.

With the exception of the odd letter-writer to the Press, Nicholls had the public and the media, too, eating out of his hand. The term 'rave review' might have been invented to describe his displays. Now, he seemed to be taking advantage of talisman status to act as he pleased. It is hardly a coincidence that this was the period when Pressmen began to frame sentences like, "Gwyn Nicholls has *consented* to play in next month's International game." To 'consent' is to do someone a favour.

It may well be agreed that as a star player of the twentieth century's first decade Nicholls cannot be judged by standards which obtained in later eras. The business which he had to run in order to make a living was still in its infancy. Its boss could not claim broken-time payments for representing his country. Let all this be conceded; he had every right to make himself unavailable. But what was surely discourteous and unacceptable was to leave withdrawal until the eleventh hour.

It is possible, of course, that Nicholls genuinely believed that the leadership and coaching which he had brought to the Welsh team meant that it ought to be able to function without him (as at Swansea the previous month). He had begun to talk almost mystically about 'the spirit of the side', a theme which is developed in his book.

In 1997 and 1998, competition between local Councils hopeful of being selected as the venue for Wales' new Assembly kept readers of the Welsh Press in a constantly frenzied state of mind. Ninety-five years earlier other, similar, corners were being fought as an 1873 proposal to found a National Library near the new University College of Wales at Aberystwyth regained momentum. The revitalised project's scope was now widened to embrace a Welsh Museum, and battle to determine a venue was energetically joined. Aberystwyth re-emerged strongly as a contender; the entry of Caernarfon to the lists and interest expressed by Swansea broadened the competition. Cardiff's Mayor set up a Fund as an earnest of his town's aspirations, making it clear that the new national institution would be accommodated on land in Cathays Park cheek by jowl with the handsome new Town Hall and Law Courts that were shortly to be built there.

Gwyn Nicholls now demonstrated that his allegiance to Wales and its causes did not end with Rugby football. The grand match between East Wales and the West of England which he organised in aid of the Fund drew a crowd of 20,000. Played at Cardiff Arms Park on 6 April, it was won by East Wales 18-7. The Mayor received a cheque for £92.16s.1d (£92.80p) and wrote to Nicholls, "...please allow me to say how greatly I appreciate your public-spirited action in organising the...football match in aid of my 'Cardiff Fund'.

Given his broad-based concern for Welsh Rugby, another match played at Cardiff that spring probably gave Gwyn Nicholls equal satisfaction. In the first-ever Schoolboys International match Wales overwhelmed England by 23 points to 5.

Welsh Rugby was soon to know some of its finest hours, including a meeting with the greatest challenge to confront it. But Gwyn Nicholls was hinting that he might now leave the game. Could Welsh success endure without his guiding influence? Did the Principality's fortunes at Rugby depend on the involvement of a single man?

At this juncture it is worth quickly indicating the strength of Welsh Rugby as perceived by other nations, first by the French, new to the game but eager to improve. *Le Matin*'s Rugby writer saw a visiting Swansea XV play Stade Français in Paris: "These Welsh are astonishing, in the manner they manoeuvre over the ground. The ball flies from hand to hand, man to man. Having reached the extreme right it comes back to the left."

Wrote the correspondent Arthur Budd in *Athletics News*: "Despite being handicapped by natural disadvantages of isolation [*sic*] Wales have, in a dozen years, not only grasped the salient points of the Rugby game but have become our pioneers." An Irish journalist had this to say: "Full well I know from years of experience that the team which can last best of any combination is the Welsh. Their training does it. When other nations are exhausted and spent forces the Welsh seem to get what the athlete terms his 'second wind' and they move on, an irresistible force." And from Scotland, a tribute in the *Glasgow Herald*: "Welsh play has always been distinguished by originality. The 'thinks department' is never allowed to rest. Evolution is more than a theory with the cream of Welsh players: it is a practice. They have led in these matters for ten years and still lead. There is no limit to the possibilities of Rugby Football in their hands."

But now, as the 1904-5 season loomed near, they seemed likely to be without their inspirational leader.

Fourteen

As Cardiff kept growing so, inexorably, suburbia shouldered its way into the vales of the Ely and Rhymney rivers which flank the Taff, and northwards in the direction of villages like Tongwynlais and Taff's Well. New housing was snapped up as immigrants kept pouring in.

The export of coal continued to be the engine which drove the local economy. Despite the stiff competition from Penarth and Barry – where David Davies had created a well-equipped port – it was rumoured that a score or more of the coal traders and shipping magnates who enlivened the Exchange in Bute Town each morning had reached millionaire status. From Westminster came warnings that the bonanza could not last for ever; one or two far-sighted local businessmen expressed regret at an over-dependence on the 'black diamonds'. But serious or widespread concern did not exist.

Such confidence was mirrored in the public buildings rising in Cathays Park. The capstone of a new Town Hall tower was fixed in position by the Mayor in 1904. On an adjacent plot Law Courts were taking shape, while the elegant South African War Memorial (not to be confused with the later Welsh National War Memorial created in 1928) stood nearby. The University of Wales Registry had been the first building to be erected in the Park. It was soon to be followed by a major College project over on the eastern boundary, while a county hall for Glamorgan would complete this first generation of buildings. What went up was both impressive and easy on the eye. During the twentieth century Cathays Park has evolved into Europe's, if not the world's, outstanding civic extravaganza.

Cardiff RFC had not been idle while this aggrandisement was taking place a few hundred yards from the Rugby pitch. Along with its sister cricket section within the Cardiff Athletic Club, the Rugby committee undertook the erection of a pavilion where players could change and clean off; and where officials and guests could talk business and socialise. A double-fronted building, it stood close to the River Taff at the junction of the cricket and Rugby football areas of Cardiff Arms Park. There was a gymnasium for indoor exercise, with space and headroom for 'touch and pass', hand-ball and physical jerks. As winter wore on Gwyn Nicholls and his fellows could luxuriate in the twelve-foot-square communal hot bath after training. There would follow feasts of buttered toast and kippers cooked at the coke fire lit and stoked by ground staff. Nicholls remarked to Charles Arthur that "It is a wonder that the Club has done without such a building for so long." Part of it was ready for use during the cricket XI's match against E.M. Grace's team in June 1904.

As the years went by the pavilion served as a handsome backdrop for many a group photograph of cricket and Rugby teams. Sadly it fell victim to heartless redevelopment when space was needed in 1934 for a double-decker North Stand overlooking the Rugby pitch.

The outlay on the gymnasium bore witness to the prosperity of Cardiff RFC. Now the club's international reputation received a tremendous boost through the selection of Percy Bush and Rhys Gabe to tour Australia and New Zealand with the 1904 British side captained by an abrasive Scot, D.R. Bedell-Sivright. His other Welsh personnel were Teddy Morgan, Willie Llewellyn, and A.F. Harding plus the as yet uncapped W.F. Jowett, T.S. Bevan and Tommy Vile.

In his *History of the British Lions* Clem Thomas says simply that Gwyn Nicholls was 'unavailable' to tour, and there is no documentation accounting for the star's absence. However, since his laundry venture with Bert Winfield was not only cementing foundations but also actively expanding, it is reasonable to surmise that the Wales captain did not feel he could take another summer off.

Furthermore, Nicholls may have privately decided that there was no Rugby glory remaining to be won in the southern hemisphere. He had toured there in a side which had seen off the opposition by three Tests to one. The Kiwis' record against Australian opposition was impressive, but not so as to suggest that they could give the British Isles a run for their money.

Further, the New Zealand appendage to the tour comprised just five games; fourteen had first to be played in Queensland and New South Wales. For Nicholls it was a case of 'been there, done that.'

He would have read with satisfaction match reports which told of the British Isles' sixteen victories in succession (including three Test defeats of Australia) before the move across the Tasman Sea. Now, however, after a couple of hard-fought provincial victories, the tourists went down to New Zealand at Wellington by nine points to three. They also met defeat at the hands of Auckland and could only draw with Taranaki.

The British reaction, which would have long-term consequences, was not to work out reasons for their failure but to explain it away. A consensus emerged attributing it to staleness and a surfeit of competitive Rugby. Bedell-Sivright also thought that lavish hospitality had been their undoing. As he had broken a leg in the first game, at Canterbury, he personally may have found it hard to avoid this generosity.

The captain and his manager Brian O'Brien had been mandated to identify and finalise key aspects of the forthcoming tour of Britain which their hosts would undertake, including its schedule and the opposition to be met. In discussion, however, there seems little doubt that the New Zealand negotiators were riled by the dismissive attitude of the British management and their unwillingness to concede that the better side had won the Test. This had two results: first, it sharpened the determination of the 'Colonials' to dent the Home Countries' pride in 1905. Second, because the English and Scottish tourists clung to excuses after returning home, their respective nations were not fully alerted to the strength of the challenge New Zealand could and would offer. Indeed, when the time came for the SRU to underwrite the games in Scotland with financial guarantees they totally refused (and were paid back in spectacular fashion for this ungraciousness).

But for the Welsh the experience had been salutary. When Teddy Morgan (who had taken on-field control after Bedell-Sivright was hurt) and his compatriots got back to Wales there were major topics for intensive discussion and analysis. Urgency was heightened by awareness that the big, exciting challenge posed by New Zealand lay a mere twelve months ahead.

There were new experiences to relate, some tactically meaningful. Others were just piquant, for example, some of the terminology fabricated as a sport evolves. In our time the New Zealand midfield includes two five-eighths, a term coined when the 'Father of Otago Rugby', coach Jimmy Duncan, adjusted the alignment of his Province's back division during a game. The change had to do with the positioning of the two players between the (scrum) half back and the three quarters.

After the match, in which the experiment had been a success and seemed sure to be made permanent, Duncan and his men debated what the players who had occupied the new positions should be called. Reasoned one bright spark, "A half back is 4/8ths; a three quarter 6/8ths; these two in between must be 5/8ths." So they have remained for a century of New Zealand Rugby.

The tourists spoke back home of the exciting *Haka*, a traditional Maori war dance calculated to unnerve the enemy and invoke support in battle from the gods. And tactically, there had been a first encounter with the 'wing forward' game as played by New Zealand's 'Rover'. The role was one which Dave Gallaher, who would skipper the 1905 All Blacks, had undertaken since his conversion from the front row in August 1903. This was the most valuable insight brought back home by the Welsh tourists, to be comprehended and considered by the national 'think tank'.

Gwyn Nicholls doubtless marked and digested what his friends had to tell him. As it happened, he had heard independently in a letter (which is held by his grandson Gwyn Williams) about New Zealand's tactical innovations from a cousin named Henry Austin Gazzard who now ran a building business in Wellington. Evidently the two men were not relatives who kept in touch, for Gazzard begins, "You will no doubt be surprised to hear from me and...will see from the above address that I am in New Zealand." In closing, he sends "kind regards to Uncle Hartley"

Gazzard, who had been in the Antipodes since 1898, had seen Nicholls play in Australia in 1899, had witnessed New

Zealand's 1904 victory over the British Isles, and more recently watched the defeat of South Island by a North Island XV led by Dave Gallaher. About the latter's play he was paranoid:

> Gallaher was continually offside and, except once or twice, was not penalised. He was allowed to do the same thing against Britain; and if your referees allow him the same amount of liberty, I do not care how many half backs you play... he will keep the ball from your three quarter line. ...I have written about him because all say he is the most dangerous man in the team.

But was there now any point in such intelligence being directed at Gwyn Nicholls? During the late summer of 1904 he wrote informing Cardiff RFC of his retirement from the game, a decision which also denied Wales his future availability. At an October 'smoker' in the new pavilion to welcome Bush and Gabe back from abroad he declined to comment on the finality of his decision; certainly at this time he was not in training. What Charles Arthur writes in his *History* is that at the start of this season "Gwyn Nicholls had retired from active football." But then he added cryptically, "for the time being." It may be that Nicholls himself and a small group of confidants knew that what he was really doing was taking a 'sabbatical'. His business partner Winfield also missed much of the new season.

With or without Wales' hero life, and Rugby, had to go on. The first half of Cardiff's season produced three defeats and eleven victories: not bad considering the absence of Nicholls, the prolonged rest that Bush had awarded himself, and Gabe's insistence on making a very gradual return to the fray (he was evidently up to speed by 10 December when he scored a crisp try at Blackheath). As the New Year approached, with the opening Four Nations game scheduled for 14 January, 1905, one concern dominated the general anticipation. Selectors deliberated, journalists speculated, common-or-garden fans simply wondered: had the last been seen of Prince Gwyn on a Rugby field?

All these parties could have been forgiven for deciding that it mattered rather less after England had been dismantled again at Cardiff. The Welsh ran in seven tries, which would remain the greatest number conceded by the visitors until Wales scored eight in 1922. Nicholls was at the game and would doubtless have been gratified to see his hallmark clearly stamped on Wales' performance, with five of the tries being scored by backs and three of those by wings.

Willie Llewellyn, automatically named by Wales' selectors as captain whenever Nicholls was absent, scored twice in Edinburgh as Wales gained a first success at Inverleith, but the going was harder than at Cardiff. Scotland led until just before the interval through a try by the burly tight forward Anthony Little, soon to be snapped up by Wigan Rugby League side after winning this single cap. Llewellyn levelled the scores; then, near the end, *The Scotsman* wrote: "The ball moved with bewildering rapidity between Owen, Trew and Dan Rees and reached Llewellyn again. The Welsh skipper put his head back and ran his best...eluding the grasp of Forrest he scored the winning try."

A second step had been taken along the road to a Triple Crown, but the Scottish Press was not well pleased and the "downright dirty, caddish tricks of the visitors" were condemned. Unwilling to take such criticism lying down the Welsh retaliated with allegations of violence perpetrated on Harding, Hodges, Owen and Trew, while Rhys Gabe really went to town on the Scots. He told reporters that, leading a foot-rush by his pack, Scotland's captain W.P. Scott had booted him on the backside as he dived in to check the drive. For six months, Gabe claimed, he could not sit down and had to take his classes at school standing up.

Earlier, we have conjectured that little was more likely to put Gwyn Nicholls on his mettle than the idea that he was no longer Number One or, worse, that his country could manage without him. Now, the Welsh team which he could claim to have moulded, and its star performers, were getting tremendous praise in the Press. He would also have taken note of a comment by 'Forward' in the *Western Mail* on the new Irish cap Basil MacLear's great performance as Ireland whipped England 17-3 at Cork. Wrote the columnist, surely with a strong ulterior motive, "He is one of the greatest centre three quarters playing today – if not *the* greatest. I will ask my readers to suspend judgement until they have seen him at Swansea."

Surprise, surprise: by 18 February the *Western Mail* was reporting: "Gwyn Nicholls is ill at ease in his retirement.... He will probably play at the Arms Park today against Newport...taking the place of young half back Jim Auckland who has a broken collar bone." Sure enough, on the morning of Monday, 20 February, 'The One and Only Gwyn Nicholls' screamed a headline. The report described a series of sizzling breaks by the Cardiffian which created two tries for Rhys Gabe in a 21-0 defeat of the visitors. The sequence of events now has Nicholls featuring in Glamorgan's victory over Yorkshire, who were touring south-west Britain. The Cardiff centre was not an original choice: a player called McGregor was side-lined to make room for him. Glamorgan won the game; Nicholls dropped a goal. Was pressure brought to bear on the Glamorgan county selectors – in the national interest – to pick Nicholls? Not initially named in Cardiff's team against Penarth on 25 February, he was quoted in the Press as stating, "I'm not a candidate for the Welsh team to play Ireland". But: Cardiff's team to play Penarth was changed. Nicholls was in it.

Finally, on 8 March, the thirty-year old veteran of nineteen international matches was selected as a (non-travelling) reserve for the Wales XV to play for a Triple Crown. Additional spice was added to the Four Nations cauldron by Ireland's 11-5 victory in Edinburgh, which meant that they too could win the Triple Crown. Sent to cover the game, 'Forward' once again built up MacLear: "We shall not see his equal in the Welsh three quarter line" – a prediction printed a couple of days before the championship decider, when it seemed that Nicholls was unlikely to take the field.

But he did. The bait laid by 'Forward' had worked. Despite the victory, however, which brought the Welsh a fourth Triple Crown, the day is remembered by the great centre as "one of the most unpleasant experiences" of his life. Once again Nicholls allowed himself to be manoeuvred by circumstances into a position which would provoke strong opposition and rancour in certain quarters – as had happened in summer 1900 when he upset Viv Huzzey over the issue of the Cardiff captaincy. Once more, vacillation and a weak will on his part brought acrimony in its wake.

This time it was the whole of west Wales that he enraged. In the midfield Wales had chosen Swansea's Dan Rees to partner Gabe, with his uncapped clubmate Frank Gordon as a nominated reserve. On the morning of the match Rees notified the WRU of his inability to play. Rightly or, as it turned out, wrongly the selection committee decided that the five-times-capped Rees was standing down to give his clubmate the cap; and, instead of bringing in Gordon, called up Nicholls.

Years later the latter recalled the repercussions, including the angry reaction of the Swansea crowd: "Gordon was a player worthy of his cap and I for some time refused to accept the invitation to play. But on being told definitely that they [the WRU] would not tolerate a man standing down for another, and even if I persisted in my refusal they would not play Gordon, I at last consented. I may say that the committee's request was augmented by an appeal from most of the players, and this was what swayed me. I write this because even now I am occasionally twitted on the subject by some of my Swansea friends."

Some of the pent-up rage and frustration that Cardiff can stoke in Swansea bosoms was vented on the man who had so often been acclaimed at St Helens: "I expected a bad reception from some of the rougher element in the crowd but was hardly prepared for the bombardment of mud and oranges while being photographed with the team beforehand. It was a trying and unpleasant experience. Every little mistake I made was seized upon by the onlookers to demonstrate their displeasure."

The crowd was somewhat mollified by the result of an entertaining, open match from which Wales emerged with a 10-3 victory and another Crown. The tries which won the game were scored in the first half by stand off half Wyndham Jones of Mountain Ash, in his only game for Wales, and Teddy Morgan, George Davies placing two conversions. Later, medical evidence was cited in the Press to the effect that Dan Rees's illness was a genuine, and painful, bout of pleurisy. That summer he signed professional forms for Hull Kingston Rovers. Luckless Frank Gordon stayed in Swansea's ranks but never did win an International cap. And the dangerous Basil MacLear of Ireland? He was tackled out of contention that day. By a certain E.G. Nicholls.

A restorative footnote to Nicholls' 'unpleasant' end of season experience was Cardiff's first game against a French club when Stade Français came to the Arms Park on April 3. The story has it that after the Welsh side built up a big lead Nicholls suggested that the French should be allowed to score a try by way of encouragement. For a time they were too excited to take the chances offered to them, until at last a centre managed to race in under the bar. Immediately his hand was shaken by Gwyn Nicholls who said, "You ran very fast then!" The Frenchman tweaked his moustache, grinned and replied: "Ah! But M'sieu Nicholl – you no run fast that time."

A final sweetener in the summer of 1905 was Gwyn Nicholls' wedding on 21 June to 'Nell' Thomas, a Docksman's daughter whom he had met some years earlier at a coming-of-age party for Bert Winfield. Said the *South Wales Echo*,

> A marriage which was quite a big event in South Wales football circles was solemnised on Wednesday afternoon by the Rev W.E. Shaw at Roath Park Presbyterian Church, between Mr E.G. Nicholls and Emmaline Helen, youngest daughter of Mr and Mrs Philip Perch-Thomas of Penylan Road, Roath. The bridegroom is not only the greatest three quarter Wales has produced but was also captain of the invincible Welsh XV.

The paper named the best man as Mr H.B. Winfield, the 'old' Wales full back (he was all of twenty-six years of age) while among the bridesmaids was the bride's sister 'Queenie' Thomas, later to become his wife. Also present were Alec Timms and Willie Llewellyn, "the Welsh captain only when Mr Nicholls is unavailable". On what authority, one wonders, did the newspaper print that?

After a reception at the Park Hotel the couple left for a west country honeymoon, Nell proudly wearing both a wedding ring and a special one from her husband set with diamonds and rubies. It is a reasonable speculation that the first night was spent at Weston-super-Mare's Grand Atlantic Hotel, which advertised aggressively in the Welsh Press. Weston was a resort which the family came to favour for summer holidays in later years. The couple's final destination was Newquay.

Gwyn Nicholls had already moved from his bachelor rooms

to a newly-constructed semi-detached residence in the northern suburb of Whitchurch, still within walking distance of the Laundry. This was the address to which the newly-weds returned. Boasting front and rear gardens, three ground-floor reception rooms and four bedrooms the house was in every way a suitable home for an up-and-coming businessman and his wife. In the absence of their name from the title deeds it seems likely that the property was rented from the builder. But the couple were allowed to call it 'Westbury' after Gwyn's birthplace; the ceramic plaque bearing the name is still to be seen on a gatepost.

Thus in many ways, Nicholls' thirty-first year had proved unforgettable. More matters of moment awaited his attention before 1905 would end

Fifteen

At the other end of the world, downright common sense had underpinned the evolution of New Zealand Rugby. In 1895, following some seasons' internecine skirmishing, factions in the North and South islands merged to found a national Rugby Union. This parturition had been both painful and prolonged, in the light of which the new body's resistance to the advances made to it in 1899 by Australia are better understood.

The 'furthest Colony', however, had needed to show much patience before getting its chance to make a debut on the world sporting stage. It will be remembered that just before the 1899 British side's departure from Sydney the necessary guarantees were announced for a New Zealand tour of Great Britain – 'Home', as it was still termed by expatriates in those days. Since then, the time lapse of half a decade had been frustrating. The visit of Bedell-Sivright's side compensated somewhat for the delay, and certainly whetted the appetite for battle.

Give or take a Christian Cullen or Bob Burgess, the outstanding characteristic of All Black Rugby as perceived in the British Isles is not so much genius as total thoroughness, which dates back to the earliest days. As soon as January 1905 G.H. Dixon was named Manager for a tour of Britain not due to start until nine months later. New Zealand's meticulous preparation for the expedition continued with a fund-raising progression around their country by a select squad which played top provincial sides. This also served as a series of trials, in which tour candidates could be earmarked or eliminated. There was even a trip to meet dogged opposition across in Sydney. In August a 27-strong party was named to travel 'Home', to be captained by Dave Gallaher and coached by Jimmy Duncan.

It left New Zealand with the words of Prime Minister Seddon ringing in its members' ears: "I want you to do your very best in the Home Country. But we don't care if you lose all your other matches as long as you beat Wales." Unerringly he had pointed to the team's primary mission. But why? And how?

It may simply be that, as Triple Crown winners three times since the turn of the century, Wales were perceived as the strongest of the northern hemisphere nations and therefore the side against whom New Zealand would need to prove themselves. Or was there some 'getting even' involved? Had Welsh members of Bedell-Sivright's touring side the previous year been patronising about their hosts' quest to become a world Rugby power? Certainly Percy Bush was a cheeky chappie whose mischievous chatter may have got under thin Kiwi skins.

On the long sea voyage attention to detail continued to be scrupulous. Once the passenger liner *Rimutaka* had rounded Cape Horn and left cold, squally weather behind there was scrummaging, jogging, and sprinting along a 40-yard sector of the deck which was reserved for the players. Passing practice was intense; boxing gloves and a punch-bag were also used. The tourists clearly ate well, and it is recorded that many put on weight between Auckland and Great Britain.

Their liner called at Montevideo and Tenerife before reaching Plymouth on 8 September to be welcomed by a group of RFU officials. There followed a journey by train to Newton Abbot and the town's Globe Hotel, from which the party emerged each day to practise vigorously and harden themselves up with contact training. There was the chance to break in new boots and try on kit for size.

In 1905 this consisted of black jerseys, stockings and shorts, the latter having superseded white breeches a few years previously. The only non-black parts of this outfit were its white collar and bootlaces, plus the silver fern emblem on the left breast. White rings around the stocking-tops were a later, minor amendment. Here, then, was a subfusc strip which positively invited the nick-name 'All Black', a term reserved in this book for men and teams from 1905 on.

In his volume *Haka!* the great New Zealand radio commentator Winston McCarthy offers two explanations of its actual origin. First, after one of the tourists' victories a newspaper headline was meant to read 'All Backs', implying that the

tourists' forwards were playing like backs, only for a typo-
graphical error to cause it to read 'All Blacks'. But McCarthy's
preferred version is that the term was coined by a *Daily Mail*
Rugby writer called J.A. Buttery. This view is supported in
Chester & McMillan's *History of All Black Rugby*: writing of the
match against Hartlepool Clubs a month into the tour they say,
"In the *Daily Mail* report on this match [by Buttery] the term
'All Blacks' appeared probably for the first time in print.... As
early as 27 September the same paper had used the term, 'the
Blacks'".

While there is certainly something aesthetically agreeable to
onlookers about black silhouettes upon a meadow-green background, such a romantic view would hardly be shared by
players who have experienced the All Black dynamic at close
range down the century. To them, the aura of the dark uniform
has an element of the sinister about it. Packs of black-garbed
forwards embody a menace that eight men kitted out in white,
or even fiery scarlet, cannot transmit. A hostile task-force which
eschews colour in favour of monochrome means business.

This is how it was from the very start, when on Saturday 16
September New Zealand travelled into Exeter for their country's
first match on British soil. Skipper Dave Gallaher had hoped,
and told journalists of his ambition, to win a majority of his
side's club and County fixtures. They, and local officials, had
patted him encouragingly on the back and advised his tourists
to do their best against the reigning champions of the south
west. But at tea-time on that first Saturday the pride of Devon
lay shattered by fifty-five points to four. New Zealand had run
in twelve tries; their full back Gillett touched the ball just twice
in the game. The news defied credence in Fleet Street, where
sub-editors corrected what they thought must be an error in
transmission to read "Devon 55, New Zealand 4".

Despite their long sea voyage the New Zealanders still
possessed more than a residue of the match fitness they had
built up before leaving home. In contrast, the British season in
those far-off days did not move from first gear until October;
the Devon XV was manifestly unfit and short of co-ordinated
practice. Notwithstanding, the gap which had become apparent
between the two sides' relative ability was huge. Billy Wallace,

described in the records as a 'utility back', scored three of the tourists' tries, converting eight and landing a penalty. For Devon, Lillicrap dropped a late goal.

The All Blacks remained in the west of England for the next two fixtures, defeating Cornwall 41-0 at Camborne and posting a similar result at Bristol. This was the first fixture to be viewed by a voluble party of New Zealand supporters who had caught up with their team. Interest, and no doubt concern, had suddenly intensified too on the other side of the River Severn. The Welsh Rugby Union's secretary Walter Rees headed a group of visitors who included Llewellyn and Gabe.

The tourists went through September with five victories; not until 7 October did they concede a try, which fell to the Durham wing Clarkson. Their fixtures began to attract record crowds. Names like Jimmy Hunter, George Smith, Bill Cunningham and Fred Roberts were on every Rugby follower's lips. Above all their skipper Dave Gallaher, he of the impassive mien and bandit moustache, was winning a massive reputation – not only as a leader and motivator but also as a bogey-man whose tactics were controversial.

The visitors brushed aside all opposition aside with contempt, and by the eve of their first International match, against Scotland, British Rugby could be said to be in shock. New Zealand had conceded only 15 points in their nineteen consecutive victories, piling up an astonishing 612 themselves.

Ninety five years on, the teams of Great Britain and Ireland are well used to cataclysmic reverses at the hands of the former Dominions. In 1905 what was happening to the best XVs in the land was a new experience, numbing to their members and to spectators. Jaws dropped. Brows creased. Eyes widened in disbelief. Not since 1066 had an invading war-band been able to disembark with such impunity upon British soil, bent on conquest and the rape of reputations.

The Kiwis' ruthlessness was leavened with a high entertainment content deriving from the continuity of their game. England's captain in the Thirties, Wavell Wakefield, had seen them as a boy: he later wrote, "They emphasised the necessity for physical fitness, and with the accompaniment of intensive backing-up...they ran riot." Their approach differed from anything to be seen in the northern hemisphere.

The shock-waves certainly penetrated South Wales. But during that autumn there were distractions. On 23 October 1905, exactly four years after its Foundation Stone was laid, Cardiff's new Town Hall was scheduled for opening. It never acquired the title, for the Government chose that day to elevate the ancient settlement beside the Taff to city status, with a chief citizen who would henceforth be known as a Lord Mayor. In 1905 the office was held by Alderman Robert Hughes, who quickly received and accepted an invitation from his opposite number in London to join the Lord Mayor's Parade in November. Thus Cardiff's First Citizen found himself cheered by onlookers who lined Embankment, the Strand and Fleet Street. His successor William Crossman became Sir William when Edward VII visited the new City in 1907.

But with the approach of winter the limelight moved from Cathays Park to the arena beside the Taff and the great match it was to stage. Interestingly, whereas today's schedulers of major tours attempt to set up an ultra-high-profile farewell game, such showmanship had yet to be cultivated in 1905. The All Blacks' visit would end with matches against club sides and a Glamorgan County XV; but what was arguably the acme of their tour (had not their Prime Minister told them so?), the game against Wales at Cardiff Arms Park, would precede these four matches by taking place on 16 December. Had the clubs not proved to be so strong all could have ended in anti-climax.

Elsewhere, New Zealand's wins continued. The Welsh were twitchy. Surely these giants in black were not the same men who, a year before, had laboured to overcome Bedell-Sivright's 'tired and stale' British side? Alarm bells tolled at the news that the tourists had scored seven tries in a 32-0 victory at Blackheath. Wrote 'Observer' in the *South Wales Daily News*:

> No Welsh side can beat the 'Heathens' on their own ground by anything like the 32 points with which the Antipodeans won.... Can seven forwards focus as much force on a scrimmage as an eight? If so, the eighth man is obviously more use outside the scrum than in it.... Gallaher was occasionally offside.

As a matter of fact a recent Cardiff win at the Rectory Field had been by 24-0 – not that far removed from 32-0. However, such jittery journalism indicated the Welsh mood as the All Black juggernaut moved through the Home Countries.

More scare-mongering concerned the fitness of the dynamic Teddy Morgan who was reported as having a heart complaint that would oblige him to retire. The little wing retorted angrily in the Press, explaining that his final medical examinations were pending and that he would miss a couple of matches in order to concentrate on his studies. "I will play against New Zealand if selected," he told journalists.

It was a former team-mate of Gwyn Nicholls and captain of Wales, T.W. Pearson, who now began the latest campaign to lure the former back to the colours. By this time Docks Engineer at Newport, Pearson wrote strongly on November 6:

> The only chance of Wales winning is if Gwyn Nicholls turns out. And there is an unanimous wish among the members of the Welsh Union that the great centre should do so. Having always taken great care of himself, at 31 he is still in his prime. It is understood that Nicholls himself has a sincere desire to play.

All this may well have been true. The fly in the ointment, however, was the continued absence from the Rugby field of the man in question.

It is clear from the book which he later published, however, that Nicholls had seen the tourists play, probably as a member of the group which travelled to Bristol with Walter Rees in September. Further opportunities to study All Black tactics followed at Gloucester and Taunton, where there is no doubt that he found the controversial role played by the New Zealand captain Dave Gallaher challenging. A summary of its virtues and shortcomings follows; and it is important to remember that Gallaher played consistently within the Laws as interpreted by his own Rugby Union at the time (and up until 1930).

Early in its Rugby history New Zealand had shrunk the pack to seven men who packed down 2-3-2. The eighth forward's role was, initially, to stand beside scrums protecting the "half back" (or scrum half) from opponents. Hence, he was part of an obstructionist tactic. Soon it was noted that the half back found it difficult to put the ball into a 2-3-2 scrum and then get behind a quick heel in time to deliver good possession to his outsides. So the eighth forward, who became known as a 'winging forward' or 'rover', was charged with putting in the ball. Even when it was not New Zealand's put-in, Gallaher's policy was to stand in the same place. If the opposition struck successfully for the ball he and the All Black scrum half could execute a pincer move with every chance of taking out the latter's opposite number.

Gwyn Nicholls thought that the wing forward concept offered "too many temptations for obstruction...to expect any but a saint to resist them...and saints are rather out of place in Rugby Football".

Removing his tongue from his cheek, he adds:

> I question whether the New Zealand wing forward (off-side scrum half as he too frequently is) is quite as useful as the New Zealanders fancy he is.... It must not be forgotten that, as he is of necessity always on one side of the scrum he has little or no opportunity of detecting the ball's passage out on the other side and is consequently totally unable to get round in anything like time. Then he is often liable to be misled as to the location of the ball and, being in a feverish anxiety to anticipate any untoward occurrence, is frequently likely to be pulled up for over-running the ball and getting offside.

Writing unusually candidly for a true-black Kiwi, Winston McCarthy says in *Haka!* "...the criticism levelled at Gallaher and Gillett in the wing forward position in 1905, and indeed at all of New Zealand's wing forwards up to the 1930s, was fully justified."

The fact is, however, that the 1905 All Blacks were permitted to employ the 'rover forward' freely and effectively in their thirty-two games in Great Britain and the three that followed in France and Canada.

As for Gwyn Nicholls, slowly but surely the results and scores reported from beyond Offa's Dyke, and the tribulations of England's clubs and Counties, were rekindling competitive fires within his breast. Against all expectations, the challenge presented by 'the Fernlanders' (as the popular Press sometimes labelled the tourists) was turning out to be one which truly merited a serious response from Wales' senior Rugby citizen. He still had currency, with both selectors and supporters. Further, Cardiff were enjoying a splendid season; if Nicholls could get fit he might take part in two matches against New Zealand. But for the time being he continued to lie low.

New Zealand were not enjoying themselves in Edinburgh. Suddenly, together, a number of unacceptable aspects of Rugby tours were manifesting themselves, starting with the tedious journey north from Bedford. Not until late on the Thursday evening before this first Test did they arrive at Waverley rail terminus and troop wearily up the flight of steps to check in at the North British Hotel.

They awoke to a freezing morning, with snow lying on the hills above the Scottish capital. When manager Dixon went with Gallaher on reconnaissance to Inverleith it was to find that, unbelievably, the Scots had learned no lessons from their maladroit handling of the match with Wales in 1899: an unprotected Inverleith pitch was bone-hard. Watery November sunshine, low in the sky, softened its surface just sufficiently for the tourists' management to agree that the game could be played.

It turned out to be the closest match for the visitors outside Wales. At ten minutes they fell behind for the first time on the tour, when Scotland's scrum half Ernest Simson dropped a goal; and although they took a lead through unconverted tries by Frank Glasgow and George Smith, half time found them trailing again after John MacCallum's try. A gruelling second half ensued and a mere five minutes remained when Scotland's luck ran out. Smith's second try restored New Zealand's lead, Bill Cunningham rubbing in the tourists' superiority with a fourth before the final whistle. The faithful Kiwi supporters' road-show yelled and cheered its jubilation: more than one Press reporter noted how many of the Scots in the 21,000 crowd turned their backs on the field at the end and trooped in sullen silence from the stadium.

In truth, there was every reason for the tourists to brand Edinburgh as forgettable. No official welcome had been extended to them. Scotland declined to award their players caps for the game, a decision that the 1905 New Zealanders no doubt found offensive in the light of their record. The match ball, which Francis Glasgow had secreted as a souvenir beneath his jersey, was retrieved from the All Blacks' changing room by Scottish Rugby Union Secretary Jock Smith. Finally, though the SRU treated its players to dinner, the New Zealanders ate alone at their hotel.

Their next experience was scarcely more enjoyable. Only 8,000 were at Hampden Park – a ground able to accommodate 100,000 – to see the tourists defeat West of Scotland 22-0. Again there was no post-match hospitality, until some Queens Park soccer officials stepped in and took the tourists to a glee club. But Mr Dixon and his men had the last laugh. In lieu of a guaranteed sum from the two matches played in Scotland the SRU had offered the net gate. As a result the All Blacks' pocketed £1,700, or about four times what they would have collected from a guarantee.

The *Western Mail*'s sports pages for Monday, 27 November, 1905, made momentous reading. Its reporters were now following the All Blacks' every move, and from Dublin came accounts of their match against Ireland. A second tense and hard-fought Test, watched by a 16,000 crowd, had ended with the tourists victorious. Though at first sight a 15-0 margin appears comfortable it comprised only three tries, each converted by the reliable Wallace. Welsh journalists suggested that the small stature and weight of Ireland's pack, fatally, had been unable to compete against New Zealand forwards who included men like 15-stone Fred 'Fatty' Newton of Canterbury and Auckland's 6 feet 3 inch tall George Nicholson.

Bracketed with the news from Ireland was a report on Cardiff's match at Swansea. In its preview two mornings earlier the *Western Mail* had lamented, "Too often Cardiff leave their hearts behind at Landore." The writer was noting how the 'Metropolitans' habitually left home full of energy and optimism, only to collapse feebly at the St Helens stadium.

For this he was imputing blame to the dispiriting entry by rail into the town from the east, through the then nauseous Lower Swansea Valley. The area, at whose heart lies the suburb of

Landore, has been rehabilitated and greened up in recent decades; but in 1905 it still bore the disfiguring marks of the world's 'copper capital'. A score of foundries and copper-related works belched dark satanic smoke and foul odours into the atmosphere and discharged evil amalgams of poisonous waste into the luckless River Tawe.

Perhaps on this occasion the Cardiff players closed their eyes and placed handkerchiefs over their noses as they passed through Landore. The fact is that for the first time in eight years they beat their western rivals, by seven points to nil, thus relieving them of a ground record which had lasted for three seasons.

But the really big story was the *Western Mail*'s 'lead': "The Welsh captain, Mr Gwyn Nicholls, is back in strict training after his absence from the game".

Nicholls had enjoyed high success with Cardiff. He had led Welsh XVs which had won Championship titles and Triple Crowns. He held more than his share of caps. He had been a winner Down Under. If he was getting fit again, that could mean only one thing: his hunger for success and glory was undiminished. A new gauntlet had been thrown down. He would pick it up.

Sixteen

In Limerick the tourists won their twenty-third game, 33-0 against Munster, before enduring a rough crossing from Dunlaoghaire to Holyhead. This was followed by the tedious rail journey to London where the moon was shining brightly before they checked into their hotel, with a Test against England less than 48 hours away. George Dixon gave his men a rest day before the match, but decreed an early start for Crystal Palace on the morning of 2 December to beat the crowds who would throng to the big game. Officially, the attendance is recorded as 45,000, but unofficial sources put it at 75,000. A huge number of spectators had penetrated the ground without paying; others handed over £10 for tickets on the black market. Again, observers from Wales were present, though not in force since the Welsh selectors were holding a Final Trial at Cardiff.

The roving activities of Dave Gallaher (who decided to play in this game despite a minor injury) had sparked an agonising debate in England (and also Wales): should they hold firm to tradition and field a mix of eight forwards and seven backs? Or would it pay to meet New Zealand's rover tactic with a loose forward of their own? At Crystal Palace England opted to replicate the All Black line-up, selecting the Oxford Blue John Raphael as their 'Gallaher'.

No matter where Raphael had spent his afternoon, it would have made no difference to the result. Nor could success be achieved through the presence in England's ranks of two players whose Rugby upbringing had been in Wales – Llandovery-born D.R. Gent and J.L. Mathias who hailed from Pembrokeshire. New Zealand led 9-0 at half time, adding a further six points in the second half to finish winners by five unconverted tries to nil. At least the English looked after their conquerors, dining them out at the Trocadero Hotel.

'Forward' of the *Western Mail* was beside himself with appre-

137

hension in the Monday morning edition. "Saxons Routed at Crystal Palace", screamed his headline. Below it he asked nervously: "Have we fifteen players in Wales capable of playing better football than that wonderful combination of athletes from the far south? – and beating them? Therein lies the root of all the anxiety which holds such a spell in our land."

Then he comforted himself and his compatriots: "England were the weakest side I have seen sporting the red rose. Cardiff would have beaten them even more decisively than New Zealand."

The All Blacks now moved back into the English shires, defeating Cheltenham, Cheshire and Yorkshire before heading for Wales. The margins of victory were 18-0, 34-0 and 40-0, so that since their narrow victory over Scotland they had gone seven games without conceding a point, running up 177 themselves. This makes palpable nonsense of suggestions in the English Press that the All Blacks were stale when they came into the Principality.

The build-up to the Test intensified in south east Wales, with the Welsh team selection attracting its time-honoured mix of plaudits – and brick-bats. Aberdare's leviathan, Dai 'Tarw' (Bull) Jones, capped nine times, was held by some to be playing below his best. Willie Llewellyn, a scorer of sixteen tries for Wales and a vice-captain when required for Nicholls, had recently hinted at retirement in order to set up in business. Some took this as a sign of less than total commitment, maintaining that his place should have gone to Hopkin Maddock of London Welsh. This attitude is worth contrasting with the tolerance, even deference, shown to Gwyn Nicholls at times when his availability was about as predictable as the weather.

A dominant talking-point concerned the selection of Cliff Pritchard, then of Pontypool, to neutralise the threat posed by Dave Gallaher. Strictly speaking, Pritchard was a midfield player, good enough to have stood in twice for Nicholls at centre for Wales. However, the edge-of-scrum role which he was now being asked to perfect – in less than a fortnight – did not require the physical bulk of the 'Rhondda forwards'. In the new position Pritchard was to fill, nimbleness and vision were requisites. The Welsh would refer to him as an 'extra back'.

In the Welsh Trial Gwyn Nicholls was reported as having 'done little', but neither was he guilty of errors. No dissenting voice or pen was raised at his recall to the Welsh side, of which he was duly given the captaincy. With this in mind he had been applying his formidable Rugby brain to dissecting other aspects of New Zealand's game besides the 'rover' tactic. He had observed, for example, how the tourists contested line out ball: "One All Black goes for an opponent jumping for the ball; another goes for the ball." Having noted what went on, the captain and his pack could develop an effective counter-strategy.

Perhaps the most valuable conversation Nicholls had in the build-up to the Test was with A.F. Harding, his former Cardiff clubmate who now captained London Welsh. This yielded a double bonus. First, the two men were able jointly to work out how their forwards should pack down and push at the scrummages. I paraphrase the way Nicholls put it across:

> Three-strong British front rows have been going to pieces in front of the All Blacks' 2-3-2 formation...the latter have hung back, before slipping their heads, the one inside and the other outside the outer opponent's head. So they have secured a 'loose head', as they call it.
>
> In our front row, three men will pack, in a 3-2-2 formation. But: the last two will wait to see which side the ball is to be put in – after which the Welsh forward on that side will bind himself to the other two outside the New Zealand loose head. Thus that gentleman's manoeuvres will be bottled up and our spare man will then fall back, to give our pack a 3-4 arrangement.

Nicholls later wrote, "But our forwards had to work very hard. The All Black front rank were tremendously hard pushers, owing to the inward motion of the two side-row men". This squeezing effect lay behind what was called the New Zealand 'wedge', which could fragment an opposing pack unless it was sternly countered. Nicholls also warned his men how the tourists 'screwed' a scrum – 'wheeled' in today's parlance – and discussed with them how this might be prevented.

The other invaluable outcome of Harding's visit to Wales was on 9 December when Cardiff had a fixture with Blackheath. Thanks to the London Welsh skipper's cordial relationship with the 'Heathens' the latters' collaboration was secured in staging what was, in effect, a dress rehearsal for the Welsh back division that would play against New Zealand: all except the Swansea scrum half Dicky Owen were on duty, and Blackheath went down by twenty-four points to four.

On icy December turf Nicholls was tackled heavily at one stage and left the field rubbing a shoulder at full time. By Monday, however, he was quoted in the *Western Mail* as being satisfied that the bruising had eased, and that he would be fit to play in five days' time. The Welsh camp breathed again. The excitement and tension were rising.

Cardiff was bracing itself for an invasion – not only by unbeaten All Black Rugby players but also by a veritable multitude of fans determined to see the game. The Great Western Railway station stood ready for fifty excursion trains scheduled to arrive from far and wide. They included one chartered by Irish enthusiasts, who would come into Wales through Milford Haven. The Taff Vale Railway promised twenty five special outings from the Valleys. A group of striking Monmouthshire miners said they would walk to and from the match. The great Bute Docks were to be closed at 10 a.m. on Saturday to allow employees to attend. Clearly the hotels, bars, restaurants, night clubs and places of entertainment in the new city could look forward to a bonanza.

For its part the Welsh Rugby Union was greatly troubled on 11 and 12 December. First, without warning a severe frost hardened the turf at Cardiff Arms Park; the Union put down as much straw as it could buy from local farms and hoped that the mid-winter temperature would rise.

Secondly, a disagreement arose over the refereeing of the match. Walter Rees had offered New Zealand a choice from four officials – two Irishmen, an Englishman and a Scot. Through Mr Dixon the tourists threw out this quartet and submitted four other names (one of whom was a current *bête noire* of Welsh Rugby, none other than Mr Findlay of the SRU whose singular rulings had cost Wales a Triple Crown or two). This second group of names did not find favour with the WRU, and accordingly a neutral country was asked to make the appointment. That is how a certain John Dallas of Scotland assumed control of Rugby football's World Championship, 1905 vintage.

There cannot be a true Rugby fan who does not know of the controversy surrounding the Cardiff Test in which the 1905 All Blacks suffered their single defeat, and a ruling by the referee which Kiwis still condemn. We will look more closely at Mr Dallas's contribution in due course, and his disallowing of the equalising score claimed by New Zealand; but one or two theories which are wide of the mark can be dismissed at this point. First, the referee was not a middle-aged has-been who was unable to keep up with the play. Aged twenty-seven, he had won his single International cap a mere two years earlier, scoring a try in the victory over England which clinched a Triple Crown for the Scots (not the greatest friends of the Welsh at this time). There is no reason to doubt any of this young man's rulings in the 1905 clash on grounds of unfitness.

Secondly, Winston McCarthy was surely carried away (as he often was, wonderfully, in commentary) when he wrote that the referee wore "his ordinary walking clothes, shoes, high collar and all". Contemporary pictures of big-match referees show men sensibly garbed in shorts, or at least breeches, and open necked shirts. Blazers, yes – this dress persisted until after World War II. But walking shoes? No. There is plenty of pictorial evidence indicating that by 1905 referees, like the players, wore boots with 'pegs', bars or 'studs'.

Having settled the refereeing issue the WRU turned to more routine matters. It announced that 42,000 spectators would be 'catered for'; that is, the crowd number was to be capped in the interest of safety and the gates closed, with a posse of mounted police enforcing discipline. Pictorial evidence indicates a plenitude of trees and lamp-posts in Westgate Street offering vantage points to frustrated fanatics.

In 1905 there were two main entrance gates to the ground. At one, opposite the Angel Hotel, spectators would pay a shilling to reach the north or west terraces. Entry via the County Club gate, opposite Guildhall Street, cost two shillings and channelled people to the east terrace and the covered enclosures on each side of the grandstand. The latter's 1800 seats were reserved for officials, VIPs and committeemen of various Welsh clubs. Programmes would be on sale, hot from Rees's Electric Press, while pre-match entertainment was to be provided by the

Band of the Second Battalion the Welsh [sic] Regiment.

Wales held a number of special squad training periods in the week leading up to the game. Together with Cardiff colleagues Gabe and Nicholls, Percy Bush completed a club triangle in midfield so that, although he was a new cap – the only one – it proved easy to integrate him into the tactical master-plan. Further, he had gained experience of the All Blacks' methods and tactics with the Bedell-Sivright tourists, leading some writers on the game to say that "the All Blacks feared Percy Bush above all men." However, despite his undoubted ability, there is no evidence that he cut much ice Down Under.

All in all, then, the Welsh kept a low profile and let the All Blacks capture the headlines. The tourists arrived at Cardiff, with their one hundred per cent record, at five minutes to six on Thursday, 14 December. Crowds lined the streets and cheered them all the way to their headquarters at the old Queen's Hotel in St Mary Street. Chester and McMillan write that it was the biggest crowd to have greeted the New Zealanders, and the party considered the welcome the most memorable extended to them.

The New Zealand management was quick to oblige the local Press by holding a news conference attended by George Dixon and Dave Gallaher. From the outset their reported public statements and attitudes to the task in hand were challenging and provocative. Mr Dixon told journalists, "The Welsh forwards seem too small to do well against our robust fellows, especially young Deans [a back] who weighs fourteen stones.... As for Bush my captain, Mr Gallaher, outplayed him in New Zealand last year and will do so again. He is the world's keenest footballer."

Gallaher himself spoke up proudly: "We were told before leaving New Zealand that we would not win a match here. Well, we have swept all before us and proved that our standard of football is infinitely above yours."

The New Zealanders ran out on the Friday morning before attending Cardiff's newest showpiece, the City Hall, for a civic reception. As they entered the Parlour players were presented with a medallion by the Lady Mayoress. It depicted Cardiff's coat of arms and an elegant silver fern. The visitors said their thanks with a fiery version of the Haka.

The Lord Mayor told them, "North, south, east and west – this is being looked upon as the match of the tour." Mr Dixon was in a more diplomatic mood than he had been the day before: "Never have we seen such unmistakeable keenness. On this tour we have done our best and enjoyed a fair measure of success. Thank you for entertaining us, and for the mementoes you have given to our men." The tourists mingled with local luminaries and signed autographs. Some unnamed players said that it would be galling to have come this far unbeaten only to lose a hundred per cent record.

Gwyn Nicholls later confirmed a certain 'unease' which had been detected in the All Blacks' camp by a team-mate (probably Gabe). The young tourists were reminded how the British side in the Antipodes the previous year had lost its unblemished record at Wellington. They appeared keyed-up and ill-at-ease.

But how was the Welsh camp? And its leader?

We do not know how much sleep Gwyn Nicholls enjoyed on the eve of the match. Did he push back the bedclothes, stand at the window and gaze into the night? Was he conscious of an awesome burden piled across his shoulders? He had begun to preach his near-mystic gospel about "the spirit of the side"; would it inspire his fourteen fellow 'chess-masters' of Rugby?

There was Bert Winfield, an ultra-dependable last line of defence, with a screw-kick that could soar half the length of the pitch. Teddy Morgan and Willie Llewellyn could scorch touch-lines like greased lightning given a vital half-a-yard's space by Nicholls and Rhys Gabe. Outside the miniature man-of-steel Dickie Owen would be Percy Bush, re-positioned in Cardiff's ranks as a stand off half by his captain.

And the forwards: 'Boxer' Harding and J.F. Williams who had been in the Middlesex side defeated 34-0 by New Zealand now thirsted for revenge. Charles Pritchard owned a shop. Jehoida Hodges was the thinking man's forward, Dai Jones his pupil with the big muscles that made the theories work. Line out expert Will Joseph was from Swansea's ranks, while the man from Newport, George Travers, was a specialist hooker.

Finally, there was the ace in the hole, Cliff Pritchard, the Pontypool undertaker. His contribution at the start of the game's second quarter would be crucial, and in the end decisive.

But could the skipper himself meet this greatest of challenges on the morrow? In three short weeks of training he had gone conscientiously on stamina-building runs, sprinted, done his press-ups and watched his diet. But experience would have told him that he was desperately short of match practice: the capacity to take a big tackle, or 'hit' as the moderns have it, get up from the turf, and return to the action as if nothing untoward had happened.

And could he still command these veterans of his? Would they be led by him? Or did they see him as old hat, doomed to be a liability against the thrustful young All Blacks as he sought to re-kindle glory and glamour from the embers of his career? Willie Llewellyn once said, "He was a born leader and captain to whom we instinctively looked up, though he was only a few years older than any of us. In a hard match, a word – or merely a look – from him was as effective as string of orders from other people." If Gwyn had heard those sentiments, he could happily have closed the curtains and gone back to bed. But they were not spoken until thirty-six years had gone by, in a 1941 radio broadcast two years after his death.

Promoted President of the Board of Trade only days before, David Lloyd George told London reporters, "I sincerely hope Wales will win. I will send them a telegram if they do."

The day promised to be that big.

Seventeen

Anyone who has played or watched Rugby in South Wales can imagine the Cardiff weather as dawn broke on 16 December 1905, a few days before the winter solstice. There was no sunrise as the Severn Estuary's Welsh shoreline grudgingly turned from black to a sullen grey. Out on the water towards Somerset dimly-seen tramp steamers and colliers queued to enter the docks on the high tide, occasionally making their presence known through a thin mist with blasts from fog-horns that reverberated around Penarth's cliffs.

Now the day gathered momentum. Cockerels in the farm-yards of Grangetown, Llanedeyrn and Caerphilly Mountain called to each other, and answered. Sleepy paper boys dragged themselves from bed and threw on woollies and flannel pants before speeding off on their rounds. Milkmen took jugs from doorsteps and filled them from ladles which they dipped into giant churns carried on horse-drawn floats. Postmen left the handsome Westgate Street headquarters of the Royal Mail to service the letter boxes of central Cardiff and its ever-widening suburbs. As road users, they needed to be wary of the city's fleet of tramcars, now 131 strong, which conveyed Cardiff's service sector employees to their offices and shops from terminals like Gabalfa, Victoria Park, Clive Street and the Pier Head. An occasional motor car (£175 ex-works) threaded its way between the bicycles, traps and cabs.

It is safe to say that talk of the afternoon's great game was on every male citizen's lips, and those of many a female too. Welsh Rugby's testing-time was suddenly at hand: the Barbarian was at the gates, if not inside them. Since Ireland's victory of 1899 Wales had won eleven home games from eleven; but now there was a real possibility of the Welsh fortress being stormed for the first time in the twentieth century.

Some fans disguised apprehension through attempts at

145

humour. 'One Who Knows' wrote to the *South Wales Daily News* offering free advice on how to beat the All Blacks: "Give the Welsh forwards elastic jerseys under which to conceal the ball," he recommended. "Pinch the pea from the referee's whistle. Pump laughing gas into New Zealand's side of the scrummage." A reader in Cheshire wrote, "This County's Rugby club attributes the severity of its 34-0 defeat by New Zealand [the previous Saturday] to the unnerving effects of the All Blacks' war-cry. To obviate this, Welsh players should invoke in unison the spirits of Druids who haunt the famous Anglesey village of Llanfairpwllgwyngyllgogerychwyrndrobwllllantysiliogogogoch."

While not going to such lengths, Tom Williams of the WRU told reporters that the home team should sing the refrain of the Welsh Anthem after the New Zealanders had given their war-cry, adding that "it is the wish of the Union that the spectators will join them in the chorus. This will be a fitting prelude to the game."

The *Western Mail* cartoonist sought to reinforce the siege mentality of the moment by representing Wales as a youthful-looking infantryman equipped with rifle and fixed bayonet and – surreally – wearing the tall beaver hat favoured by Welsh ladies during the previous couple of centuries. He is positioned in 'the last ditch'; in other ditches can be seen successively the upturned feet of a Scotsman, an Irish pixie, and John Bull. The final gallant defender is preparing to beat off the assault of a fiery-looking native (whose ethnic make-up, it has to be said, suggests the African continent rather than Australasia), also equipped with a rifle and bayonet.

The newspaper's leader column played on the gravitas theme: "Never in the whole history of Rugby Football has so much interest been taken in a match, so much speculation indulged in as to the result." By now the English Press were in the city, and their big-match previews in the Fleet Street newspapers were united in giving Wales no chance. 'Captain' Fitzgerald, in the *Sporting Life*, wrote typically:

New Zealand will win their match with Wales by their international average, about 14 points, if the Welsh forwards can hold the tourists' seven. If the latter are, however, masters in the scrum then our Colonial friends will win by a good bit more than their international average.

But local writers reminded their readers that no Welsh XV had ever been as well prepared as this one, and that "all were in perfect condition, including the veterans" – chiefly, that is, Gwyn Nicholls, but also big Dai Jones who had been limping earlier in the week. So 'Forward' in the *Western Mail* felt able to write:

> The great majority are of the opinion that our kinsmen will return as Invincibles to their far distant island home in the South Seas.
>
> As against this huge mass who pin their faith in the little silver fern, there are a few optimists – only a few – who are daring enough to hope and believe that the leek will be too strong a vegetable for that delicate plant, and that Wales will succeed where England, Scotland and Ireland have failed.

New Zealand had three injury problems which affected selection but could not be said to have materially weakened their XV. After a heavy tackle by Maclear in Limerick George Smith's injured shoulder ruled him out and Stead and Cunningham were also unfit. The tourists opted for Wallace on the wing, with Gillett at full back, and put Mynott in Stead's place at first five eighth. Gallaher, absent from the Dublin game, resumed his rover role, while Newton replaced the injured Cunningham at lock. In the morning a few members of the party strolled along St Mary Street and The Hayes sampling goods for sale in the shops. Others preferred to relax with a newspaper or mail from home in their hotel rooms, perhaps avoiding an atmosphere which some of them found oppressive.

This midwinter day was turning out well for a big Rugby occasion. The threat of frost or snow had been receding steadily since the week began, and the Cardiff Arms Park pitch promised to be near-perfect for the first match between Wales and New Zealand. The sun was finding it hard to shine through clouds that remained dull and grey; and as the afternoon wore on spectators would have difficulty peering through the gloom at distant action. But there was no wind; this was the kind of day when the constant straining and heaving of forwards in conflict generates steam that hangs as a pall above set-pieces and mauls.

The Welsh were turning up in force. By 10.30 Westgate Street was choked with fans bent on gaining admission to see the champions of two hemispheres meet head-on. Kick-off time was still four hours distant, yet at both entrances there were already queues: that opposite the Angel ran four abreast along the pavement opposite the Castle and into High Street. The area was patrolled by Chief Constable McKenzie, controlling his seventy-seven men from a vantage point on horseback.

Within the ground he had posted a further sixty-eight constables, on whose advice he ordered the gates to be closed at 1.30 p.m. But he could not stop Hansom cabs parking beside Cardiff Arms Park's perimeter wall, where enterprising drivers charged would-be spectators anything from 3s to 5s to climb aboard and stand on tip-toe to glimpse the Rugby action.

The scene was set. The audience was rapt. Battle was about to be joined. A bond born of rivalry was to be forged, between two small nations whose sporting ambitions ran concurrently. Characterising encounters between them would be a *frisson* which would last for three quarters of a century. It still exists; if it is now only vestigial that is not New Zealand's fault.

At the Millennium, New Zealand's basic Rugby ethos remains a powerful cultural factor, with the capacity to fascinate small boys and hold them in its thrall. Each of them wants to become an All Black. An occasional athlete strikes Olympic Gold, a golfer tops the leader-board, a great soprano thrills the world. But if such phenomena are brilliant comets, Rugby football is the unchanging sunshine which permits New Zealand's citizenry to bask in reflected glory.

At a pre-match function in 1905 the country's Agent-General in Britain, W.P. Reeves, eloquently outlined to an invited audience in Cardiff how the foundations of Rugby prowess had been laid in the Colony. His audience nodded understandingly as he described:

A land and a climate which breed a fine, hard race. In winter there is just enough daylight for Rugby to be played; unlike cricket it does not take up too much time. In three or four hours players can get into town for a match and back to the farm again.

In summer there is competition between cricket, tennis, boating and swimming. In winter, there is a lack of variety, so most play Rugby. Hence, skills are not spread over several codes.

New Zealand is also split into Provinces and settlements, divided from each other by comparatively empty tracts. This isolation increases local feeling and competition.

Mr Reeves might have added the other element which motivated the 1905 All Blacks and, one suspects, all their successors. Through history, 'Colonials' have experienced a consuming desire to show the 'old country' that they have made good in the wider world.

As against travelling to the end of the earth in order to create an identity, the Welsh have sought to preserve one – in a land at which they began arriving as an admixture of Iberians and Celts 4,000 years ago. Often it has been hard work co-habiting an island with Saxons; protecting the homeland against cruel and acquisitive Normans; latterly trying to absorb and convert newcomers who enter Wales for diverse purposes with little intention of acknowledging, let alone integrating into, a distinct ethnic community; and, in practice, living with an 'occupying power' (the English) whose presence has been ostensibly benign; but also suffocating. Like New Zealand, the Welsh had points to prove.

On the Saturday morning the home team, as was the case until the nineteen-seventies, made their own ways to the match venue at Cardiff Arms Park. Those from outside Cardiff came by train, before reporting to the new pavilion beside the River Taff. At around half past one their opponents trooped past them en route to the visitors' first-floor dressing room.

Downstairs Nicholls' men pulled on their red jerseys bearing outsize ostrich feathers, black shorts cut to three inches above the knee, and club stockings. When they posed for a team photograph it could be seen that some players – Dicky Owen and Charlie Pritchard for example – had threaded new white laces into their boots. WRU President Sir John Llewellyn came to the changing room to wish them good luck. A minute or so ahead of schedule the All Blacks clattered downstairs and out into the December afternoon.

Nicholls thus had precious moments in which to address his men. Mere games of Rugby cannot compare in import with military actions like Thermopylae, Agincourt, or Alamein. But on this day the Welsh captain's rallying call was a miniature masterpiece by a great leader:

> Gather round, men.
>
> The eyes of the Rugby world are on Wales today. It is up to us to prove that the Old Country is not quite barren of a team that is capable of giving New Zealand at least a hard fight. It has been suggested by some of the English papers that they come to Wales more or less stale; but as they played two English Counties last week and won each match by forty to fifty points with half their best players resting for today's game the staleness is not very apparent.
>
> We have already discussed tactics. So it only remains to me to appeal to you to be resolute in your tackling. You all know what New Zealand are like if they are given latitude. They throw the ball about, and their system of intensive backing-up makes them very dangerous.
>
> So there must be no hair-combing. Every man in possession must be put down, ball and all. As for the forwards, you already know what to do to get the loose head.
>
> Come on! Let's get out.

The scarlet of Wales was brilliant against a sombre backdrop as Gwyn Nicholls and his men followed the All Blacks out from behind the north terrace. The torrent of sound was awesome. It seems certain that the 42,000 gate allowed for by Mr Walter Rees had been exceeded by several thousand; the Rugby historian John Billot states that 47,000 got into the stadium, a figure which is endorsed by Chester and McMillan.

The crowd was well-stewarded, and there was to be no trouble such as had occurred during the 1899 match with Ireland. Before the start New Zealand performed their Haka, to the huge delight of onlookers. As expected the Welsh replied with their relatively new anthem. The *South Wales Graphic* reported:

> The singing of 'Hen Wlad' in reply to the Haka fired Welsh blood as nothing else could have done.

It went on:

Even when Wales were hard-pressed and victory seemed likely to be snatched from their grasp, the refrain 'Land of My Fathers' would persist in floating above the ground, putting new life into our men.

Referee Dallas whistled the game into action a couple of minutes after half past two. It soon became clear that this was not a day when the New Zealand machine would function smoothly. Spanners were thrown into its works from the opening minutes – more than once by Nicholls, who was leading by example. His first big tackle drew a grunt of anguish from the Taranaki first five eighth James Hunter, who groaned, "You're too old for this game – why don't you give up?" Nicholls also stopped Wallace in the Welsh 25, "...lifting him bodily, bearing him back yards, and dumping him down hard," reported the *South Wales Echo*.

At the scrummages Wales were capturing a lion's share of possession, following the counsel from Nicholls that virtually guaranteed them loose heads. 'Rover' Cliff Pritchard had clearly given thought to his strange role and was neutralising the threat from the two All Black five eighths. Dicky Owen laboured nobly behind the seven forwards despite taking a pounding from the New Zealand pack under which one of his ribs was cracked. In the first quarter he consistently fed Percy Bush, who imaginatively probed the tourists' back-line for weaknesses, keeping it under pressure.

Moreover Mr Dallas was exerting an authority on the play which, it would appear, New Zealand had not experienced before. The one cap he had won for Scotland, plus many outings as a Watsonian, had alerted him to the less legal ploys available to artful scrum feeders, one of which was to put the ball in with a spin calculated to favour his hooker. Say Chester and McMillan, "Dallas wasted no time in showing his disapproval of Gallaher's feeding of the scrum and penalised the New Zealand captain frequently." Assuming that the referee was a sensible and reasonably balanced individual, this suggests that Gallaher may have profited from much polite and tolerant home refereeing in the tour's first twenty-seven games.

So the two great sides sparred, punching and counter-punching, through the game's opening stages. Having adjusted to the pace Gwyn Nicholls was now on the look-out for an opportunity to use the ruse he had devised with Dicky Owen during training. It would involve the Welsh 'rover' Cliff Pritchard; and would demonstrate the captain's genius for exploiting stratagems to the full and extracting more from them than even their inventors had thought possible.

The chance came at twenty-five minutes and Nicholls gave the nod to his diminutive Swansea scrum half. After hooker George Travers had won the strike at a scrum near midfield just outside New Zealand's 25-yard line, Owen gathered and darted to the Welsh right, where Bush and Nicholls appeared in support. New Zealand's forwards rose from the scrum and began moving left. Their number probably included Gallaher.

But now Owen checked and, as arranged, spun the ball back infield towards Cliff Pritchard. The Welsh 'rover' was expecting the pass, which would be his first; but this was still a risk-laden ploy whose success depended on the All Black forwards being off balance and the Welsh pack having the self-restraint not to attempt an interception of the pass. Pritchard did well to snatch the ball from ankle level before picking up speed from a standing start.

Having drawn the All Black centre Bob Deans, he passed to his left where Gabe had accelerated to top speed. McGregor came in purposefully from the All Blacks' right wing, but could not prevent the Cardiffian finding Teddy Morgan, the Welsh left wing. This deadly finisher put New Zealand's full back Gillett into two minds with the merest suggestion of an infield side-step before taking the outside route to the corner. Pandemonium! – even though the conversion attempt by Winfield floated just to the right of the target. Wales led.

It was to be the try which decided the game, crowning a move which was carried out as planned at very high speed. Characterised by the flair Welsh backs had been showing for a decade, it also contained a new use of the 'rover', as a pivotal element in the attack. But in no way did it put the result beyond doubt, since well over half the match remained to be played.

For the most part man-to-man marking was exceedingly tight, and it is clear from sundry accounts of the play how closely the back divisions lay up on each other. Thus the fate of the game centred on the ceaseless duel between the tight forwards. In the third quarter New Zealand won a stream of possession which frequently tempted Hunter to test Winfield with up-and-unders which were chased by his colleagues, but the Cardiff man was equal to every demand made on him.

With his amazing capacity for putting lack of match practice behind him Nicholls, too, was clearly at his best. He continued to tackle magnificently; and made the game safe for his side in the dying moments by picking up a dangerous loose ball not far from the Welsh line, brushing off challengers, racing to the 25-line and firing a good screw kick into the opposition half. He also created a scoring chance for Harding, which the big London Welshman could not accept. But a last counter-attack by the tourists in their bid for a Grand Slam kept spectators in an agony of suspense, and the jubilation when Mr Dallas blew for time was laced with huge relief.

The All Blacks' great record was no more; on their own soil Wales were still unbeaten after six years. Their delirious supporters invaded the pitch and carried off Nicholls and try-scorer Teddy Morgan, who shouted at his bearers, "We knew we could bring it off!" The tourists' sad captain Dave Gallaher told reporters how the Welsh singing of their anthem had 'impressed' his team before the kick-off; perhaps he meant 'affected'. A German visitor was quoted as saying, "The Welsh fought as if their lives depended on it. The field reminded me of an arena in ancient Rome." Willie Llewellyn could not explain how he had dropped a pass that was awkward but would have brought a try. Bush dwelt on a drop at goal which missed by inches.

After dining with their opponents at the Queen's Hotel, with Sir John Llewellyn in the chair, the tourists made many Welsh friends and admirers when they left their headquarters to walk along Cardiff pavements and chat with fans. However, there were still four major fixtures in Wales to be played before the end of this momentous tour, and it appears that the New Zealand manager had rounded up his charges and got them all to bed by 12.30 a.m. For their part, the Welsh were receiving heroes' welcomes as they arrived home; on getting to Pontypool off the midnight train Cliff Pritchard was serenaded by 'Men of

Harlech', 'Sospan fach' and 'Land of My Fathers'.

It had been an amazing afternoon. Despite his disappointment the leading New Zealand journalist C.C. Reade reported:

> The game was absolutely the finest I have seen in the history of
> Rugby football. By the end of the day the play of the Welshmen
> became a revelation. They demoralised the New Zealand defence with
> their deadly and persistent onslaught on the blind side of their oppo-
> nents' formation. The development of that attack, swift as a knife
> thrust, was a creation of genius.

And the Welsh skipper? Said Nicholls: "A clever captain or
team must keep up their sleeves one or two attacking ideas
which every player understands something of and which can be
put into operation whenever an opening occurs. That happened
against New Zealand."

It made the final score three-nil. This was, and would remain,
Gwyn Nicholls' finest hour. Afterwards he and Gallaher shook
hands. Later he traded his jersey for that of his opposite number
– whose scalp he had also secured.

There is, of course, an aspect of the game on which we have
yet to touch. After the final whistle the New Zealand centre Bob
Deans had walked from the pitch, and exchanged jerseys, with
Rhys Gabe. He told Gabe, without rancour, that he had scored
a legitimate try which referee Dallas had disallowed.

Obviously this became a talking-point after the game, in days
before players were prevented from making undiplomatic statements or observations within ear-shot of the media. Deans, a
vulnerable twenty-one year old, was button-holed by the same
Daily Mail journalist, J.A. Buttery, who had coined the 'All
Blacks' nickname. The next morning at his prompting and, no
doubt, via his expense account the young man sent a telegram
to the *Daily Mail* stating: "Grounded ball six inches over line.
Some of Welsh players admit try. Hunter and Glasgow can
confirm was pulled back before referee arrived – Deans". Close
to a tragically early death from peritonitis two years later, the
centre repeated his claim to the score disallowed by Mr Dallas.

The successive beatings given to Wales by New Zealand in

the second half of the twentieth century make a 0-3 reverse ninety-five years ago seem almost irrelevant. From 6-0 and 13-6 in the mid-sixties, via 19-0 and 33-12 in the first Tests on New Zealand soil, the All Blacks' winning totals have soared to 52-3 and 54-9 in the nineteen-eighties; and since their last defeat by the Welsh, in 1953, they have averaged 28 points per game in fourteen consecutive victories over the nation which once could stop them in their tracks. Thus a main motive for setting down these latest thoughts on the 'Disallowed Try of the Century' is the uniquely fascinating case-study it amounts to of conflicting evidence, and how witnesses can err about where they were or what they saw at a particular moment.

It is wholly unlikely that the controversy can be laid to rest, or ever will be. But there are elements in it which point towards the correctness of the Centenary book on Welsh Rugby *Fields of Praise* by David Smith and Gareth Williams: "The Deans 'try' was in all probability, and so far as can be reconstructed from contradictory evidence seventy five years later, not a try."

Reports of the exact time of the incident contradict each other, though it seems safe to state that it occurred late in the fourth quarter of the match. Having won a line out on their right a little way into New Zealand's half, the Welsh forwards fly-hacked the ball past the All Black scrum half Roberts but were unable to prevent Wallace from snapping it up and heading infield from his position on the left wing. He evidently cut between Gabe and Nicholls, to find only Winfield barring the way. Although wrong-footed, the Welsh full back recovered, prompting Wallace to respond to a call from Deans on his left and pass the ball rather than risk being tackled in possession. As he fed his centre Wallace was grounded by Llewellyn, who had covered back.

Though now at full speed Deans chose not to head for the corner flag which he might have reached comfortably. Thinking no doubt of the need to score near the posts to facilitate a match-winning conversion he veered infield slightly, only to be tackled a short distance from the Welsh line. As a result the ball could not be played and the referee blew for a scrum. The Welsh lifted the pressure.

So much for the – undisputed – bare bones of the incident. It is the case that many of the people who subsequently went public on it cannot possibly have seen its climax with any clarity.

In those days the Press sat at trestle tables near the touchline, at ground level. From here, at half way, it was possible to write authoritatively about lines out, scrums and line kicks. But to adjudge a try claimed some sixty yards away was scarcely feasible for the most eagle-eyed of the media pack. Likewise, although the touch judges, Ack Llewellyn and New Zealand's W.J. Stead, thought the score was valid the try was claimed "a few yards" from the Welsh posts, or perhaps thirty yards from the nearer touchline. Their testimony is interesting but hardly definitive.

Turning to those closely involved, Wallace wrote many years later that, as he approached Winfield, "The full back was standing about the 25-yard line". That would have been where the New Zealand wing was tackled by Llewellyn, as he passed to Deans. Wallace could still state that the centre "just grounded the ball six inches over the line." Not good evidence.

All the Welsh deny the try, with the exception of Teddy Morgan, who had come racing back from the Welsh left flank. In *Rugby Football Up To Date*, published in 1921, Morgan wrote "As I tackled him [Deans] *a few yards outside* I distinctly saw *the white-goal line underneath me*. Yet when I got up off Deans' legs he was holding onto the ball (with two others of our side) which was grounded about a foot outside the line." The two sets of italicised words appear to contradict each other.

At a 1924 Dinner the then New Zealand captain Cliff Porter persuaded Morgan, present as a guest, to confirm on a menu card that "Deans scored in '05" which he obligingly did. Yet in a 1953 BBC radio discussion in which Winston McCarthy took part Morgan would not say Deans scored but "thought he might have".

To add to this uncertainty, in the book *Rugby Players who have made New Zealand Famous*, written by R.A. Stone and published in 1937, Percy Bush is quoted as saying that Gabe and Harding together caught Deans, and "on this occasion Deans came down... with the ball underneath him just two inches outside the line." Gabe himself also claims the tackle, and often stated how he had to hold tight to Deans as the New

Zealander tried to 'wriggle' – the inference being that he had failed to touch down over the line. Willie Llewellyn, at an advanced age, also put a case for having brought Deans down, but is likely to have been confused; the true victim of his tackle, was surely Wallace.

For the record, Gwyn Nicholls also considered that Deans had failed to score, hinting that there may have been a 'momentum' touch-down, which was illegal at the time. However, it is time to quote the opinion of the only person present whose view mattered a jot. Thirty years later, possibly prompted by the WRU at the time when the Third All Blacks were in Wales, Mr Dallas wrote the definitive statement, as follows:

> I was astonished to read in the newspapers following my return to Edinburgh that Deans 'scored' a try which I 'disallowed'. When Deans was tackled he grounded the ball six to twelve inches short of the goal-line. At that moment he could neither pass nor play the ball. As I passed between the Welsh posts my whistle went shrill and loud. It is true that when I got to the spot to order a scrum the ball was over the goal-line, but without hesitation I ordered a scrum at the place where Deans was grounded. I never blew my whistle at the spot itself. It had already been blown. Deans did not score.

Many touring sides in the British Isles since 1905 have found it difficult to accept that, on a Rugby field, a referee from any Home Country can be wholly neutral where another British side is involved. They cannot credit the healthy, but demonic, rivalry between the nations. That is why it is worth finding space, finally, for an interview given to a Welsh newspaper by a Rugby follower from England. It is in the form of a cutting (probably from the *South Wales Echo*) which survives in the papers of Nicholls' Ontario-based grandson Gwyn Williams, quoting a Yorkshireman, C.R. Fretwell. His view of Deans' approach to the line was good, and he must have been standing near the north-east corner flag:

> I can see the scene now. Deans stretched at full length, his arms out in front of him reaching for that white line while despair and misery flood his face – inches short. If Wales wished I would go into a witness box and swear to it: I, a Yorkshireman and a northern Rugby League enthusiast. Deans did not score. And he knew it as he lay there.

So the final record of the First All Blacks' tour bears just a single blemish: played 35, won 34, lost 1.

During the rest of the twentieth century New Zealand have taken many savage revenges.

Eighteen

At an informal news conference on the Sunday morning Gwyn Nicholls told Pressmen of the black cat which had strolled into the Victoria Laundry while he and Winfield sat in his office passing the time and steadying their nerves before the big game. Both players had made sure of stroking it. The reporters scribbled enthusiastically, but were less pleased when the Wales captain announced his withdrawal from Glamorgan's XV to meet the All Blacks in midweek. Another six of his victorious Welsh team followed suit.

Among them was Willie Llewellyn who, as anticipated, had decided that he must retire to further his business. Clearly he was going out at the top, and he never contemplated the comebacks which Nicholls made. As for the captain, Nicholls spoke of the need to rest a 'rheumaticky' shoulder (the one he had hurt against Blackheath) in order to be fit to play for Cardiff against the tourists on Boxing Day. The Rugby world could assume, it appeared, that he would play another Championship season for Wales.

On the following morning (18 December) the *Western Mail* said that the prestige of Wales had been enhanced tremendously. An anonymous 'Old England International' wrote in the paper's columns: "There is something uncanny about a Cardiff crowd, which knocks an invading team off its balance. It may be the cheers; it may be the singing; there is a Celtic electricity in the air which, while it loosens our sinews and weakens our joints, has a marvellous astringent effect on the home team." In London the *Evening Standard*'s late-edition placards on Saturday evening had generously read, 'Cymru Am Byth! – 3-0'. On Monday *The Times* was very fair, while the *Yorkshire Post* said "Wales would have scored three or four tries in the first half had it not been for superb New Zealand defence."

Other Englishmen chose this great occasion for British Rugby to parade their spite. The *Sporting Life* felt that "a draw would have been a fairer result" and had no compliments to offer the Welsh. The *News of the World* said: "The tremendous speed of New Zealand was always a menace to the Welshmen." When the Deans 'try' was claimed, its reporter was evidently among the group which failed to work out exactly what had gone on: "Wallace went through the Welsh back division like a mackerel through a shoal of herring," he wrote. "It looked as if nothing could stop him. But he failed." Wallace?

The *Daily Telegraph*, however, can claim to have printed the most astonishing and crass line of that Monday morning: "Whether they [the Welsh] are as good footballers as the New Zealanders have shown themselves is a question which, the Principality apart, would be answered by most good judges of the game in the negative."

Whoever wrote that, in days before 'by-lines' identified responsibility, can be bracketed with the English critic E.H.D. Sewell, who stated in the *National Review* the following February: "Wales were met when the New Zealand team was at its weakest.... Wales have set about strengthening her forwards by the introduction of a 'miner' element into the pack, a move undoubtedly good from a Welsh point of view but of questionable good to the game as a whole." Clearly the embers of class distinction in sport were being fanned by this man; but Sewell got his come-uppance when Gwyn Nicholls told the *Western Mail*: "In Wales the miner and the dock-worker have as great a chance of playing for their country as the man from a university. Rugby in Wales is democratic. All depends on a man's ability."

Dave Gallaher had no complaints to voice after the match, about either the refereeing or the result. He said, "It was a rattling good game played out to the bitter end, with the result that the better team won, and I am content".

At Swansea New Zealand relieved the below-strength Glamorgan XV of an unbeaten record stretching back five years, though not without a struggle, and were given an even harder game the following Saturday at Newport where they snatched a

17. Summer 1905: just married, Gwyn and Nell Nicholls pose with the wedding party. Standing left, is Nicholls's best man – his business partner Bert Winfield.

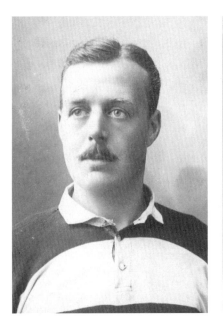

18-21. Three great protegés of Gwyn Nicholls who represented Cardiff and Wales. Top left, Percy Bush; right, Rhys Gabe. Bottom left, Bert Winfield. Bottom right is the remarkable Walter Rees, an unflappable Hon. Secretary of the Welsh Rugby Union for fifty two years.

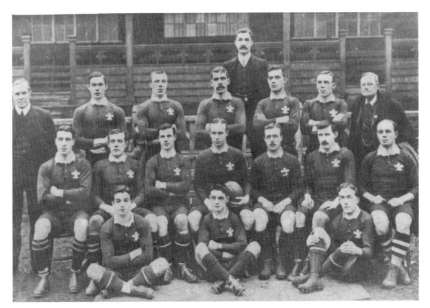

22. The Wales XV which Gwyn Nicholls led to victory over New Zealand on 16 December 1905. Teddy Morgan, scorer of the solitary winning try, sits cross-legged, front left.

23. 3-0! The fans are over the moon.

Those Terrible "All Blacks."

"Your turn next old chappie."

24 Cartoonists contributed to the hype and 'those terrible All Blacks' indicate that the game is up for John Bull – sure enough England lost by five tries to nil.

25. A tartan-stockinged Scot, an Irish pixie, plus Mr Bull have been upended by the All Blacks, and a beaver-hatted Welsh soldier guards the Home Countries' last ditch.

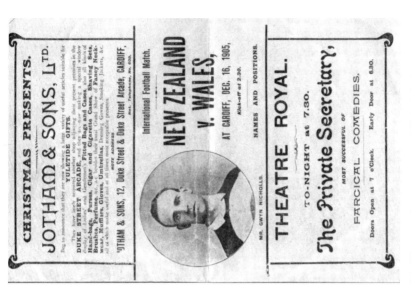

27. The match programme: Nicholls's finest hour.

26. The rugby fraternity everywhere rubbed its eyes in disbelief at a famous victory. Once again cartoonists sought to express the range of emotions engendered. But how did the All Black manage to snap a horn off the goat?

28. Welsh hopes were high as the self-styled World Champions took the field at St. Helens in 1906 against the First Springboks.

29. Under Paul Roos the tourists posted a sensational 11-0 victory, with tries by Loubser (seated second left), 'Klondyke' Raaff (centre, back row) and Joubert (centre, cross legged) who also placed a conversion. Nicholls's final game for Wales was, sadly, his worst.

30. On 1 January 1907 Cardiff, under Percy Bush (seated centre), took revenge for Wales' defeat, plunging South Africa to what remained until recent times her biggest reverse. In a final first class appearance Nicholls scored the first try in Cardiff's 17-0 win.

31. For once Gwyn Nicholls could not be lured out of retirement to play. But as a Cardiff committee man (extreme right, standing) he watched Cardiff Past's game against Cardiff Present aimed at raising funds for the dependents of the 439 miners who died in Wales' worst ever pit disaster at Senghenydd, fifteen miles north of the city, in 1913.

32. & 33. A series of 'action' photographs illustrated Gwyn Nicholls's publication of 1908, *The Modern Rugby Game*. The poses are forced; but the techniques they portray cannot be faulted.

6-3 victory. Nicholls had recovered fitness by Boxing Day when more than 40,000 spectators crammed Cardiff Arms Park to see if the Blue and Blacks, who had won eleven games in the first half of the season and drawn the twelfth, could emulate the national XV.

Cardiff certainly had chances, particularly in the second quarter, which could have brought them victory. 'Old Stager' contributed a match report for Charles Arthur's book, which makes it clear that Nicholls' steadying influence was invaluable in the face of New Zealand's whirlwind start with his frequent 'saving', a term reporters of the day used when referring to falling on the ball. The Cardiff captain Percy Bush was having a very positive game, narrowly missing with a drop at goal and setting Nicholls up for a try: "a mighty groan of disappointment went up when it was seen that the ball had canted off his knees, the Welsh captain having come up at too great a pace."

Cardiff's combined play led to a score at twenty-five minutes after J.L. Williams had made ground down his wing and cross-kicked for his support forwards led by Northmore and Neill. Both handled before an injection of pace by Gabe took him up to Wallace, who was at full back for the All Blacks on this occasion.

Nicholls had tracked the movement energetically and, as Wallace committed himself to a tackle on Gabe, was well positioned for a scoring pass. The try was scored far out, but 'Old Stager' commends the Wales skipper for his discretion in not attempting to run around behind the posts. Winfield added two points with a conversion which went in off an upright. For the first time outside the Tests New Zealand were behind.

Despite the loss of Jim O'Sullivan with a broken collar bone, the All Blacks were level at half time. Hunter and Deans in the midfield combined well to send Thompson over near the corner flag and, after requesting some spectators to make room for him, Wallace placed a fine conversion for a 5-5 score-line.

With just ten minutes left an indiscretion by their skipper cost Cardiff at least a draw. A wild kick over the home side's goal line by the New Zealand forward Seeling seemed to pose no threat and all but one man in the stadium thought the ball would be kicked dead by Bush. That one man was George Nicholson who had followed the ball on what seemed a hopeless quest – and when Bush dallied and ultimately missed the ball with his boot, the giant Aucklander was at hand to pounce for a try also converted by Wallace: ten-five.

The greatness of Nicholls was never better shown than in the game's dying seconds as Cardiff gave everything in a bid to get on terms. He received possession some thirty-five yards out and went between Deans and Stead with a tremendous burst of pace. Once again the luckless Wallace was drawn, and this time it was Ralph Thomas whose path to the corner flag was clear. But Winfield's kick was inches wide, the final whistle went, and Cardiff had to be content with a mere consolation prize: becoming the sole British team to score two tries against the All Blacks.

The visitors ended their British tour at Swansea where a try by Fred Scrine, playing as the extra back, kept them in arrears until ten minutes from time. Then Wallace gathered a loose ball 40 yards out and dropped a wonderful, if wind-assisted, goal to snatch a victory which gave New Zealand thirty-one wins out of thirty-two games in the UK, with 830 points for and a mere 39 against. The five-match Welsh leg had been transparently the hardest, containing the one defeat and with a cumulative score-line of 29 points against 17.

As a result of the All Blacks' tour Rugby football had come of age and was clearly destined to establish itself as a top-ranking sport for playing and watching. In this first decade of the twentieth century France would be admitted to the annual European tournament, which consequently became known as the Five Nations Championship, while South African, Canadian and Australian sides would follow the 1905 New Zealanders on tours to Britain. Test Rugby between them also took off.

Gwyn Nicholls had already experienced some of the most eventful seasons the game would know until it went open in 1995. After his leadership had brought victory over the champions of the southern hemisphere, his own career might well have fallen victim to anti-climax. Instead, more great days lay in store for the Prince of Centres. And one, in particular, that he would prefer not to have dawned.

Nineteen

The Victoria Hygienic Laundry at Llandaff North continued to flourish. Gwyn Nicholls had brought the same urgent approach to running it which he had shown as captain of successful Welsh XVs. Just as his assessment of employees' merits was shrewd, so the section leaders appointed by him proved successful. Mrs Main, for example, the woman chosen to run the plant, managed a hundred staff adroitly as the business grew. A Mrs Taylor, responsible for the packaging of clothes for return to customers, was described by Trevor Lewis as "a stickler for perfection". The successful formula which Nicholls and Bert Winfield had devised was also working at Cadoxton and Bridgend.

These were all vital considerations which smoothed the way for the former to opt for resuming and extending his first-class Rugby career. With hindsight, it can be stated that it was some distance from being the best decision he ever made.

The day after they beat Cardiff, and before victoriously concluding the British leg of their tour at Swansea, the New Zealanders were present to see the Barbarians defeated by a Cardiff XV which did not include Nicholls. However, he turned out against Moseley on 6 January, 1906, bent on sharpening his fitness for the match with England seven days later. The Welsh selectors duly selected him and re-appointed him captain.

Since the start of the 1904 Championship campaign, in which they drew with Wales and defeated Ireland, there had been nothing for the English to celebrate. While Wales were winning Triple Crowns and defeating All Blacks, the wearers of the rose had known the indignity of a wooden spoon and a whitewash. There had also been the five-try hammering by New Zealand.

Before announcing their team for the first International match of 1906, to be played at Richmond, the RFU already knew how their opponents would line up. In Wales there had been an on-going, and audible, debate about the validity of perpetuating the loose forward, or 'rover', experiment. Although it had made a vivid, specific contribution to the winning try against the All Blacks, some influential critics felt that the selection of an eighth man behind the scrum was essentially a negative tactic: all very well if containment was the objective, but something that might diminish, not enhance, the attacking potential of the Welsh back division by over-crowding the midfield.

However, when the team was named Cliff Pritchard of Pontypool was again chosen as a loose forward. It would appear that, as skipper, Nicholls had got his way. He admitted to having reservations about New Zealand's exploitation of the novel 'position' they had created, and its defensive limitations. However, he is on record as stating that "a third, or flying, half will greatly assist in the successful development of [new] manoeuvres...by providing infinite possibilities for a wide variety of re-shuffled positions." That is, the loose forward created extra options.

England's team selection, in contrast, was no doubt influenced by the memory of John Raphael's experience against New Zealand at the Crystal Palace in December, which could scarcely have borne less resemblance to Pritchard's afternoon at Cardiff. Chosen as a 'rover' the Oxford-educated barrister had a disastrous afternoon in a role to which, as a centre, he was unsuited and with which he was wholly unfamiliar (as, of course, were most Englishmen at this time). The RFU therefore reverted to a traditional schemat of seven backs behind an eight-man pack.

The plan was that, in order to counter the numerical advantage which Wales would enjoy outside the scrum, the speedy Charles Hammond, nick-named 'Curly', would be withdrawn from the pack to take up a loose-forward position whenever danger threatened on or in England's 25. Unfortunately this half-measure was doomed to destabilise the efforts of his seven colleagues whenever the need arose for him to leave the pack.

The other extraordinary selectorial gamble concerned the choice of no fewer than seven new caps to face a nation which could reasonably claim unofficial world champion status: Hodges, Kewney, Kelly, Mills and Dobbs were the forwards, Hudson and Jago the backs. Raphael, incidentally, was retained as a centre, and at stand off half D.R. 'Dai' Gent was awarded his second cap. Evidently a great opportunist, the Llandovery-born 23-year-old had discovered, to his surprise, while at St Paul's College, Cheltenham, that he was English. This did not prevent him accepting a Welsh Trial in 1905; but when his country failed to acknowledge his calibre by selecting him for the National XV he made himself available to the RFU. England capped him, no doubt in a spirit of gratitude, five times between 1905 and 1910. Gent later wrote on Rugby for the *Sunday Times*.

Predictably, the home side went down by sixteen points to three, failing for an eighth year in succession to defeat the Welsh. The latter, who had been using a dedicated hooker for some seasons, now supported Travers with six specialists in their own positions who, admits England Rugby historian John Griffiths, "more than held the efforts of the England pack." There is clear evidence for this in that the two early Welsh tries fell to forwards, Jehoida Hodges and Charles Pritchard finding their way to England's line.

In the second half Teddy Morgan crossed for Wales, Winfield placing a second conversion, while Arthur Hudson scored an unconverted try for England. But the game's highlight was credited to Gwyn Nicholls, in action against the old enemy once more after missing the 1905 fixture and setting up a superb try for the London Welsh wing Maddocks (winning a first cap as Willie Llewellyn's successor). John Griffiths writes: "The Cardiff centre beguiled the English three quarters Hind and Raphael with a swerving run and drew the full back, Jackett, before sending his wing clear."

It was to be Prince Gwyn's last game against the *Saeson* but even in the autumn of his career he was still able to draw the level of praise which only Gould had experienced before him, and which would be reserved for a small elite during the rest of the century. Commented the *Sporting Life*: "Nicholls was the pivot on which the system worked. His generalship in attack, and skill in defence, mark him as still the greatest centre playing at present." The *Daily Chronicle* said, "Inspired by Nicholls the Welsh passing was swift, insidious, fluent, kaleidoscopic." Its correspondent could not resist adding, "England's XV was like a steam roller with puffs and snorts and a man in front to give not warning, but indication, of its approach."

In the *Western Mail* 'Forward' assessed the skipper's play as faultless, expressing the hope that he would not retire before the season's end. Besides noting six All Blacks in the crowd on the eve of their departure for France, the correspondent drew attention to 'spaces' on the terraces. Rugby, he observed, did not seem to command the same interest at London venues as it did at other English centres and at Cardiff. Well, maybe; but a major factor keeping spectators away must have been the series of beatings given to successive England XVs. Losing sides quickly shed support.

In post-match interviews Nicholls was, as usual, the soul of tact: "The result hardly does justice to England... there was not a thirteen-point difference between the teams." But in subsequent reflections he stated why he thought that the English were going through such an unproductive period. He believed that training and playing together was the true secret of such teams as the New Zealanders, South Africa and the big Welsh club and International fifteens: "In contrast, an England XV is more or less a scratch side. The men are drawn from a great variety of clubs playing various styles of games, and almost totally unfamiliar with each other". Again the words reveal Nicholls as a Rugby thinker decades ahead of his time. It would be another seventy-five years before the English began to stamp a (highly effective) uniform style upon their game.

Wales had certainly peaked against New Zealand with the selection of an extra-back or 'rover'. The risk was undertaken, however, in the knowledge that New Zealand were committed to the same line-up, so that a seven-man Welsh pack would not be outnumbered by the opposition. Their defeat of the All Blacks persuaded Wales that the system had merit. What would happen, however, when seven Welsh forwards found themselves up against an orthodox, eight-man International pack?

This was a question which was not answered at Richmond because of the England forwards' feeble display (weakened even more from time to time as Hammond disengaged himself for his loose forward role). Now, in contrast, the Scottish side selected to visit Cardiff for the 3 February Test not only presented a bigger threat but also included most of the men who had gone down narrowly to New Zealand at Inverleith. They knew all about the loose-forward tactic and the seven-man pack, and how to draw their sting.

Scotland's visit coincided with signs of staleness in the Wales XV which manifested themselves even in a 9-3 victory. Cliff Pritchard, Maddocks and Hodges scored unconverted tries, to which the visitors' only reply was a MacLeod penalty goal. But press reportage makes it clear that the victory was far from decisive.

Though doomed to defeat, the Scots tore into their Welsh opponents from the outset, out-playing them at every phase and especially at forward. The *Western Mail* correspondent was aghast: "It was hard to believe that this was the same Welsh pack that had played so well against New Zealand". It was taken apart by Scottish forwards who performed like men possessed. Ironically it was the kicking, covering and tackling of the extra back – 'rover' Reggie Gibbs well supported by stand off half Billy Trew, which enabled Wales to turn crumbs of possession into winning points. The former was to win fifteen more caps, mainly as a wing, while Trew's career was to last almost until the outbreak of World War II. The important point for the future of the Welsh game was that both were acolytes of Nicholls, able to perpetuate his vision of a style that would be fulfilling to its exponents, attractive to spectators, and success-ful at both club and International level.

Not, however, at Ireland's expense in 1906. With a Triple Crown at stake across in Belfast the reactionaries on Wales' selection panel got their way, and an eight-man pack was selected for the Balmoral Showgrounds encounter. But three of those forwards – Powell and Westacott of Cardiff and Llanelli's Tom Evans – were newcomers to International Rugby who failed to last the pace: 'cracking up terribly' to use the vernacu-lar of the day. With Trew relegated to the reserves Gibbs was the sole stand off half, and had a nightmare of a game. Even Gabe made defensive errors.

Nor could the great Gwyn Nicholls save the day in what was his final Championship match. Ireland's captain, Charlie Allen of Derry, knew the significance of the occasion, and in his pre-match talk invited his men to give The Prince something special by which to remember the Emerald Isle. Nicholls was thus a prime target; and later admitted that seldom, if ever, had he been tackled so consistently and violently.

But what was astounding about Ireland's 11-6 victory and its try-count of three to two was that well before the close both of their half backs had been removed to hospital by ambulance, Ernie Caddell with a broken leg and Willie Purden because of damaged knee ligaments which would to force his retirement from the game. The thirteen Irish survivors gave three cheers for Wales' skipper as he left the field at the close, but doubtless Nicholls' grin of acknowledgement was forced. His International winter, which had begun so triumphantly, had ended in discontent.

Nonetheless there were ample consolations. Not least, he could look back on a career in Championship Rugby which had seen him on the winning side fifteen times in twenty-two games. On six occasions he tasted defeat; and there had been a draw with England. Teams led by him had usually scored heavily; the Rugby they played had been much admired.

Twenty

Although the thought of club matches must have seemed anti-climactic Nicholls turned out a few times for Cardiff in the dying days of the 1905-6 season, as on 31 March when three first-team players were unavailable through injury for the home game against Gloucester. Faithfully as ever he delivered the goods, helping to ensure a 15-0 win which included three tries and a dropped goal.

Hence, ultimately, he could claim a substantial in-put to what ranks among the three best seasons in Cardiff's history, alongside 1885-86 and 1947-48. Later in the year, at a ceremony in the Park Hall to salute the final record of twenty-nine wins, two draws and the single defeat by New Zealand, the Lord Mayor presented gold watches to nineteen of the players who had contributed to it. The twentieth was Gwyn; but on this occasion, as team-mates had already given him a gold watch on the occasion of his wedding, he received a silver salver.

It is hardly open to doubt that, as a former captain, Nicholls would have been very much inclined to assist the preservation of the Blue and Blacks' unbeaten record against clubs. On the other hand, he evidently still sought to be persuaded and cajoled. He wanted to be assured that his presence was vital. He needed to hear people say that, without him, calamity threatened. An anonymous team-mate told the Press, "Gwyn is actually very anxious to retire from the game altogether. But, as he is playing now as well as he ever did, his friends cannot refrain from persuading him to play an occasional game...and Gwyn is such a good fellow at heart that he yields to their entreaties." The modern term to describe such behaviour is possibly, 'Playing hard to get'.

To what, then, can this trait be ascribed? A healthy but repressed conceit on Nicholls' part? Perhaps he positively relished the prostratings and blandishments of Pressmen and the lobbying of selectors beseeching him to fend off defeat by 'consenting' to play. Had he grown to relish annual, long-drawn-out courtships such as these? Did being lionised prove an irresistible stimulant? – one in which he exulted, and which massaged his ego?

Or was the greatest player of his era simply weak-willed? – one who could be influenced against his better judgement and manipulated by administrators thirsting for the sweet taste of yet another Triple Crown or bent on ensuring a packed house for the next match played at Cardiff Arms Park? That is, had Nicholls become someone who now hankered after peace and quiet, yet could not bear to let adherents down?

There is a third possibility, which is that as he moved into his thirties Nicholls told himself that, while the Laundry must now take priority, as business thrived there would be occasions when he could reasonably take an afternoon away from the office to enjoy some Rugby – and that if club, or country, asked him to turn out, then he should oblige them. This theory, however, does not take into account the skill and fitness levels which the centre had to reach when he made his sudden, ostensibly random sorties out of retirement. For ten years he had been ranked as the world's best three quarter; now, there was just too much at stake to justify following his fancy by playing an occasional game to make up numbers or boost the morale of fourteen lesser men.

My inclination, therefore, is towards the first hypothesis, one that accounts not only for his sporadic re-emergences into the first-class game, but also for other aberrations. Nicholls was now not only a mature adult, but also a very calculating one. Hence I suspect that every time he 'consented' to appear again for club or country, he made sure that he had trained hard out of the public gaze to achieve a good level of fitness. Probably, trusted members of the Press became aware of this too, and indeed may well have become part of the plot. In those days the 'scoop' was not a be-all and end-all.

And, yes, Nicholls probably did enjoy the hysterical relief with which Wales habitually greeted the news that, yet again, Achilles would leave his tent and enter the fray.

There is also the question of motivation. Historian Danny Davies states that the star was still appearing for Cardiff at the end of the decade. What accounts for a love affair with Rugby football which kept him active, at one level or another, for twenty years? After passing the age of thirty, why had he stayed in the game at all, let alone succumbed again and again to its appeal after making solemn declarations of retirement?

Since he could take Rugby, or sometimes leave it, we can be sure that the game itself was not an obsession with him. But the hold it exerted on his intellect and his imagination was powerful. In *The Modern Rugby Game* he wrote that when a side is of all-round excellence, "players are fully capable of taking any of their fellows' places. They are thus able to judge the best move which the man in the centre of the picture can adopt and will, therefore, act as if the same idea had occurred to them."

Even if we doubt whether Dickie Owen, the Swansea midget, could have stood in for big George Travers as a hooker, it is true that such interactive possibilities fascinate certain types of Rugby devotee in our own day, for instance those who become coaches. Further, never more so than in its formative years, Rugby football's framework and tempo has always offered a challenge to men of an original and inventive bent. As we have seen, Nicholls can claim to have refined the three-quarter game, whose template was laid down by Frank Hancock, by spelling out the principles of good ball transference. His influence on the evolution of play behind the scrum was profound.

But his vision penetrated further than back divisions. He worked on ploys involving cross-kicks from the wing to involve forwards following up at speed. His influence prompted the selection of specialists in the three rows of the Welsh pack. He argued for running, handling forwards (New Zealand had grasped this possibility at about the same time). In addition to its complex tactical advice, his text-book includes pictures which show him not only taking and delivering passes but also catching the ball at a line out! It deals with detail, such as the advisability of putting the boot to a muddy, rolling ball rather than trying to pick it up and risk knocking on. Simple? Yes; but, again, someone had to say it first.

In other words, Nicholls clearly took great delight in creating and exploiting every kind of manoeuvre that might arise as thirty men battled to control 7,000 square yards of playing field. He was among the first to appreciate that, all other things being equal, the player with brains and acumen would always finish on top in the game of Rugby football.

In a Welsh context there must also have been gratification for Gwyn and his team-mates at being under-dogs whose bite proved again and again to be as good as their bark. This was not so much the case in club Rugby: here, English sides were little more than chopping blocks for their top Welsh opponents. As a national entity, however, despite its 'black diamond' economy and buoyant national morale, Wales was still accorded a patronising, country-cousin status within the United Kingdom. 'Gallant Little Wales' is a phrase which Nicholls, along with the Welsh Press, had recourse to often. Then, victories in games where they had been written off beforehand were doubly satisfying.

There existed, too, a 'national' cause which Nicholls could have ignored but did not. He acknowledged it.

It will be recalled that he and his family were among thousands of English who arrived in south-east Wales during the late nineteenth and early twentieth centuries. Immigrants into Wales have behaved in intriguing ways. Fifty years before, the Irish imported to build Lord Bute's docks fenced themselves round in churches and Catholic schools rather than take to their breasts the Welsh culture and values which they encountered.

Many of the Anglo-Saxons who arrived from the English West Country and Midlands fifty years later simply ignored the distinctive ambience of Wales, thinking and behaving as if they were still in England. Such latter-day Colonials were quick to enliven the *Western Mail's* correspondence columns, as some still do today. In 1906 they were busily deploring the compulsory teaching of Welsh in Cardiff's schools, which had been sanctioned by the Council. Educational loyalists hit back. Such a level of controversy sold lots of newspapers.

Other immigrants have perceived Wales as some kind of 'club', of which it can be useful to claim membership (or sometimes deny it). But Gwyn Nicholls, who left Gloucestershire as a toddler, without any ethnic or emotional hang-ups about what it was to be English, went wholly beyond this. Influenced, no doubt, by club and International team-mates from the Valleys and western Wales he seems to have embraced total Welshness and what it implied graciously and with conviction. There is no evidence that he learned the language; but he writes approvingly of it in his book, in the context of circulating coded information and signals during a game: "Welsh players, most of whom speak Welsh, have a ready-made code of our own." Invariably, when referring to the National XV, he uses 'we' and 'us' of the Welsh, never 'they' and 'them'.

Significantly although Gloucestershire, as we have seen, used the Cardiff centre's place-of-birth qualification to secure his services occasionally for County Championship matches, as far as can be ascertained no enquiry about his availability ever came from England's selectors. In 1908 Wales discarded the brilliant forward 'Boxer' Harding – born at Market Rasen in Lincolnshire and, like Nicholls, committed to Wales as an immigrant. Some members of the RFU were not slow to speculate whether he might now fancy a couple of games for the country of his birth – an initiative which was vetoed before receipt of a reply. But in the case of Nicholls the attempt was never made. It was well known where his loyalties lay.

Twenty-One

So much for the aspirations and values which mattered to Gwyn Nicholls in public life, and especially in Rugby football. The private man now became a father for the first time, when Nell presented him with a son, Ivor. Later, the baby would be followed by Erith and Geoffrey; none of the three is still alive. Ivor captured much limelight when making his first social appearance at the 1906 wedding of Bert Winfield to Nell's sister 'Queenie' – Elizabeth Perch-Thomas.

The Winfields had two daughters, Dorothy Picton (who celebrated her ninetieth birthday in 1998) and Enid Williams, later to win three hockey caps for Wales. Now, in widowhood, they share a property in north east Cardiff, where they spoke to me vividly and with affection about Gwyn Nicholls. The recollections are of their uncle in middle age; but the salient facets of his personality were established in his thirties. What the ladies had to say remains valid.

They remember him first in Whitchurch where, after early married life at 'Westbury', he moved to a mini-mansion called 'Craigside' situated in Heol Don, close to the then Taff Vale railway station at Llandaff North, even nearer to the Laundry. Soon the infant Dorothy came with Bert and Queenie to live at 'Ryelands', also in Heol Don. The family would soon grow with the arrival of baby Enid.

Both sisters experienced Nicholls' basic generosity. He thought nothing of slipping them ten shillings for pocket money. Later, when they were sent away to school, such subs arrived by post. Enid has letters that open, "Dear Bill", which derives from 'Sweet William', his pet name for her. Unable to account for it, she could only speculate that it had something to do with Gwyn's awareness that Bert would have liked a son: a kind of clumsy acknowledgement.

On Cardiff RFC's committee their uncle ensured that local

charities and good causes benefited from the club's surplus funds. In 1908, for example, a handsome sum of £262 (worth many thousands of pounds today) was given to Cardiff Royal Infirmary. Often Nicholls would start the ball rolling by dipping into his own pocket.

Such generosity lasted throughout his life. Shortly before he died in 1939 Enid and her husband, in early married life, needed a guarantor for the house they were proposing to buy for £850. Though in the end his backing was not required, Gwyn was quick to tell the couple that he would stand surety.

So much is not to suggest that he was considered a soft touch by his young relatives. Among the weapons with which he would admonish them was sarcasm. A friend once remarked to him in front of the two nieces: "Don't they have beautiful faces!" "I've no idea," came the response. "They wear so much make-up that I can't claim to have seen them." He could be stern: the Winfield girls' cousin Geoffrey had a talent for getting under his father's skin, often by 'borrowing' his clothes. "Take my tie off," they remember Gwyn occasionally snapping. Then, as the boy made his way sheepishly upstairs, "While you're at it, take off my socks, too." But he also lent support if it was needed: when Geoffrey was at Christ College Brecon, his father would often drive the tortuous road across the Beacons to cheer his son in action for the School XV.

Enid Williams also remembered how her uncle could make her feel abashed. Once she tried to rid herself of a boy-friend by telegram: "Sorry," it stated. "Can't See You Again." Gwyn told her: "That's a coward's way out." Enid added, "He could give you a Look. You knew he disapproved." This echoes comments on their captain by the Rugby players in the broadcast of 1948.

On working days at the Laundry the sisters remember him as habitually dressed in a suit, whose waist-coat boasted a watch and chain. If they saw him in plus fours and a ratting cap it meant that he was looking forward to a round of golf or an outing in his motor car, which seems to have been a Lanchester. A woollen sweater with holes in it was his dress for gardening or attending to his bee-hives and rose-beds.

Much of the ladies' testimony is supported by another female member of the family, Claire Whythe, who lives in Cowbridge, and also spoke of her uncle. She is the daughter of Nicholls' brother-in-law Philip Perch-Thomas and Hilda, née Williams, who was born into a prosperous Docks family. The crash of 1921 bit deeply into the fortunes of Williams Bros, and in due course Hilda suffered a breakdown which necessitated her hospitalisation. Young Claire was sent to stay with Uncle Gwyn and Aunt Nell while her mother was treated and convalesced. Like others who remember him, Claire spoke immediately of her uncle's generosity: "What are you going to do today, Claire," he would ask at breakfast-time over the top of his newspaper. "Well, anyway – here's something to spend." And he would dole out half a crown, twelve and a half pence – then a small fortune for a little girl.

The Nicholls' own children were grown up by the time little Claire was sent to them, so that she became the main beneficiary of her uncle's enduring generosity. She remembers him buying her a 'Fairy cycle', an early and expensive predecessor of today's mountain bikes. In the house she was allowed to listen to the 'wireless' (the radio), which incorporated a radiogram on which the new-fangled 'gramophone records' could be played.

Claire's random memories include the night when, after accidentally locking himself out, her uncle propped a ladder against the wall in order to re-enter his house through a first-floor window. His efforts were suddenly lit up by the beam of a torch, shone by an alert local bobby on a security patrol. Fortunately, the constable was a Rugby fan who, once he had identified who was attempting to break and enter, put a large boot on the ladder's bottom rung to steady it.

Once, attracted by a black jersey in the Nicholls display cabinet, with a silver fern stitched into its left breast, Claire took it out and wore it to nearby shops. She remembers ruefully the telling-off which she suffered on her uncle's return for daring to trifle with the Rugby apparel of the late Dave Gallaher.

Such were the day-to-day highlights in the later life and times of Gwyn Nicholls, the proud family man and successful entrepreneur. Back in the summer of 1906 it seemed that an even-tenored future was in prospect: adoring his wife, loving and disciplining sons and a daughter, spoiling nieces. Taking in washing for a great sector of south east Wales. Enjoying an occasional cigarette and glass of whisky. Throwing himself into life's trivial pursuits, as when he entered a fancy-dress competition in a shift and night-cap as 'Ready for Bed' and, to his great surprise, won a prize.

There was no suggestion of his cutting himself off from Rugby football, and he continued his membership of Cardiff RFC's committee. But the roar of the crowd as he split a defence, the thrill of leaving an opponent sprawling in the mud, the acclaim which greeted yet another Championship triumph – these were features of his life-style which, it seemed, he would not experience again.

In the autumn of 1906, when Rugby emerged from aestivation in South Wales, Prince Gwyn was absent from the field of play, neither offering his services for club fixtures nor, as it seemed, in training. He had made unexpected come-backs before; but this time, he told admirers, he had really hung up his boots.

Hmm. It was a story which Wales had heard before.

As Gwyn Nicholls, the Cardiff club, and Wales were scaling heights of greatness around the turn of the century, a third great southern hemisphere nation, South Africa, had acquired a taste for football's handling code. Just as graduates of Oxford and Cambridge had taken the game out into many parts of Britain so, south of the equator, it was through the students of Stellenbosch and the University of Cape Town that Rugby football moved away from the Cape Peninsula and seized the imagination of young men in its vast northern hinterland. "The game's popularity" wrote A.C. Parker in *The Springboks* (1970), "spread like a prairie fire". By 1890 Western and Eastern Provinces, Natal, Transvaal and Border all boasted powerful, well-run Unions.

The National XV's record improved steadily as support grew. W.E. Maclagan's first British touring side of 1891 played nineteen games, including three Tests, and won them all. Yet a dozen years later a party led by Scotland's Mark Morrison met defeat in seven of its nineteen provincial games and lost the

Test rubber 0-1 with two games drawn. Happily for South Africa both its peoples of European origin, those of Dutch descent and the British, had fallen under the game's spell and played it with equal pleasure, commitment and expertise. The ability gap between these colonists and the Old World they had left behind was closing fast.

The Rugby fraternity had to curb its passion for sport while the Anglo-Boer War of 1899-1902 followed a painful course. A number of players destined to enhance their country's Rugby reputation in the new century were soldiers as Transvaal and the Orange Free State fought, and lost, their struggle against Natal and the Cape Colony. For a number of years 'South Africa' still comprised these four groups, whose amalgamation into a single state was delayed (until 1910) by protracted negotiations tinged with the bitterness of the Boer camp; but when the fighting stopped all of Africa south of the Zambesi was British-controlled.

Less than a year later, in 1903, the visit of Morrison's men signalled the resumption of sporting ties between colonists and the Homeland. To the British it seemed a natural way of emphasising that life had returned to normal, and that this was how things would be from henceforth. The Boers' Rugby lobby made sure that political grievances were not allowed to prevent the development of what was becoming the national sport: even the *Pretoria News* had to admit, "South Africa is disunited about every subject under the sun, but in hearty agreement about Rugby."

This tentative locking of shoulders symbolised an end to hatred and hostility, and was now firmed up by an approach from the RFU in London. It invited South Africa's Rugby Board to send their team on a reciprocal tour to the United Kingdom in 1906. The latter body debated earnestly whether their playing strength was adequate to undertake a 28-match schedule including four Tests, before boldly accepting. It was a momentous decision; no-one on earth would have dared to predict that the Springboks were to become giants of the game, who would not lose a Test series to any Rugby-playing country, anywhere in the world, for half a century.

The SARB's lengthy selection meetings were preceded by trials – despite which it appears that confusion about players' identities led to some first choices being left in South Africa while the wrong men made the trip. Finally, after kitting out, a 28-strong party left Cape Town on 27 August 1906 on board the liner *Gascon*. Managed by C.H. Carden, it was captained by Paul Roos, a Western Province schoolmaster and lay preacher. Their men followed the fitness routine that was by now well established for touring teams undertaking long sea voyages. The *Gascon* docked at Southampton on 19 September, where newsmen were told that the South Africans were happy to be known as 'Springboks'. Soon they were in action, opening with a 37-0 victory at Northampton over East Midlands.

Meanwhile, despite the absence of Gwyn Nicholls the new Rugby season in Wales was proving attractive. Gabe, Trew, Travers and Teddy Morgan were still in the game and had reached maturity, while men like wings John Williams and Reggie Gibbs were new crowd-pullers. Although promising to become a good team again, under Percy Bush for the second winter running, Cardiff were slow to hit their stride, meeting three defeats away from home before Christmas at the hands of Swansea, Devonport and Llanelli.

The Welsh kept a weather eye on the South Africans' early progress through England; but initially, unable to credit that any side in the world could replicate New Zealand's wonderful record in Britain twelve months before, their mood was sanguine. After seeing the tourists' second victory, a 29-0 defeat of the Midlands at Leicester, one anonymous correspondent suggested that Wales should be favourites at 10-1 on to win the 1 December Test at Swansea.

In other respects the tourists were getting what may be called a good Press. 'Forward' wrote in the *Western Mail*: "Individually they are not as good as Gallaher's All Blacks...as they stepped out you missed the half-jaunty New Zealand air. Their smile was more forced. They do not chew gum. As for their dress, their black knickerettes are cut longer, while they wear a green jersey on which a Springbok with a crumpled horn is in evidence. Their black stockings are topped with white hoops."

The first loud warning noises about their calibre and potential emanated from Plymouth, where the Springboks beat Devon 22-6 for a seventh victory from seven. Hamish Stuart, who had now moved from Wales to the *Daily Chronicle*, stated that in his view they were "quite as good" as the All Blacks. Perhaps anxious not to give his old readership heart attacks, however, he still maintained, "There was nothing in the South Africans' play to forbid Welsh hopes of repeating their success of last season...the Colonials lack finesse, though they are to be feared for their physical power." Another Fleet Street pundit, E.H.D. Sewell, hinted that the Springboks' display surpassed the form shown by New Zealand.

On the same afternoon a strong Glamorgan XV, with many prospective Welsh caps in it, could only draw with Gloucestershire. A reporter wrote, "Supporters are exhorting their players to improve, or else Wales will never beat the Springboks." The panic button had been pressed; and such palpable jitters were accentuated when the tourists won their eighth and ninth matches against Somerset and Middlesex without conceding a point.

Beginning with a visit paid by Cardiff's Lord Mayor to Neath, signs now began to surface that yet another 'Bring back Gwyn' campaign was being put under way. The First Citizen had travelled west to present the Dewar Shield to its 1905-06 winners, Neath Schools, to whom he commended Gwyn Nicholls as a role model. He then added, out of the blue, "I hope he can be prevailed upon to take the field for Wales against the South Africans...this would ensure their being beaten" – loud applause. Enthusiastic calls of "Hear, hear!" followed as he added, "I would like to take the message to Cardiff that Neath's Rugby-lovers want Nicholls to be selected and to play." It is impossible to believe that such words were wholly ingenuous.

Something was afoot. Within days Nicholls was named in the Glamorgan XV to play South Africa on 31 October. 'Old Stager' reacted in the *South Wales Daily News*, "This season he has not played, and recently reiterated his absolute retirement...his selection will cause a flutter." Did the veteran critic mean a healthy quickening of the pulse, or a feeling of dismay?

For once, it may be that he was unhappy with the reintroduction of a man whom he had admired so much, for he continued: "As Nicholls cannot go on for ever he will probably take the view that his successors should be given their chances."

In the event the centre made no move to prove that he could still hold his own at the highest level. For example, he could have turned out for Cardiff against Swansea on 20 October, but did not. Instead, after a few days he told the Glamorgan selectors that he was unable to accept their invitation. Further, when covering the South Africans' arrival for their first games in Wales, Reuters added that "Gwyn Nicholls has decided to give up football and will not play for Wales in the International match."

The tourists told newsmen of their disappointment that the great centre would not take the field to test their backs' mettle. However, Nicholls was not slow to call at their Welsh headquarters in Cardiff's Royal Hotel to pay his respects – to find that the manager was out refreshing his memories of the city. Mr Carden had lived in Cathedral Road as a child when his father was serving with the 41st Regiment of Foot – the Welch Regiment – and had even sung in the Cathedral choir as a pupil at Llandaff Cathedral School; when he was fifteen the family emigrated and settled at Port Elizabeth. Returning to the team hotel Mr Carden was told by his distinguished visitor, "I fear your team will meet its Waterloo in Edinburgh."

Although the rank and file South Africans declined to speak with Welsh Pressmen, Nicholls' readiness to be interviewed out on the pavement was some compensation. "Scotland, with most of last year's team, will defeat the Springboks," he opined. "Also, I should think the Irish forwards will be too good for them."

These comments were probably made by him on October 26, with the Welsh Test five weeks away. When asked if, given the unexpectedly strong threat South Africa posed to Wales, he would change his mind and emerge from retirement he was still insisting, "I have finished with active football and shall do my best to resist whatever pressure is brought to bear on me."

He was present to see South Africa beat Newport 8-0, with tries by the brilliant wing Stegmann and a conversion by Doug

Morkel. The Black and Ambers were censured for not exploiting the power of their pack and keeping play tight. Ominously for Wales the tourists' back division moved the ball swiftly and accurately, winning acclaim from 'Monkey' Gould, called in beforehand to help prepare Newport.

On the losing side was Charlie Pritchard, who was to suffer criticism for allegedly disclosing the Welsh scrummage techniques which had outsmarted the All Blacks a year earlier. Despite their win at Rodney Parade, it was suggested, the tourists had failed to grasp the importance of securing the loose head, and as a result were consistently thwarted: on the Springbok put-in the Newport tight head prop would kick the ball away until referee Gil Evans lost patience and told scrum half Dobbin, "Try the other side" – thus affording Newport the loose head. Pritchard is supposed to have explained this to Paul Roos.

That the South Africans, ten games into their tour, could be so naive was always hard to credit. The story was given the lie in *The Carolin Papers* (1990), compiled and edited by Lappe Laubscher and Gideon Nieman, and based on an accumulation of papers relating to the 1906 tour discovered in an attic by Punks Carolin, son of the Springboks' vice captain H.W. ('Paddy') Carolin. The find included a tour diary, letters sent to friends in South Africa and subsequently returned to the writer, Press cuttings, photographs, match programmes and menus from post-match functions.

Among this material is a letter written by Carolin to his friend Leslie Cox on 10 September making it perfectly clear that the tourists had done their homework. They had worked out, and understood, how "Gwyn Nicholls and his men countered the New Zealand loose forward tactic and minimised the effectiveness of the New Zealand formation". The letter includes sketches showing scrummage formations which would ensure an equal contest for set-piece ball. Doubtless Roos listened intently to what Pritchard had to say at Newport; whether he learned anything from it is another matter.

It may be that the refereeing fraternity pricked up their ears however. Before long it became an offence to block the entry of the ball to a scrummage.

The Springboks now faced what they – rightly – thought would be their biggest hurdle so far, the match with Glamorgan. Nicholls had declined selection, Bush was absent unwell, an unimaginative Swansea stand off half called Toft would run the Glamorgan back division. But it was still full of class, and in addition the County pack was strong and aggressive. Forty thousand eager spectators packed Cardiff Arms Park. The gates were closed early.

Alas for home supporters, the points that mattered came in the game's first seven minutes. First Dobbin and de Villiers combined to send Stegmann outside Maddocks and Winfield to the corner; and five minutes later Dobbin, again, crossed the gain-line to send the brilliant Stegmann in once more. Neither try was converted but Glamorgan straightaway faced an uphill struggle for more than seventy minutes. Evidently they achieved and maintained parity during this time; but all that resulted was a try by Will Joseph. Also memorable was an abortive thrust by Maddocks, who seized a South African knock-on and cleared the defence only to be halted by a whistle-blast for the visitors' infringement from referee A.O. Jones – who had failed to play advantage. Six-three at the end; South Africa knew they had been in a contest; but their record still read, played eleven, won eleven. In four weeks' time it would be Wales' turn to take them on. By Monday 2 November all tickets for the match had been sold.

The tourists moved off for a series of games in England, Scotland and Ireland. They were due to return on 28 November to prepare for the 1 December Test.

A few days after their departure, debate about the Wales team selection had moved away from the Gwyn Nicholls situation to other issues. Should the versatile Reggie Gibbs be chosen as a loose forward? Who was best qualified to lead the home team?

Suddenly, Nicholls-mania rose to fever pitch again.

The great man had been spotted training at the Arms Park by a sharp-eyed reporter on 14 November. 'Mr Gwyn Nicholls May Play' said a headline. "At practice," read the story, "Nicholls looked as alert and speedy as ever, and had not lost one whit of form."

Next there appeared, in the *Western Mail*, the following extra-ordinary statement: "[Nicholls] had not been unwilling to play [for Glamorgan versus South Africa], but was restrained by friends." If this was the truth, what exactly had Nicholls been trying to convey to the Press for the previous two months – not to mention Welsh selectors and erstwhile team-mates? Possibly 'dissembling' is the politest word for his behaviour at this juncture.

An interview was carried in the newspaper's next edition:

Reporter: Will you play versus the Springboks?
Nicholls: My intentions are the same as before.
Reporter: Let's assume the WRU pick you...
Nicholls: That's all we can do, assume it.
Reporter: So: we leave it as an open question?
Nicholls: As far as I am concerned, yes.

The reporter, no doubt in desperation, concludes with the view, "I am left with the impression that he is ready to play if required."

Yet after eight weeks of the season, Nicholls had still to step onto a Rugby field in earnest. Would he be required? In the circumstances, a good question.

Twenty-Two

The Springboks continued along their winning way until they reached Glasgow for the game with Scotland. Here, as predicted by Gwyn Nicholls, they went down to a first defeat, by two unconverted tries from Purves and MacLeod to nil. The tourists were certainly weakened by the absence of skipper Roos, who had sustained what was described as a broken collar bone in the match with Oxford University (though, as he returned sixteen days later against Ireland, the injury seems unlikely to have been more than severe bruising). Further, half back Gert Mare gallantly played through to the final whistle against the Scots with a broken bone in his hand. South Africa's manager was not pleased about Scotland's use of the boot as part of their traditional dribbling game, and his report to the SARB records a kick to Brink's ankle which kept him out of the next game, a toe-cap applied to Stegmann's side, and a kick under the jaw which rendered Marsberg unconscious for "about fifteen minutes."

However, the tourists put these setbacks firmly behind them, crossed to Ulster, and beat Ireland 15-12 in Belfast. The home side did their country proud, and it took an opportunist try by Stegmann ten minutes from time to settle things in South Africa's favour. The Springboks moved south to Dublin where a game against the University XV took the heat off them as they contemplated their engagement at Swansea.

And now, suddenly, in Wales the new Nicholls saga surged to a breath-taking, totally unexpected, climax.

First, on 21 November Billy Trew withdrew from the Glamorgan XV that was to meet Monmouthshire in Cardiff the following day. Who 'consented' to replace him? None other than the greatest retirer in Welsh Rugby history. Prince Gwyn had not yet abdicated.

As bewildered journalists tried to come to terms with confirmation of the latest *volte-face* Nicholls told the *Daily Mirror*, "I should like to have a shot at the Springboks. If everything goes off as I wish, and I have a chance of testing myself to the full in this game I shall...turn out against them." 'Old Stager', though he was not the journalist who broke the story, knew enough to add, "Gwyn Nicholls has kept himself in condition by constant training since the season began."

The hints, the suggestions, the supplications, the clandestine suppers with selectors over steaks and claret, maybe even some influence brought to bear upon Nell Nicholls – all these elements of the overall strategy had now been successful: Nicholls had been prised out of retirement. But, at 32, could he still deliver a response to the robust challenge clearly presented by the Springboks? At International level, would he survive the physical power and crunching tackles of the tourists' midfielders? Could he defend adequately against a South African three quarter line adjudged to be faster than any in the UK?

Thus in more than one very important respect, the inter-County match was virtually a final Trial, attended by all the Wales selectors. Nicholls took the opening minutes by storm, catching the ball from the kick-off, accelerating as vividly as ever, and initiating a passing movement which ended near the Monmouthshire goal line. Soon he slid a scoring pass to his wing Maddocks. In the second half, stated reports, he defended well as the opposition tried bravely but ineffectively to stay in the game. Glamorgan ran out winners by 23 points to 3; just a few hours later Nicholls was named as right centre and captain of the Wales side to meet the First Springboks.

Among the four new caps under him would be the high-scoring Johnnie Williams, Cardiff's left wing, who now played regularly outside Rhys Gabe. The selectors were later to be censured for preserving this link by switching the experienced Teddy Morgan from his usual left wing to play outside Nicholls on the right.

All in all, the days preceding the game were tense ones for the Welsh side, with undercurrents of discontent disturbing team spirit. Notably, as had been the case in March 1905 when his last-minute inclusion as replacement against Ireland cost Frank Gordon a cap, Nicholls' presence upset some members of the

Swansea club. This time their indignation was fuelled by his retention of the captaincy; admirers of Dicky Owen had expected the little scrum half to get the nod. An unofficial move to persuade Owen and his clubmate Will Joseph to withdraw was hastily quashed by the All Whites; but the atmosphere was evidently strained. No-one in Wales questioned Nicholls' pedigree and experience; however, in some quarters he was now perceived as Yesterday's Man.

To make good his lack of match practice the skipper turned out for Cardiff against Penygraig, contributing to a 22-3 victory. 'Forward' wrote in the *Western Mail* that it was gratifying to see the old star in such form; "...[Cecil] Biggs operated on Nicholls' wing, taking his centre's stream of marvellous passes with unfailing accuracy." 'Old Stager' was moved to come off the fence and offer cheering words to Wales' hero: "A genius in attack, a rock in defence, a sportsman to the end, and the most unselfish player that ever wore football boots. In his case unselfishness does not mean self-effacement, but gains the reward it deserves in the shape of goodwill and the good wishes of fellows."

The Welsh prepared together at Cardiff in their now customary fashion, while the South Africans trained at St Helens. The latters' methods attracted a great deal of interest, not least because of the seven Rugby balls which were used to intensify the practising of skills. The forwards' machine-like precision caught the eye of watching Welsh critics. Afterwards, when Paul Roos gave a brief news conference, his "pronounced Dutch accent" was commented on by reporters. So was the strict training regime of the tourists; invited to a banquet by Swansea Town Council they declined, asking for a light snack instead.

It is worth quoting two South African reactions to their Welsh experience. First, a couple of paragraphs from manager Carden's weekly report to the SARB written on the eve of the Test:

> ...the interest in tomorrow's match is so enormous that it is difficult to describe. Some idea may be formed when one learns that 49 special trains from all parts will run into Swansea for the match.
>
> I visited the ground yesterday, and the arrangements for seating are on a hitherto unprecedented scale for any International. Thousands of

seats are piled tier upon tier all around, and workmen are erecting more.

It was amusing to see about 500 spectators perched on the stand to view a few of our men practising."

In a letter home Paddy Carolin released some pent-up frustration and emotion as he reflected on the team's arrival in Swansea:

Ever since we came to this country, and everywhere we have been, every man, woman, child, dog, cat, hen and even parrot has told us to look out for Wales. It is very kind of them to warn us, but it is fearfully monotonous.... Well, after tomorrow, no matter what the result, they won't be able to say 'look out for Wales', and it is a good thing too. Personally I have had enough of that and will blow the next man's brains out who says, 'Look out for Wales'

The tourists would be without some star players the following day, notably their leading try-scorer Anton Stegmann who was nursing a leg muscle strained in Belfast. They were cheered, however, by the return of Paul Roos, wearing a large shoulder-pad to protect the bone that was on the mend. Two or three members of the chosen XV, ill at ease in the damp Swansea climate, had coughs and sore throats.

On the eve of the game the Springboks sent a message thanking their Welsh hosts for the warmth of the welcome, adding in Afrikaans: "Ons weil graag die Welsh team speel, en wensch dat die beste team zal win" – "We are looking forward to playing Wales and hope that the best team will win." Next morning they awoke to bright December sunshine streaming in across the Bay.

Right up until kick-off, Welsh correspondents who had seen the Springboks only once or twice as well as experts who had followed the tour closely felt that a home victory was the game's likely outcome. This view was fortified when Wales began at a furious pace, pursuing Will Joseph's kick-off to the tourists' 25 and pinning them there. The first hint of disappointment came when a panic fly kick by full back Marsberg ballooned its way to the unmarked Gwyn Nicholls – only to be knocked on three yards from the visitors' line.

South Africa weathered the storm and began to launch

attacks of their own, clearly enjoying a firm St Helens surface which would have reminded them of pitches back home. Their wing Loubser was caught by Teddy Morgan at the Welsh corner flag and, after narrowly failing with a long penalty attempt, full back Steve Joubert opened the scoring. After their forwards delivered a quick heel, South Africa moved the ball smoothly left for the diminutive Stellenbosch student to make an extra man and reach the corner flag. Japie Krige sent Loubser in for 6-0 at the interval; the crowd began fearing the worst.

For Gwyn Nicholls it had been the poorest forty minutes of his Rugby career. Soon after his early failure to exploit Marsberg's error he was heavily tackled by Krige and kicked on the shoulder by Brink as he tried to get up. In later years Percy Bush was to say that this affected the skipper more than he admitted; but Nicholls never blamed the kick for his succession of mistakes and bad judgements. He and Gabe were tightly marked by a Springbok back-line which lay up closely on their opponents; and evidently, for once the vaunted Welsh pair had no answer to the tactic.

Nicholls' more glaring errors included losing his footing and finishing up on his back after making a rare clean break. He missed tackles. He knocked on, again, after Joubert had failed to take a Garryowen. And, if he and the crowd were hoping that things would improve in the second half, they were to be disappointed. At fifteen minutes he caught a high ball safely, only to jerk it away in the direction of no-one in particular. Brink came speedily onto this heaven-sent possession, dribbled for a few yards, and sent 'Klondyke' Raaff in for the third, decisive South African try which Joubert converted.

Nicholls' agony was compounded when, rather than feed the unmarked Teddy Morgan, he tried to crack the Springbok defence himself – only to be smother-tackled inside the opposition 25. Near the close he broke in the grand old manner, but when Johnnie Williams appeared outside him it was to be sent a wretched pass which fell to the turf. Though still trying hard at the end, Wales were worsted by 11 points to nil.

This first defeat at Swansea in 11 years left supporters of the 'world champions' dumbfounded and distraught. A number of them made a point of helping the small band of Springbok travelling fans carry Paul Roos from the field; but the majority departed the scene downcast, in a strange, eery silence. Reuters said, however, that "when the Springboks left the ground and were driving back to their hotel through the streets of Swansea, they received a great ovation and such was the crush of those desirous of congratulation that they could only proceed at walking pace."

Many reasons were proffered by Rugby critics and players alike for the failure of the Welsh. They were over-confident, wrote Paddy Carolin in a letter home. Their forwards had been feeble, thought many writers. The selectors had made mistakes. Such was the respect in which Gwyn Nicholls was held, however, that hardly any critic chose to highlight the centre's failure to live up to pre-match expectations. Only the Reuters Special Football Service correspondent, in his despatch of Sunday 2 December, was bold enough to state that the Welsh defeat was "probably due to the selection of too many old players...the Welsh backs were altogether lacking in resource, and Gwyn Nicholls was a failure." In his letter Carolin wrote, "On his form it was hard to imagine him as the really marvellous player he must have been in his palmy days."

'Old Stager' contented himself by observing, "He omitted to do many things which, had he been in his prime, could hardly have failed to end in a score."

Nicholls did not avoid Pressmen after the game, though refusing to be drawn into discussion of his own contribution. He stated, "I will probably turn out for Cardiff against South Africa on New Year's Day." He told reporters that, because his injured shoulder was giving him pain, he was travelling back to Cardiff immediately to have treatment. He would thus, perforce, miss the Dinner given by the WRU for the tourists, at which Charles Pritchard would speak for him.

In his book *Springboks in Wales* John Billot evokes the captain's journey home: "Gwyn Nicholls, head bent, sat miserably in the train; not broken in spirit or humbled in pride, for he was a man of immense character – but sick at heart, feeling he had let down his team and his country."

Years later he felt able to be candid about his poor afternoon. In 1931 during a function for the Third Springboks he admitted:

> It was a rotten performance on my part. I missed a sitter early on, attempting to pick up a twisting ball with the line clear instead of dribbling over it. I must have forgotten the precept, 'Keep Your Eye on the Ball.' Young players please note – watch the ball until it is absolutely grasped."

Because the Springboks' last game in the British Isles was scheduled to be against Cardiff on 1 January 1907 he was to have a chance to make amends – though not, it must be emphasised, in the extraordinary way in which he now sought to impress the tourists.

A note in the Papers of Paddy Carolin, referring to the Dinner after the final match against Cardiff, says: "I sat next to Gwyn Nicholls...he told me that on the night of our victory at Swansea over Wales a meeting was held of the Welsh Rugby Union at which he was instructed as captain of Cardiff [sic] in the intervening month between the Test and the Cardiff match to select a XV and train it in such a way as to secure a victory and Welsh Rugby's rehabilitation". While there is no way that Carolin could have invented such a story, it is possible that Yesterday's Man did. It simply does not make sense.

For the WRU to have adopted such a course, on the night of Wales' crushing Test defeat, would have been a knee-jerk reaction highly untypical of the stolid administrators of the day. Secondly, while their captain of that afternoon was on his way back to Cardiff licking physical and psychological wounds, the WRU committee and Secretary Walter Rees must surely have been at Swansea entertaining their guests, hardly calling off-the-cuff meetings two hours away in Cardiff. Finally, given the never more than lukewarm relationship between Cardiff and the WRU, the latter would not have dreamed of interfering in the club's preparation for a major fixture.

Alas, the yarn must have been dreamed up by Nicholls in order to impress the wide-eyed young South African vice captain seated next to him. All remaining doubt can be removed by referring again to the 1941 radio programme about Nicholls. The transcript of the conversation, in which Percy Bush took part, has the 1906-07 Cardiff captain stating that Nicholls announced his retirement from Rugby, again, after the Test match and stuck to his decision despite the appeals of the Cardiff committee to make himself available for the club's match with the tourists. Said Bush: "So I went to see him. At first, he was adamant, but when I pleaded with him that the prestige of Wales demanded his presence...adding that it would make the difference between winning and losing, he replied: 'well Pierce-Eye, as you think Cardiff can beat them I will play, as you wish it.' "

This seems a far more likely explanation of how Nicholls came to play against the tourists again.

To be fair, it also seems probable, and rather more in character, that he was unwilling for one of the new, regular Cardiff three quarters to be dropped so that he could play. To accommodate his wish the club named Reggie Gibbs as an eighth back or 'rover' and announced that their pack would comprise seven forwards only.

Under the blue skies which accompanied a frosty Christmas week Cardiff lost to Llanelli, who in turn went down to South Africa in a scrappy match notable for indecisive and inaccurate refereeing. However, Blue and Black morale for the club's game against the tourists on 1 January 1907 was restored by a 35-0 victory over the Barbarians (Nicholls played and scored a try) and grew stronger when the weather suddenly changed. The temperature rose, a west wind blew ever more strongly across the Taff, and heavy rain began to fall unremittingly. Some fifty labourers were hastily brought in to remove the tons of straw with which the pitch had been insulated against frost – when, inevitably, their heavy boots turned the turf into a tract of marshland. South Africa were doomed to play the last match of their brilliant tour on a playing surface more suited to reptiles than Rugby players. Afterwards, both Paul Roos and Mr Carden stated that it was the worst pitch of their tour: in effect, a swamp.

Hence for the players, as would be the case in 1960 and 1969, Cardiff was a wholly unpleasant experience – doubly so for the losers. Spare a thought for the 28,000 spectators who paid £1,100 to be present at a stadium where, on three sides, there was no shelter whatsoever. But as the game ran its course, these fans would mind neither the wind nor the rain.

For one hugely positive aspect of the Nicholls era was that in good weather and bad, Welsh crowds were consistently able to gorge themselves on Rugby football's haute cuisine. In the new century there had already been Canadian and New Zealand challenges to the Welsh XV; the equally charismatic Springboks had won their Test; later in the decade Australia would mount a colourful and only marginally less successful challenge.

The fact that these virile and powerful Dominion sides played the clubs of Wales as well as the National XV underlined the formers' status as the strongest in Britain. They were to enjoy this standing (in curious contrast to Wales' fluctuating fortunes) until the last decade of the twentieth century. This pre-eminence guaranteed compulsive entertainment for the members of top clubs two or three times every month, not just a few times each winter.

It should be remembered that the experience offered by the Rugby game – turbulent, thrilling, colourful, emotional; bent on maximising its spectator appeal – was still relatively new. It is not too extreme, I would argue, to compare its impact (along with Association Football) to that of television half a century later. Big Rugby had become, literally, something new to look at, in a new way. The man on the terrace was an integral part of a fresh phenomenon: a 'mass audience' witnessing combat and courage, applauding artistry and tactical finesse.

There had been no 'grand-stands' at Hastings, Waterloo or Trafalgar from which to watch men in battle. Hence the novelty of being able to watch two miniature armies hitting hell out of each other – mimic strife, as it was dubbed by some – had become spell-binding. Never mind the weather: spectating was the in-thing.

Especially on a day like this.

For there were precious things at stake: Welsh pride, craving restoration after Swansea; the prestige of Welsh back play; a consuming ambition to deprive the tourists of their unbeaten record in Wales. Above all, the unspoken but omnipresent knowledge that The Prince of Centres himself had something to prove against opponents for whom his claim to greatness had yet to be authenticated. The tension at Cardiff was great, the crowd's expectations enormous.

After Roos began the New Year by losing the toss, South Africa's inexperience of the most wretched kind of Atlantic coast weather was compounded by their opponents' immediate exploitation of it: using the wind to keep the ball behind the luckless tourists, preferring to dribble than to handle, and putting wicked little grub-kicks along the greasy, treacherous pitch. In contrast, the Springboks were wholly out of their element. Their slippery hands, streaming eyeballs and squelching footwear could not cope with what was not so much a contest as an ordeal.

There were early mishaps which prevented Cardiff gaining a quick lead, notably a knock-on by Gibbs. Soon Biggs dropped a scoring pass and was in collision with the covering South African forward Millar. Both men were badly hurt, and although they returned after receiving attention they were passengers for the remainder of the game.

More than any other player Nicholls needed to shine. A golden chance to do so came when, after twelve minutes, his lengthy punt enabled Cardiff to force a scrum fifteen yards into the tourists' half. Inspired by Billy Neill, the home pack won possession. The ball was moved rapidly to the midfield. Nicholls received a long pass, about ten yards into his own half.

Now he put behind him the sad memories of Swansea, moving onto the ball at a speed that left the South African centres leaden-footed and took him between them like an arrow. The Springboks' full back Marsberg, whose tackling throughout the tour had been brave and faultless, was disposed of with a powerful hand-off. Said Percy Bush, "Gwyn sped on to score one of the most important tries in Rugby history." The crowd roared; Cardiff's players crowded around their veteran centre to shake his hand; the Springboks rubbed mud, rainwater and disbelief from their eyes as they waited for the conversion attempt – which Bert Winfield placed from an awkward angle.

Gibbs beat three men on his way to Cardiff's second try, Winfield kicked a penalty goal. In the second half Frank Williams and Gabe scored the tries that killed the South

Africans off. At the end it was 17-0 to the Welsh side.

In Cape Town, whose locals had become used to acclaiming the triumphs of their country's Rugby task-force, a throng waited in the moonlight to hear the Cardiff score-line. "After their surprise," wrote a correspondent, "they gave Wales and Welsh football a sporting recognition which I wish your Rugby enthusiasts could have heard." The South African Rugby Board sent a telegram from their HQ: "Heartiest congratulations to Cardiff and all Wales on brilliant victory".

Suddenly, Gwyn Nicholls had rehabilitated himself – not least in the eyes of his own countrymen. Wrote 'Old Stager', "I doubt whether in the whole course of his career he has ever played a more strenuous game...one and all of the South Africans exhausted superlatives in their assessment of his contribution to their defeat." At the post-match Dinner in the Queens Hotel Paul Roos made special mention of Nicholls:

> It is only human to be disappointed in having been beaten...but I am glad for one man's sake that you had such a glorious success, and that is our friend Gwyn Nicholls. My reason for saying that is that some newspapers were unfair in going for him after the International match at Swansea.

Nicholls accompanied the Springboks to the Great Western Railway station, and was among the crowd who sang 'Auld Lang Syne' and the National Anthem to the departing tourists. Roos and his men caught the 19.10 hours Fishguard to Paddington express; they were to play in Paris and defeat a French XV 55-6 before returning home.

His two games against the First Springboks had taught Nicholls a final, vital lesson, one that also needed to be digested by the Welsh selectors. To stand shoulder-to-shoulder with younger opponents, who were pitted against you and desperately craved victory, you had to be fit. It was not necessary to be in the first bloom of youth; but the wisdom and experience of three decades needed to be supplemented not just by physical conditioning but also by regular participation if a man was to influence the course of a game and not let his side down.

Now, at last, there was acceptance of these imperatives. At 32 Gwyn Nicholls had reached the end of his Rugby days, certainly

Test matches. Gradually, and thoroughly, he let it be known –
this time for sure – that he would not don a Wales jersey again.
If it is true that, in the past, friends and fans had worked to lure
him out of retirement for key games, this time they did not
succeed. Gwyn had played a superlative part in bringing about
the Springboks' only defeat outside the Tests; his admirers were
content that this was the right moment for their hero to exit
Rugby at its highest level.

Nicholls informed the Welsh Rugby Union that he was, at
last, in earnest and that there could be no more procrastination.
They got the message.

Announcing the team to play England at Swansea on 12
January later Secretary Walter Rees stated tersely, "Mr Gwyn
Nicholls was not considered for selection."

Twenty-Three

Having gone to the lengths of playing himself up to full fitness, Gwyn Nicholls appeared for Cardiff whenever invited during the remainder of the 1906-7 season, crossing for seven further tries. In May he attended a ceremony at which silver cigarette cases were presented by Cardiff to the XV which had beaten South Africa. The club also gave a silver knife, fork and spoon to his small son Ivor.

Now, rather than coming to any sudden halt, his Rugby career gradually and gently faded away as the years and seasons went by. In response to an entreaty from the new Cardiff captain Rhys Gabe to "play a game for me" he again went into training at the start of 1908. Early in January Mr Lloyd George paid a visit to the Arms Park, expressing a wish to watch Nicholls in action, only to be disappointed by the star's absence on the grounds that he had not yet reached full fitness. As President of the Board of Trade, LG was invited to start the game against Blackheath on 25 January, propelling a feeble kick in the direction of Gabe, who promptly called a mark.

It was 29 February before Nicholls, now 33, felt ready to turn out, but an occasion well worth waiting for. The announcement that he would be in the Cardiff XV to meet London Welsh put thousands on the gate recorded at West Ham that day. Charles Arthur described this as a match that "calls for comment":

> ...by reason of that 'Prince of Three Quarters' Gwyn Nicholls turning out for Cardiff. He scored a try early in the game and was easily the best man on the field throughout...his form this day really astonished his fellow players and spectators by its brilliance.

In April 1908 Nicholls evidently had another burst of energy, appearing and scoring two tries against Gloucester, contributing to a 24-11 win over Leicester, and turning out against Cork who had especially asked that he should play a farewell game against them. Though unwilling to be considered for a place against the visiting Australians, whom Cardiff thrashed 24-8, he travelled to Bordeaux with the club in February 1909 (a journey which, in those days, took all of five days there and back) to play the current French champions Stade Bordelais. The Welsh visitors won by twenty-one points to five; the Prince was hailed as man-of-the-match for his three tries.

In the evening of his career Nicholls built up his total of tries for the club to 111. The Danny Davies book has him making the last of 242 appearances for Cardiff in the 1909-10 season, though it is not made clear which was the final game of all. This was also a time when he tried his hand at refereeing; and it is a sign of the huge respect in which British Rugby held him that in 1909, after only a few matches with whistle in hand, he was given charge of the most prestigious fixture the game's calendar then had to offer – the Calcutta Cup match between England and Scotland at Richmond. The Prince of Wales was in a crowd of 20,000 who saw a marvellous game, won by Scotland 18-8 but with no suggestion by the losers of sub-standard refereeing. As the participants left the field, however, Nicholls called to an acquaintance, "Wasn't I awful!" He never refereed again.

However, he sat on the Cardiff committee from 1905 until just before the outbreak of War. His association with the club had begun when it was little more than a local team less than twenty years old; by the time he ceased to be actively involved in its administration it was known and respected across the world.

The capacity of its ground had risen from 4,000, with one small grandstand, through 36,800 in 1901 to the 43,000 who could be accommodated after the redevelopment of 1912 which included a new grandstand, plus upgraded terracing above the north, east and west touchlines. Nicholls had played a huge part in the rise and rise of Cardiff RFC; and had an eye for peripheral details, too, like the preservation of his club's tradition of generosity and compassion. Thus after the catastrophic Senghenydd colliery disaster of 1913 Cardiff Past played the Present to raise funds for the bereaved. Nicholls was just beyond an age to have played with The Past, but features in the team photograph wearing a stylish ratting cap.

But now, in more ways than one, salad days were over for Prince Gwyn. The First World War broke out, and a month after the start of hostilities the Cardiff club cancelled all Rugby fixtures. At a September meeting called by its President W.T. Morgan, the Lord Mayor urged his city's young men to enlist in the armed forces. Representatives from a variety of sports were present; following the formal speeches Cardiff's captain of the previous season, W.J. Jenkins, showed the way by being the first to enlist. Next day the club offices were opened as a recruiting station.

One of the reasons prompting Nicholls' resignation from the club committee was that the Laundries had perforce to be managed by a Partner, war or no war. It was the convention of the day that, faced with a situation such as he and Bert Winfield were in, the younger man joined up; this was supposed to rule out agonising arguments between friends and relatives. Hence, before the conflict was a few months old, Winfield joined the City of Cardiff Battalion, which would see action in France, leaving his partner to manage the laundries at Llandaff North, Neath and Bridgend.

Bert's letters to his brother-in-law from the Front are at once matter-of-fact and poignant. When he first crosses the Channel, he writes asking that a bank account be opened for his wife Queenie – "she must have a cheque book." In the next paragraph he says, "I shall be glad if you will send me two pounds of Frys sausages weekly, as I hear that little luxuries are very hard to obtain in France." A year later he is being introduced to gas warfare and his protective mask: "Very unpleasant, as one has a feeling of suffocation for five minutes after fitting it on." He has been taught to use 'bombs', which he describes as being the size of a lemon; he probably meant grenades.

Winfield returned; but numbers of Gwyn Nicholls' friends perished in battle. His dearly beloved team-mates Charles Pritchard and Johnnie Williams fell in France. 'Darkie' Bedell-Sivright lost his life at Gallipoli. Above all, the great New Zealand captain Dave Gallaher, indestructible on the Rugby field, was among those who died at Passchendaele. To a great International sportsman like Nicholls, these would have been emotional thrusts that penetrated to the heart; the casualties were but four of many. If he was to fall victim to a certain melancholia as the years went by, such losses may have been a root cause of it.

But the most grievous bereavements were yet to come.

Bert Winfield's wife Queenie, and his daughters Dorothy and Enid, were overjoyed at the safe return of the head of the house late in 1918. Bert threw himself energetically back into the laundry business, resuming control of the Bridgend and Neath branches. The family moved to Porthcawl where Winfield bought himself a motor cycle to travel the few miles to and from work each day. At the age of 41 he was, we may presume, a careful driver, not given to the taking of risks.

However, on 21 September 1919 he met his death as he rode home from the office. It appears that a farmer had thoughtlessly left a gate open on Winfield's route to Porthcawl. Across the road had meandered a herd of cattle into which he ploughed after rounding a sharp bend. He was catapulted from his mount, landing on his head in an era long before crash helmets were obligatory. There followed a journey – some say by ambulance, some say in a taxi summoned by Gwyn Nicholls – to the Cardiff Royal Infirmary, where he died without recovering consciousness. His partner and bosom friend maintained a vigil with Queenie until the end.

He grieved for Bert. He had lost a brother-in-law; a business friend (who had taught him the ropes); and a great team-mate, about whom the obituaries said it all: notably that Winfield always observed the priority of his position by finding touch when he aimed for it; certainly the 1905 New Zealanders would not have disagreed with that. The 50 points which he placed with the boot for Wales would at least have been doubled, wrote onlookers, had he been kicking dry balls off firm turf – his career at the top coincided with a series of wet winters. He made 244 appearances for Cardiff, and although scoring only one try the number of conversions and penalty goals placed by him is too great for even Danny Davies to compute. Winfield belongs on the top shelf of Wales full backs.

Queenie now returned to live with her parents in east Cardiff. The loss of Bert threw Dorothy and Enid into a closer relationship with Uncle Gwyn as a father-figure, forging the unusually strong bond between them noted earlier. The sisters fully appreciated the generous, absolutely fair attention Nicholls paid to every material need of his partner's widow, including arranging an income for life from the Laundry.

Soon, perhaps to put sad Whitchurch memories behind him, Nicholls moved to live at the village of Dinas Powys between Cardiff and Barry. After his long, but ultimately unsuccessful, resistance to golf's seductive appeal he bought a house opposite the local club's fifth tee in which to spend his declining years, calling it 'The Spinney'. Today, 59 Highwalls Avenue is painted a bright pink; while across the road, near the fourth green, still stands a bench commemorating the contribution to the club of Erith, Gwyn's daughter. In the days after he was widowed, the two grew to enjoy playing the course together; he is commemorated at Dinas Powys by a Cup for mixed foursomes.

Colourful memories of Nicholls the golfer were provided by local octogenarian Tom Collins who, as a small boy in the nineteen thirties, caddied for him and his partners for 1s.6d. a round (seven and a half pence). Collins, later to become a club Captain, was able to shed further light on the Nicholls persona from on-course conversations which took place between him and his various partners. Although ears needed to be kept skinned, since Nicholls spoke quietly, the caddies would hear gossip and views on a wide spectrum of Welsh topics, which included Rugby football. "We have a new player called Fender," Collins once heard Nicholls say. "He's an outstanding forward of a new breed: a back row man who, besides destroying, can run, pass and kick." At other times talk might be of the economy, and Cardiff or Penarth Docks. In conversation with stockbrokers, shipowners and industrialists Nicholls could hold his own.

Evidently, he was by no means the giant on golf courses in south Wales that he had been on Rugby fields, and modestly played off a twelve handicap. But, certainly, he left an impression on his young helper. In particular Tom Collins remembers his 'huge' hands; it seems that the handles of his clubs had to be bulked out with leather or tape before he could obtain a good grip on them. He was a very long driver of the ball, off the solid footing afforded by the rainproof Veltschoen shoes which he wore all year round; and he was capable of leaving a six-inch long divot for his caddy to replace. Collins echoes points made by Rugby contemporaries to the effect that he was 'unflappable' and never lost his temper. In sum, there is little doubt that he took great pleasure and comfort from golf and its camaraderie in his declining years.

Dating back to their honeymoon Gwyn and Nell Nicholls had warm feelings about England's west country, and Weston-super-Mare in particular, as a holiday destination. In the summer of 1923 Ivor, by now a teenager, Erith (named after her father) and young Geoffrey left for a holiday there with their mother. Needing to tie up some loose ends at the business, Gwyn stated that he would join them two days later. The weather deteriorated steeply that morning as the Cardiff steamer on which he travelled reached the Somerset resort; Nicholls sent his baggage to his hotel by cab and set off to walk there along the promenade. The seas pounding Glentworth Bay were heavy and he noted the strong undertow.

At the same time two pupils from a Bristol 'school for young ladies' known as St Joseph's were also at Weston on the first day of a week-long outing arranged by their school, which had booked accommodation opposite the Bay. They made up their minds to defy the elements and bathe which, given the state of the tide, was a reckless decision. The girls, Nellie Moore and Kathleen Butler, quickly got into difficulties as the undertow washed them away from the shore. Neither was strong enough to make progress against the current. Alarmed holidaymakers heard their cries for help.

The first would-be rescuer was "a slimly built, well-dressed gentleman", as the *Weston-super-Mare Gazette* described him, later identified as Dr Edward Ratcliffe Holborow, who practised locally as a GP. Discarding only his coat, he leaped into the sea and swam out towards the girls. The newspaper says, "With the waves so boisterous the odds were terribly against him. Yet he struck out through the surging sea and blinding spray...some say that he reached one of the girls and assisted her, only in the next moment to be swept away by a huge wave. Suddenly it was seen that he himself was in huge difficulty."

Interviewed next day by the *Weston Mercury* Nicholls said that as he was approaching the scene he saw a girl being brought to the shore unconscious. What he had observed was the rescue of Moore, to be followed moments later by that of Butler, by a strong woman swimmer and a member of the local swimming club. After being revived the two girls were none the worse for their experience. Nicholls' ordeal, however, was only just starting. Here is the account he gave to the local newspaper:

> At this moment I noticed the head of a man I had not seen bob up between the waves [Dr Holborow]. He seemed to be in difficulties...in my excitement I went over the sea wall. I managed to get to the man and spoke to him, but he made no reply – I think he was practically unconscious.
>
> I wound my arm around his and was making for the shore when a big wave submerged both of us. I must have involuntarily let him go, for when I came to the surface he had been washed some twelve yards away from me. I saw another swimmer coming out with a life-buoy, by which time I was fairly well spent as I had not been in the water for two years and had no previous experience of swimming with my clothes on. I managed to get ashore and came to the hotel in a taxi.

This typical piece of understatement by Nicholls, who was recognised by several bystanders, contrasts with the summation of the *Mercury*; "...He experienced a narrow escape from losing his life. Exhausted by the buffetings of the sea and being altogether out of swimming practice he collapsed upon reaching the shore and was removed to his hotel, where he received treatment." Sadly, although an experienced life-saver was able to bring Holborow in, the GP could not be resuscitated and was pronounced dead at the scene.

The *Mercury* report stated that Mr Nicholls had "fully revived." But as the years went by intimate friends concluded that, in truth, the experience had taken a toll of his health. The amount of sea-water that he swallowed was evidently substantial; the physical effort he expended simply to stay alive after Holborow was swept away was enormous. Also, the effect on his personality of so traumatic an episode was severe. Had he not become involved, his surviving contemporaries insist, he would have lived to a greater age.

A grievous decade for Gwyn Nicholls continued with the death the following March of his father Hartley at the age of 86. He was buried in the cemetery of Whitchurch parish church, just a few strides from the grave of Bert Winfield. A carved sentence on his tombstone reads, 'Work Done, Now Rest'. The final description of Hartley was 'retired lime merchant', and evidently he continued to operate through his later career as an agricultural trader and consultant. Compared with that of his son, Hartley's profile was low, but there is evidence of unfailing support given to Gwyn. Jane Eliza survived her husband a mere three years, and is buried at Whitchurch alongside him. Their youngest son Garnett, who never married, lies with them.

But the cruellest blow of all came in May 1928 with the death of Nell Nicholls at the age of 43. For a long time she had put up with a grumbling appendix, but was terrified by the thought of an operation. Some members of the family were aware of her condition, and the pain she suffered from time to time, but Nell had always forbidden them to reveal its severity to her husband. Now, suddenly, she was rushed to a nursing home in Penarth, where after a few days she died of peritonitis.

His niece Enid Williams sums up Gwyn's reaction in one telling phrase: "he was devastated." She still has the letter, in its black-bordered envelope, which he wrote to her soon after the funeral: "There is only one event to mention and that, of course, is too painful to say much about. The death was a great, great blow to us." She and her sister Dorothy agree that he was not a man to manifest grief or to shed tears. A black tie was the only revelation of his great sadness.

This is born out by Trevor Lewis, his right hand man at the Laundry. Of course, he mourned; but his way of dealing with his crisis was to seek refuge at work. Except when he had to deal with undertakers or parsons he came to the office in the week following Nell's death, often closing the door against an unkind world. Members of staff who brought flowers, and sympathy, were thanked quietly, not effusively.

Exactly how supportive his children were at this time is hard to assess. There was certainly love between them and their father, though the latter's character made it hard for him always to demonstrate it. On the other hand, he was a strict parent –

brought up in the Victorian era – who had major differences with all three at one time or another: there were outspoken and heated exchanges with Ivor, in which his eldest son was told in no uncertain terms that his playboy attitude to life was unsatisfactory. Later, when Nicholls was in the last weeks of his life Ivor was said to be consumed with anxiety – lest the demise of his father would mean that a Rover saloon which he had been promised as a generous birthday present should not materialise.

Erith was at a finishing school at Bruges, Belgium, at the time of her mother's death. Uncomplainingly she abandoned her course there to live in Dinas Powys and run 'The Spinney', taking up golf for relaxation. In letters Gwyn states unequivocally that her house-keeping for him was admirable. But the relationship came under strain when she began seeing a young Cardiff midfield player called Frank Williams.

Despite the caps which he began to win for Wales (finishing with fourteen) he was never liked or accepted by Nicholls, who is said to have found him too conceited for his liking. The couple nevertheless became man and wife, departing to live in Leeds where Frank obtained a teaching post. Here, in due course, there was a divorce. Erith re-married and again put distance between herself and South Wales by leaving to live in Canada with a new husband, Douglas Thomson.

Then there was Geoffrey who, as noted, habitually got under his father's skin and earned tickings-off. From remarks in the papers left by his sister he appears to have been the family iconoclast, in that category of offspring who find it difficult to live in the shadow of a well-known, successful parent. Geoffrey played seven games for Cardiff at scrum half before falling prey to wander-lust which took him first to Canada and later to Australia. He ended his days there.

If there was, then, a certain coolness between Nicholls and his own offspring, this would help to explain the unusually strong bonds between him and the Winfield girls, and his kindness towards his other niece Claire Whythe. He liked to show shy affection; he liked the opportunity to be generous; but perhaps he craved more appreciation than his children realised.

During his forties Gwyn Nicholls stood successfully for the Welsh Rugby Union and in 1925 became one of the two representatives of the East District, centred on Cardiff. Soon he had risen to become chairman of the team selection committee or 'Big Five' as it was already being called.

There is, however, little evidence of regular, enthusiastic contributions by him in debates about what band should play at big games before the kick-off, how much champagne should be served after games, or whether a referee's penniless widow should be left £4 or £5. Nor does he seem to have spoken on more significant issues like amendments to the Laws of the Game or the broadcasting of radio commentaries on matches.

In May 1928 he was clearly touched by the Union's message of condolence on the death of Nell and the wreath which accompanied it, and wrote a letter to say so; but, from this point on, his attendance record became sporadic: for example, in 1929 and 1930 he failed to attend seven meetings of the General Committee, and only his reputation effected his re-election in those years. Certainly at the time bereavement was a weight on his mind; but, more significantly, he had had enough time to assess the work of the WRU at close range. He was disillusioned with what he saw, and felt that changes were sorely needed.

For its part the WRU machine set out to frustrate his main aim, which was to establish an on-going majority of men with actual International experience on the Big Five. Not only did the 'establishment' block the reform; they also voted Nicholls off selection altogether, thereby hurtfully rubbishing his proposals that Welsh teams should be picked by men who knew the qualities needed at the game's highest level.

It is possible that he might have got his way had teams chosen by him and his colleagues been successful. Instead they underperformed woefully, failing to win a Five Nations title, going down to the Third Springboks and suffering a first-ever defeat at French hands. Thus Nicholls could not point to his own judgement as proof that his proposal would turn the tide.

Much of this has to be inferred, since the WRU Minutes record little or nothing of the in-fighting of the day. However, the rebuff was a last straw for Nicholls, who stated in May 1931 that he would not stand again for the WRU. The comment of his trusty supporter 'Old Stager' would not have left his readers any the wiser about what had really been going on:

> Player, administrator, selector: excellence in these roles does not always gain the votes necessary for re-election to the Big Five. Certain parties...have devoted their activities to securing an alteration to the composition of the Big Five. For reasons which need not be disclosed [sic] Gwyn was one of the members of the Big Five whose position was placed in most jeopardy.

The Cardiff club invited him back onto their committee as a sympathetic gesture for which he was grateful, though there is no evidence that he brought much more than great distinction to meetings. Certainly in group photographs he now looks the part of an elder, with silvery hair, a slight chin, and wearing a well-cut double-breasted suit. He still gazes away from the camera.

This cannot have been the sort of old age a man like Gwyn Nicholls had hoped for, or indeed deserved. The faithful Trevor Lewis speaks of a slow decline which set in as he turned sixty, never to be reversed. He kept in touch with old team-mates from the turn of the century like Willie Llewellyn and Rhys Gabe, and attended a memorable eve-of-match dinner and re-union in 1935, when the Welsh XV of the day repeated their forbears' victory of 1905.

But it became harder and harder to lure him out to any formal occasion; and when he did make an appearance, to give away prizes or trophies his shyness became ever more acutely noticeable. The veteran Wales and British Lions centre Harry Bowcott recalls a presentation ceremony in his playing days when he was excited at the prospect of receiving an award from the great Gwyn Nicholls. Bowcott expected that, as they shook hands, there might be a sotto voce 'Congratulations'. Instead, the handing-over took place in silence.

During the three previous decades 'the Guv'nor', as he was affectionately known at the laundries, had taken pleasure in accompanying staff on their annual outings. He would drive his tourer, and later a large Austin six-seater saloon, ahead of the packed charabancs and deliver pep talks over picnic lunches. Now he found excuses to be absent. His visits to Llandaff North, and to the plants at Neath and Bridgend remained regular but were much briefer; by now Ivor was taking the strain of running the firm (which he would do until his retirement in 1977) having put aside once-harboured ambitions to play cricket for Glamorgan. His father still drove himself from and to Dinas Powys and even as far as Neath; but Trevor Lewis noted sadly how he now accepted help getting in and out of the car.

In 1938 he began a series of visits chauffeured by Lewis to Oxford, where a nephew was in practice as a GP. He would spend several hours in the surgery with a Harley Street specialist who came from London to treat him for 'a heart condition'. On the return journey he would confide in his driver that they had 'put him through it'; sometimes he would ask for the car to be stopped because he was experiencing cramp and chest pains. They would halt at roadside inns for a drink; afterwards Lewis had to help his boss use the toilet.

Ivor Nicholls had moved to Dinas Powys with his wife Mary; and now, as her father-in-law grew noticeably weaker, it was she who ferried him to the office for visits whose duration was down to a mere thirty minutes. Early in 1939, when the Guv'nor's attendances abruptly ceased, Trevor Lewis drove to Dinas Powys for what, as it turned out, was their last meeting. His boss was dressed, but resting in an arm chair and very subdued. He told the visitor that his health was going; to which the only response could be, "Oh, you musn't worry like this". Their last conversation never took off, and Lewis departed sadly: "I knew that he would not get better," he recalls. "He was not at all the same man that I had known for all those years."

Another caller at 'The Spinney' in these last days was erstwhile caddy Tom Collins, now grown up, embarking on a career in Her Majesty's Custom and Excise arm – and eager to tell Mr Nicholls all about it. Collins remembers him apologising for not rising to greet him and grimacing "Sorry I can't get up, young man. I'm paying the penalty for letting all those sixteen-stone forwards run into me in match after match."

He would have known with satisfaction by 18 March that,

after a three-way tie in the Championship, Wales could claim top place ahead of Ireland and England by virtue of points difference. Apart from a notable, and in many ways astonishing, victory over the Third All Blacks, Welsh successes in the Thirties had been rare; now, playing behind strong packs, brilliant backs like Wooller, Cliff Jones, Haydn Tanner, Willie Davies and Vivian Jenkins were rebuilding Wales' reputation after the doldrum years. As their great antecedent's life drew to a close he could take comfort from the knowledge that such men played the game his way.

Thanks to the Winfield family's medical contacts in the English Midlands, two highly-qualified male nurses travelled to care for the now house-bound Gwyn Nicholls; apparently a recent charge of theirs had been Jesse Boot, who founded the chain of chemist shops as well as funding the early days of Nottingham University. But there was little they could do for their Welsh patient beyond ensuring his comfort and seeing that he was in no pain in these final days. He quietly breathed his last on the morning of 24 March 1939; heart failure was given as the cause of death.

A few days later the funeral service took place at St Andrew's Parish Church, a little way into the tranquil Vale of Glamorgan countryside west of Dinas Powys. In addition to Ivor, Erith, Geoffrey and their spouses, elder brother Sid – now 68 – was among the mourners. The Welsh Rugby Union was represented by its Secretary Walter Rees. Willie Llewellyn, Rhys Gabe, Percy Bush and Cliff Pritchard were there as his Welsh contemporaries from club and International Rugby; the other Home Countries and France sent mourners too.

In the cemetery just across the road a re-opened grave was now closed again over the coffin of Gwyn Nicholls, re-united with his adored Nell. "Here lies Erith Gwynne Nicholls," reads the cap-stone, reverting to the spelling on his birth certificate; "Also his dear wife Emmaline."

Many years later, the ashes of Erith would be brought from Canada to be placed with the remains of her parents in this quiet place. A few paces away is the grave of Ivor and Mary.

That April the Welsh Rugby Union and Cardiff Athletic Club jointly sanctioned a Fund to create a suitable memorial to the Prince of Centres. Its form would be determined by the amount of money raised.

Quite quickly £753 was subscribed by admirers, an amount which would approximate to £30,000 today. The Fund was then put on ice until the end of World War II, when a renewed flow of donations, plus the takings from a star-studded exhibition match, pushed the total past £1,650. This was sufficient for the commissioning of the beautiful wrought-iron gates which have enhanced the entrance to the old Cardiff Arms Park complex in the second half of the twentieth century.

The Gates were formally opened in front of a large gathering on Boxing Day, 1949. Nicholls' one-time team-mate Rhys Gabe performed the key-turning ceremony, and spoke eloquently of Prince Gwyn:

> He was the most complete footballer I have ever met, equally strong in every department of the game. He was the most difficult man to stop because of his long, raking stride coupled with a deceptive body-sway. His abiding ambition was to carve openings for colleagues.
>
> Gwyn Nicholls possessed that indefinable glamour which others did not have to the same degree.
>
> It is this which puts him on a pedestal, above all the rest.

Epilogue

Just how good, then, was Erith Gwyn Nicholls? Would he have found his way into a Welsh, or Lions, XV in 1955, 1971 or 1997? Such questions, of course, are irresolvable and open-ended, which is why they can keep fans embroiled in club-house arguments until stop-tap and beyond. Was Cliff Morgan as good as Barry John? Which was the better captain – John Gwilliam or John Dawes? Supposing Gerald Davies and Ieuan Evans had opposed each other when each was in his prime, who would have come out on top? And so on.

There is a standard, cautious answer – which is that great practitioners in one period would rise to the same pre-eminence in any era. It is a little glib. The *Western Mail* did rather better in the leader column of 25 March 1939, devoted to Nicholls and his career: "People have never seen a subsequent performance by a three quarter without measuring it against the criteria set by Gwyn Nicholls" – this written in a decade which had witnessed Bowcott, Davey and latterly Wooller. In other words, the consensus was that Nicholls was the greatest, until proved otherwise, partly because he was an exemplar of centre play.

The columnist added: "His most valuable achievement was that he lifted the game to a level which gave a view of possibil-ities...and in so doing transformed it into a finer spectacle; a more glorious game than it had been before; a rare delight to behold." What did this mean? In the same edition 'Old Stager' explained in an analytical essay, "The pioneers of the four three quarter formation left it to him to provide final proof of its virtues, subduing his own great qualities in order to perfect combination between team members." That is, the great solo try is cheered the world over; but it is the score that comes through fifteen pairs of hands that brings the house down.

The *Daily Telegraph* recalled his timing: "Neither earlier nor later than the precisely correct second Nicholls would deliver a perfect pass, which left the receiver in the most advantageous position and a try more than a likelihood". But perhaps the most penetrating contribution came in the now defunct *Illustrated Sporting & Dramatic News*. The habitually sceptical E.H.D. Sewell wrote the following about Nicholls:

> The secret of his lasting success...was that he never betrayed his intentions to the opposition. They and the onlookers...were always left in some doubt, until the thing was done, as to what was going to be done. Then, what was done seemed the only thing to do.
>
> Thus, in that historic try which he scored on 'impossible' going at Cardiff on the first day of 1907 against the South Africans, Nicholls never revealed the fact that he was going for the line himself until he flung himself over it. Moving right, with two men backing him up, a pass to either of them seemed the most likely thing to happen at any moment. Even a cross-kick towards the centre, where the pack was advancing in skirmishing order, was a feasibility. All the while Nicholls...beat the opposing backs for pace; and A.F.W. Marsberg for once, little suspecting such speed possible on such a day, quite missed his man.

Other obituarists chose to highlight the Prince's personal qualities. The Cardiff match programme published a few days after his death rated him the greatest figure in the club's history: "The biggest trait in his character was the modesty and unostentatious demeanour displayed in the midst of his triumphs."

The *South Wales Echo* dispelled any idea that he had been an austere, moody figure. Yes, Gwyn Nicholls could be serious; but he "...would not for long suppress the infectious smile that always sought expression – whether on the Rugby field or in life's weightier affairs." Welsh International scrum half and Glamorgan cricketer Maurice Turnbull said he was "a man who never lost his temper or did a shoddy thing."

And there was the tribute of D.R. Gent: "He has left a sweet and pleasant memory, for his greatness never for a moment affected his temperament off the field: that of a modest, simple, genial and sincere man whom it was always a sheer joy to meet. For years, he was the idol of South Wales crowds."

'Idol' is probably not exactly the best word. Smacking of something inert, without vitality or animation of its own, it conjures illusions of false gods and graven images. No, the panache of Gwyn Nicholls, his charisma and sheer virility surely demand the accolade 'hero'; which is to say, "one admired and venerated for his achievements and noble qualities". There is a crucial difference between 'idol' and 'hero' which the dictionaries do not highlight: the former's role is simply to be worshipped, and there is no sense in which it can be imitated or set an example which others can follow. On the other hand a hero inspires, and positively invites emulation. That Nicholls possessed these capacities can be dramatically inferred from the results Wales delivered not only under his leadership but also after his retirement, with a Grand Slam (including a first victory over France) and two Triple Crowns in the years leading up to the First World War.

Only a few men, and not as many women, win unanimous acclamation as national heroes from the Welsh. That is not particularly because we are a nation small in number. It has more to do with the multiple fractures that characterise our make-up. There is the huge, palpable divide between the North and the South. There are those who can, and those who cannot, speak Welsh. There are those who live on the land, and there are the city-dwellers of the south east. Around 77% of us were born in Wales; a substantial 23% were not.

The value-judgements of these groups are as disparate as they are idiosyncratic. Thus although time and distance favour undisputed heroic status for, say, King Arthur or Boadicea, attitudes and circumstances mean that figures of the Second Millennium like Llewelyn the Great, Owain Glyndwr, David Lloyd George and Aneurin Bevan cannot win general acceptability.

Sporting champions are, however, exceptions who prove the rule. Their feats are matters of fact, not dependant upon judgement or a political standpoint. The achievements of Meredith, Farr, Charles, Lynn Davies, Winstone, Edwards, John, Jackson and certain of their peers can be measured. The goals and tries they scored, the distances, points and punches which feature in the record books – these are beyond dispute. The worthiness of their sporting ethics and attitudes is another criterion, if a secondary one (it would seem to be the case that most Welsh champions are good guys). And they are hero-worshipped with equal fervour in Cardiff and Caernarfon, Newport and Newtown. They unite a nation. The great Welsh sides of the First Golden Era seldom if ever included personnel from northern Wales; yet when they boarded the ferry for a Championship engagement in Dublin, crowds flocked to speed them on their way from Holyhead.

Erith Gwyn Nicholls earned a place in an august company of superstars. Or should we say, perhaps, that other heroes of Welsh sport have subsequently won a place in his.

But the Rugby legacy bequeathed to Wales by him was more than the afterglow of heroism. Applied to a mere game, Nicholls' perception of his contribution as the framing of a philosophical system will strike some as high-flown. What he did indubitably achieve, however, was the moulding of an ultimate Style of Rugby football, to which his compatriots were – are – particularly well suited by temperament, inclination and not least physique. Its brilliance seized and retained the imagination of the Welsh nation, bringing pleasure to the players who adopted it and marvellous entertainment to the many who looked on and cheered themselves hoarse. It also delivered success: as their captain, Nicholls led his men to eight victories in ten games.

Subsequent generations of Welsh players at all levels have striven diligently to embrace and honour the Style. In many decades since Nicholls' day it has been beyond their grasp; a little out of reach. Yet in the Fifties and the Seventies it experienced a Second Coming, and a Third.

The Style that Gwyn Nicholls left to Welsh Rugby remains within the reach of men with vision and daring. It is no more, nor less, than a birthright.

Index

Index of International Games